DUST AND DIGNITY

DUST AND DIGNITY

Domestic Employment in Contemporary Ecuador

Erynn Masi de Casanova

ILR PRESS

AN IMPRINT OF CORNELL UNIVERSITY PRESS

ITHACA AND LONDON

First published 2019 by Cornell University Press

Library of Congress Cataloging-in-Publication Data

Names: Casanova, Erynn Masi de, 1977– author.
Title: Dust and dignity : domestic employment in contemporary Ecuador / Erynn Masi de Casanova.
Description: Ithaca : ILR Press, an imprint of Cornell University Press, 2019. | Includes bibliographical references and index.
Identifiers: LCCN 2018057157 (print) | LCCN 2018059081 (ebook) | ISBN 9781501739477 (pdf) | ISBN 9781501739484 (epub/mobi) | ISBN 9781501739453 | ISBN 9781501739453 (cloth) | ISBN 9781501739460 (pbk.)
Subjects: LCSH: Women household employees—Ecuador—Guayaquil. | Women migrant labor—Ecuador—Guayaquil. | Work environment—Ecuador—Guayaquil. | Informal sector (Economics)—Ecuador—Guayaquil.
Classification: LCC HD6072.2.E2 (ebook) | LCC HD6072.2.E2 C37 2019 (print) | DDC 331.4/81640986632—dc23
LC record available at https://lccn.loc.gov/2018057157

To all the women informal workers who are unseen and underpaid

Para las mujeres trabajadoras informales en reconocimiento de su lucha, trabajo, y sacrificio

Contents

Foreword by Maximina Salazar   ix

Acknowledgments   xi

Introduction   1

1. In Search of the Ideal Worker   21

2. Embodied Inequality   35

3. Informed but Insecure (Written in Collaboration with Leila Rodríguez)   55

4. Pathways through Poverty   82

5. Like Any Other Job?   105

Conclusion   122

Epilogue   131

Appendix: Research Methods   133

Notes   141

References   153

Index   169

Foreword

The biggest obstacle that household workers face in Ecuador is the lack of compliance with labor laws. The laws exist, but they are not acted on, and it seems that they don't matter to the authorities today. We the household workers have carried out a daily struggle (*lucha*) to achieve some changes, like respecting the eight-hour workday—so that we, like any other worker (*trabajador o trabajadora*), can work Monday to Friday—and requiring social security coverage. We have engaged in political activities on behalf of members of this occupation. For example, we lobbied for the ratification of the International Labor Organization's Convention 189. But, at the moment, there is a reversal in the observance of our guaranteed rights.

On the topic of social security, we conducted a research study, whose results are presented in this book, to see how many household workers are enrolled in social security. Then we launched another study to determine the education levels and work histories of remunerated household workers. Investigating the experiences of the workers is the best way to get real information that comes right out of their lives.

With Erynn Masi de Casanova, at first we got to know each other casually, but as time passed she has cooperated with us, supporting us in the research about social security and other topics. She was the one who trained us so that we could conduct surveys with this important labor sector. Because we didn't know how to do the analysis, we had to have a professional. She was the one who did the tabulation and analysis, as we had agreed. I also want to state that she is now our friend and comrade (*compañera*). Thanks to God and to life that we had the privilege of getting to know each other.

These collaborations between academics and activists are ways of helping others when there are not sufficient resources. This is true teamwork, and I see it as a way of supporting the organization.

Maximina Salazar
President of the Association of
Remunerated Household Workers
(Asociación de Trabajadoras
Remuneradas del Hogar)
Guayaquil, Ecuador

Acknowledgments

I owe thanks to many people who supported me in this project, which has spanned nearly a decade:

Primero que nada, gracias a las compañeras de la Asociación de Trabajadoras Remuneradas del Hogar por compartir sus historias y colaborar en el diseño de algunas partes de esta investigación y en la recopilación de datos. Su ejemplo de dedicación, solidaridad, y amistad me ha afectado profundamente.

Gracias a la Sra. Lola Proaño Yela, por compartir su casa y recibirnos con tanto cariño.

To the people who opened doors for me in Ecuador: Irma Guzmán de Torres, Jorge Calderón, Amy C. Lind, Jo Vervecken, and Magalí Marega.

To Frances Benson and the team at ILR Press, thank you for your faith in this project; it is a pleasure to work with you all.

To the Charles Phelps Taft Research Center, which partially funded the project, and my colleagues in the Department of Sociology at the University of Cincinnati, who can be counted on for both cheerleading and critique. And my writing group, without whom I would publish nothing worth reading: Danielle Bessett, Sarah Mayorga-Gallo, Rebecca Sanders, and Rina Verma Williams.

To the UC sociology graduate student research assistants who helped with content analysis and literature reviews: Jeremy Brenner-Levoy, Rocío Bueno Roldán, Sevsem Çiçek-Okay, Jeffrey Gaver, and Amanda Staight.

To the Rockefeller Foundation Bellagio Center, which provided the time, space, and inspiration to finish the first draft of the manuscript during an academic writing residency, and to my Bellagio family, who encouraged me to be bold and creative and live in the moment.

To friends who are not just brilliant scholars of social life, but also funny, loyal, and gorgeous human beings: Littisha A. Bates, Tamara R. Mose, Holly Y. McGee, Shailaja Paik, and Leila Rodríguez (who gets an extra thank you for helping me with the statistical analysis for this book).

To Juliana Sarmento da Silveira for creating the GIS map depicting workers' commutes.

To the researchers of domestic work in Latin America, who produce groundbreaking—and sometimes heartbreaking—scholarship that deserves a bigger audience.

To my family: Joaquín, Soledad, and Henry. You are home for me, no matter where we are.

DUST AND DIGNITY

INTRODUCTION

During some unusually cool and breezy days in Guayaquil, Ecuador, when the early matches of the 2018 World Cup dominated televised and in-person conversations, a national TV channel aired a series of sketches called "Sin peroles no hay paraíso." A play on the title of a popular Colombian *telenovela*, the phrase uses a term, *perol*, that denotes both a heavy metal pot with handles and a paid domestic worker. Without these workers, according to this sarcastic title, there is no paradise. In one of the sketches, a character called La Gringa, white and blond, introduces herself in English. She then describes, as she sweeps wearing a sexy maid costume, how she came to Ecuador from the United States out of economic necessity, but has grown to love the country. The moment she stops sweeping, her employer, played by an actress wearing blackface and a wig of long braids, appears and begins scolding her, swinging her hair around as she imposes her authority on the apologetic employee. The supposed humor in this sketch is built on the absurdity of a *gringa* domestic worker in the employ of a black woman. The audience knows this because, despite the declining number of full-time domestic workers in recent years, they have watched many inversions of this scene, on screen or in person, featuring people who consider themselves white berating domestic workers seen as nonwhite.[1]

This brief sketch grotesquely demonstrates key elements of the domestic employment relationship: the abuse of power, the racialization of the occupation, and the poverty that leads women to do domestic work for wages. The term *perol* itself reduces the worker to the very object she uses to do her work in the kitchen of her employers. This book, based on research conducted between 2010 and 2018, explains why domestic work remains an occupation of last resort in Ecuador (and elsewhere) and discusses how these working conditions might be improved. In exploring the experiences of paid domestic workers in Ecuador, I show how concepts of social reproduction, urban informal employment, and class boundaries can help illuminate the particular forms of exploitation in this work and explain why domestic work continues to be a bad job. If we want to improve conditions for workers, we need to pay attention to these three dimensions.

The International Labor Organization (ILO) defines domestic work to include housework; caring for children, ill, disabled, or elderly people in private homes; and tasks such as "driving the family car, taking care of the garden, and guarding private houses" (ILO 2016a, 3). An estimated 67 million people, mostly women, are employed in domestic work worldwide and 50 million of these are informally employed (9). An estimated 27 percent of the world's domestic workers live in Latin America and the Caribbean (OIT 2018, 27). Thirty percent of families in Latin America are involved in domestic work either as employers or workers (Blofield and Jokela 2018, 534). Statistics likely undercount the population employed in domestic work, because it is informal and stigmatized. Work becomes invisible when it is done off the books, by poor women, behind closed doors in private homes.

Paid domestic work is an ancient occupation, rooted in feudal economic systems, but it is part of the modern world under capitalism.[2] Historically, domestic workers cooked, cleaned, and cared for children, as they do today. However, this work has shifted from in-kind payment (room and board) to wages, and from most domestic workers living with employers to most living separately (García López 2012). Also, middle- and upper-class women have entered the workforce, relying on domestic workers to take up the slack at home. The economic transformations of the twentieth and twenty-first centuries have changed the experience and structure of work for many people around the world, including domestic workers. Starting in the 1980s and 1990s, the fragmentation of production through the breaking up of manufacturing operations and their dispersion around the globe has reduced the power of workers in formal, legal employment. Traditional labor organizations have weakened in the process (Castillo 2000), as the "typical" male, industrial, permanent, unionized laborer has become rarer (Davolos 2012; de la Garza Toledo and Hernández 2000).[3] Employment has increased in the service and financial sectors, which provide goods and services for purchase rather than producing concrete things. At the same time, we have seen growth in "atypical jobs"—precarious, part-time, or temporary—and a rise in low-earning self-employment that is also precarious (de la Garza Toledo and

Hernández 2000; Kalleberg 2009; on the "gig economy," see Hatton 2011; Kessler 2018; Lehdonvirta, forthcoming; Prassl 2018).

In Latin America, the female workforce tripled between 1960 and 1990 (Arango Gaviria 2001, 13). In Ecuador, where my study is based, the number of paid women workers increased by 80 percent between 2001 and 2010 (INEC 2014). As middle-class women increasingly engaged in paid work, domestic employment increased to fill the gap and accomplish the tasks of social reproduction, the behind-the-scenes work necessary to sustain the labor force (Moreno Zúñiga 2013, 96–97). By middle class, I mean women with a high-school diploma and probably some higher education, who often have spouses with formal employment, and who live in well-resourced neighborhoods and households with a certain degree of purchasing power. (The middle class made up 37 percent of Ecuador's population in 2015, though that number is most likely declining as the economy contracts [Gachet et al. 2017]).

The incorporation of women into paid labor in the developing world has been both a result and a driver of increased informal employment. Such work takes place at the borders of, or outside of, legal regulations, and may involve self-employment or work for wages or commission (Cortés 2000). In the "developed" world, the informal economy (where informal employment takes place) is seen as an anomaly and as separate from the formal economy.[4] But Latin American informal employment has a long history and has not faded away as some early theorists of economic development predicted. Informal work also has links to the formal economy rather than being wholly separate (Connolly 1985; Cortés 2000). In the Global South, it is often more of a survival strategy than a means for upward socioeconomic mobility; it is "unemployment disguised as employment" (Connolly 1985, 62). Underemployment is rampant in formal and informal sectors: people are working less than they would like. These employment patterns are important for understanding contemporary domestic work.

Most research on domestic work published in English in the last twenty years focuses on international migrants (Chang 2016; Ehrenreich and Hochschild 2002; Hondagneu-Sotelo 2007; Lan 2006; Mose Brown 2011; Parreñas 2001; Rosenbaum 2017). These studies often highlight global rather than local economic and demographic processes as the context for domestic work. Yet only a minority (17 percent) of the world's paid domestic workers are international migrants (ILO 2016a, 27). Another body of work, which somewhat overlaps with studies of migrant domestic workers, focuses on understanding the activities collectively called "carework" (Arriagada and Todaro 2012; Carrasquer, Torns, and Romero 1998; England 2005; Esquivel 2011; Francisco-Menchavez 2018; Gutiérrez-Rodríguez 2014; Kofman 2012; Vega 2009). Studies using a carework perspective often emphasize microlevel interpersonal interactions between employers and employees rather than labor relations and the potential for collective organizing. Taking international migration and carework as starting points for inquiry can limit our view of local labor markets, labor relations, and employment alternatives. Using migration and carework as the only lenses for examining domestic work can also obscure the question of where domestic work fits into capitalist labor processes and the organization of work more generally.[5] In this introduction, I explore three frameworks that are especially useful for analyzing domestic work, but seem to have fallen by the wayside: social reproduction, urban informal economy, and class.

Domestic work in contemporary capitalism is shaped by current economic and social structures (patterns of relationships) and by its roots in precapitalist and—in the case of Latin America—colonial forms of patronage and servitude. Ecuador, despite the socialist leanings of its most recent presidents, has a capitalist economy. The theories of Karl Marx, whose main object of study was the relationship between capital and labor, have long informed analyses of Latin America's social and economic realities. Scholars have found these theories useful in explaining the transition of primarily agrarian economies to industrial and postindustrial economies. I draw on Marx's concepts here partly because they are popular and influential in the region, and form the backbone of much of the sociology of work produced there (de la Garza Toledo 2000). In addition, these ideas have inspired reams of writing by feminist scholars on the topic of domestic work—usually unpaid (e.g., Barrett [1980] 2014; Beechey 1978, Hartmann 1979; Molyneux 1979; Picchio 1992). More important, Marx's theories of the exploitation of workers, and workers' ability to collectively resist this exploitation, allow me to explore domestic employment with an eye toward improving the lives of workers. Feminist political economy is a school of thought that draws on Marx and other theorists, but includes relations of gender and power. I see this study as an application and extension of feminist political economy because I share the goal of remaking social and economic relations in more equitable ways.

Domestic work is rooted in particular historical forms of domination. This legacy, along with informal employment arrangements, helps account for the continued exploitation of domestic workers today. In developing economies, precapitalist economic activities often continue during and after the emergence of industrial and service sector employment. Because economic development is a fragmented rather than a linear process, these activities, such as subsistence agriculture, home-based production of goods involving many family members, and paid domestic work, all continue to exist even as new occupations appear. Why is domestic work an exploitative and undesirable job? To answer this question, we need to understand its place as a practice that predates capitalism, emerging in feudalistic social relations.

Social Reproduction

Most formal employment takes place within what theorists of capitalism call production, which is the creation by waged laborers of products that circulate as commodities. More recently, formal employment outside of this traditional production process—in the service and finance sectors—has increased.[6] While not producing commodities, these sectors of the economy may participate in their circulation and do generate profit ("surplus value," to use Marx's term).[7] In order to continue, the capitalist mode of production relies on labor power being continually renewed and available; reproduction is the set of behind-the-scenes activities that makes this possible. What Marx simply called "reproduction" other scholars often refer to as "social reproduction." This renaming seems to limit reproduction to the social and production to the economic, though these two spheres are mutually penetrating and interconnected. Marx argued that "every social process of production is at the same time a process of reproduction" ([1867] 1990, 711). But the reverse is not true: domestic work, both paid and unpaid, is part of reproduction rather than production, as I will argue below.

The relationship between production and reproduction and the location of domestic work within the capitalist system matter because when labor is classified as "productive," those who undertake it have a clearly defined role in the economy. These "productive" workers enjoy legal rights and social protections not generally extended to "unproductive" workers, who engage in tasks that do not generate profit. The production/reproduction divide is important because governments regulate productive work that takes place in the public sphere, but we might not expect them to intervene in reproductive work that takes place in the private sphere of the home. So while a government agency could shut down a factory or fine its owners for unsafe work practices, it is unlikely that the same agency would sanction a private employer for allowing a domestic worker to labor under unsafe conditions. This example shows how a seemingly abstract discussion—about what kind of work domestic employment is—can have concrete consequences and shape employer-worker relations.

In addition, workers firmly located in the sphere of production can organize collectively and make claims on employers because they help them to generate profit.[8] If paid domestic work lies outside of the production process, then domestic workers may have to fight harder to get the same rights as workers involved in production. They may have to use different collective or individual strategies to obtain these rights, as traditional labor organizing may not be effective. The distinction between productive and reproductive work has implications for social protections, specifically social security. If social security is designed to take care of the labor force, then who is part of that labor force, and thus deserving of coverage?

TABLE I.1. What is social reproduction?

	REPRODUCTION OF LABOR FORCE	REPRODUCTION OF RELATIONS OF PRODUCTION
Daily*	Providing food, clothing, shelter, care (survival)	Instilling and enacting class (and gender) identities, turning people into workers
Generational*	Biological reproduction	Socialization of children, including education

*Inspired by terms used in Carrasco Bengoa 1991.

Feminist scholars care about social reproduction because it is mostly per-formed by women and is one area in which gender relations play out and thus may be challenged. What is the difference between paid and unpaid domestic work? The actions involved are identical: cooking, cleaning, caring for those who need assistance with daily tasks (carework), and household management. So what differentiates a domestic worker from a housewife or other person who engages in unpaid domestic work? The domestic worker performs these tasks for wages, does not usually belong to the kinship network of the household in which she works,[9] and works under the authority of one or more members of that household. As sociologist Judith Rollins (1985) famously put it, domestic employment is an economic relation that, unlike many others in male-dominated societies, tends to remain "between women." Some experts argue that the reason that domestic work is low-paid is that it is indistinguishable from the unpaid work that women have traditionally done in the household (ILO 2010; Gimeno 2010; Thornton Dill 1988). Domestic tasks are gendered, seen as the natural province of women rather than the work of skilled professionals.

Social reproduction can be divided into two types of activities, and two scales or levels. The types of reproduction are (1) the reproduction of labor power (defined as the capacity of the members of the paid labor force to work) and (2) the reproduction of the relations of production (defined as the class struc-tures that both connect and separate employers and workers). The two scales are daily and generational. Labor power needs to be reproduced. Laboring bodies need food, shelter, clothing, and sleep. The relations of production connect capi-tal to labor, or more specifically, capitalists to laborers,[10] and these relations are characterized by exploitation and domination. Labor power and the relations of production are reproduced daily, as people meet their day-to-day survival needs in their households, and generationally, as they raise up the next generation of workers. Biological reproduction is one component of reproduction, and chil-dren are most useful to capital when they make it to adulthood and become workers. This raises an important point to keep in mind when analyzing domestic work: the actors driving the expansion of capitalism are not concerned with *how* social reproduction happens, but are dependent on it happening. The activities of social reproduction can be performed as paid or unpaid work, or even undertaken by the state (e.g., government day care centers). State involvement in social reproduction is increasingly uncommon in today's economies, which are governed by neoliberal ideals of private responsibility for reproduction. So social reproduction occurs primarily in the family or household unit and may take different forms for households of different class positions (Benería 1979; Redclift 1985). Yet in all social classes, reproductive tasks are largely devalued and seen as women's work.[11]

Social reproduction received a great deal of attention from feminist scholars, particularly in what came to be called the "domestic labor debates," in the 1970s (Benston 1969; Dalla Costa and James 1975; Delphy 1980; Hartmann 1979; Molyneux 1979; Seccombe 1974; Smith 1978; see Weeks 2011 for an overview). These academics, many of them economists, wanted to figure out how the social (as opposed to biological) part of social reproduction fit with theories of capitalist production. After reviewing the debates over whether social reproduction is part of capitalist production or sits outside of it, I agree that social reproduction is connected to production, and that the production process relies on but does not subsume it. In accomplishing reproductive tasks, the household is not directly governed by capital and it does not produce surplus value for capital.[12] Reproduction lies outside the production process (Valenzuela and Sanches 2012). Yet it is not just the distinction between production and reproduction that disadvantages reproductive workers (paid and unpaid)—it is the hierarchy that *privileges* production over reproduction (Lerussi 2014).

The domestic labor debates, which seem to have fizzled rather than finalized, excluded paid domestic work almost entirely. What are we to make of paid domestic work as waged labor situated within social reproduction, what we could call "reproductive labor" (Lan 2006; Parreñas 2001)? As I mentioned, domestic work produces only use values for the members of the household rather than concrete things with exchange value that can be sold outside the home (de Barbieri 1978; Saffioti 1978). Domestic workers are waged laborers, but they don't have a direct relation to capital. Instead, they are paid from other workers' (or professionals' or small business owners') earnings, in what we might argue is a form of consumption rather than a capitalist employment relation. Marx did not write much about paid domestic work, though he did mention paid cooks and suggested that domestic work would increasingly become a paid service as more wives and mothers came to be employed outside the home (cited in Beechey 1978, 186). I am convinced by Latin American scholars' classification of paid domestic work as "noncapitalist," because of this lack of direct dependence on capital and the resemblance to servitude under feudal economic systems (Saffioti 1978). Yet, like unpaid domestic work, paid domestic work is indirectly useful to capital, as it reproduces the labor power that is directly subject to capital.[13]

The frequent exclusion of domestic workers from traditional labor movements and trade unions stems in part from labor leaders who interpret paid domestic work as unproductive and thus less valuable, evaluating it as unskilled labor performed by women. Paid domestic work's similarity to unpaid work that women do in the home distinguishes it from other types of work. The literature on carework takes up this issue, but largely jettisons in-depth discussions of social reproduction and domestic work as a labor process, which are crucial for explaining these workers' exploitation and their potential for collective organizing (with some exceptions: Bakker 2007; Carrasquer, Torns, and Romero 1998; Kofman 2012).

The debate over where domestic labor fits within capitalism has real implications for paid domestic workers' lives. If work is directly linked to production and profit, it can provide the workers a set of legal rights and social protections, although there is always a tug-of-war between the opposed interests of workers and capitalists. The recognition of productive work *as work* opens up avenues for worker mobilization and state regulation. In order for domestic workers' collective resistance to exploitation to be successful, they and their advocates and allies must find ways of showing that their work counts, even if it does not generate profit.

Other aspects of paid domestic work facilitate exploitation. The poorest and most vulnerable tend to perform this occupation, and the domination by employers in the home is personalized and mingled with affection. But the generally weak responses from the public world of government and labor unions to the plight of domestic workers are best explained by the marginal location of the work outside of the production process. The uniqueness of domestic employment stems from its reproductive tasks, as I have discussed here, but also from its informal arrangement.

The Urban Informal Economy

Employment in the formal economy is governed by legal regulations. The informal economy, on the other hand, is characterized by a lack of, or noncompliance with, legal regulations. Informal workers, including domestic workers, are ubiquitous features of urban life in Latin America, yet domestic workers occupy a unique niche and often experience less autonomy than other informal workers.

Their work takes place in private households, is invisible owing to "social norms and highly personalized contexts," and depends on employers, with little oversight or regulation from the government (ILO 2016a, xi).

In Latin America, the informal economy has grown along with urbanization, as formal labor markets in the cities have been unable to employ all the migrants from the countryside looking for work (Cortés 2000). Internal migrants to the cities, some of whom become domestic workers, form part of the reserve army of labor, moving into the formal economy when they can and engaging in informal work—including domestic work and informal, small-scale self-employment—when there are no formal jobs (Cortés 2000). As formal employment opportunities for the urban poor dry up, however, they may spend their whole lives working in informal conditions, and there seem to be fewer and fewer pathways from informal to formal work in Latin America. As a survival strategy, "informal employment has replaced an inadequate system of state welfare and its growth is the result of pressures from urban poverty" (de Oliveira and Roberts 1993, quoted in Cortés 2000). Urban informal employment in its current configuration is not an efficient path toward full employment for a society; at best it is a stopgap that prevents violent unrest among the poor.

The informal economy dominates in many developing countries, with 47 percent of nonfarm workers in Latin America engaged in informal work (the figure for Ecuadorian women is 64 percent; ILO 2014b). The informal economy is a broad category that includes many different types of activities, dependent employment (in which a worker has a boss), and self-employment. Jobs considered informal tend to share the following characteristics: income near or below the legal minimum wage, lack of legal registration and taxation, lack of medical coverage and other benefits enjoyed by workers in formal employment, instability or precarity of employment, and lack of union representation (Connolly 1985). Paid domestic work in most Latin American countries fits these criteria, despite legislation granting workers certain rights and benefits.

Formalization is the process by which jobs move from the informal to the formal economy, entering into systems of regulation and taxation. At a minimum, formalization entails "legal recognition as workers . . . organization and representation, and access to social protection" (Schurman, Eaton, and Chen 2017, 223). In their explorations of the informal economy, experts have often returned to the questions of whether formalization is always desirable and what formalizing informal work entails (de Soto 1987; ILO 2016a; Tokman 2007; Tomei 2011). Rather than promoting transformation from formal to informal in the blink of an eye, the International Labor Organization uses language such as "moving toward formality" to imply the unevenness and gradualness of formalization. The feasibility and goals of formalization differ by the type of income-generating activity the state is trying to regulate.[14] In general, formalizing has the goal of guaranteeing what the ILO calls "decent work" and bringing working conditions for workers in the informal economy in line with those in formal employment.

We might be reluctant to define domestic work as informal once it becomes subject to at least some government regulations. If a domestic worker registers with the social security system, for example, is she still an informal worker? I agree with Nanneke Redclift that it makes most sense to classify employment *arrangements*, rather than workers or activities, as informal (1985, 96). Despite being covered by some labor laws, domestic work is still usually arranged informally and paid "under the table" in most cities of the Americas (in cash, without reporting to labor authorities or registering workers with Social Security). Domestic workers are also disadvantaged relative to self-employed informal workers because they depend on employers for work and usually lack autonomy in their work activities.

Whereas informal economic activities in the Global North are seen as "anomalies or exceptional cases," in Latin America they are ubiquitous and are intimately connected with "fundamental problems of development, employment and poverty" (Connolly 1985).[15] In fact, scholars working in the Global South see informal employment as necessary for economic development (Tinsman 1992) and the survival of the urban poor (Cortés 2000). Rather than fighting against informality, which governments often do through crackdowns on street vending or other work activities, some experts propose accepting it as inevitable and appreciating the way it keeps many families from starving.

So the informal economy touches nearly everyone in developing countries, but who are the informal workers? Women tend to be disproportionately represented in informal employment, as recurrent economic crisis and neoliberal development policies increase women's work, paid and unpaid, in and outside the home (Benería 2003; de Oliveira and Ariza 2000; Lind 2005). Because women are overrepresented in informal employment, and because a large proportion of those informally employed women are domestic workers, in earlier statistical analyses "many of the characteristics imputed to informality refer in fact to domestic service" (Connolly 1985, 76–77). To avoid this confusion, the ILO and some governments in their reports now break out domestic work as its own category either within informal employment or outside both formal and informal categories.

Domestic worker organizations and advocates often push for formalizing domestic work,[16] which would mean not just legal parity with other occupations, but employers' compliance with labor laws. For example, in the United States, advocates succeeded in getting a "domestic workers' bill of rights" passed in several states. Enforcement, however, is still lacking. Since the early 2000s, several Latin American countries have passed laws to protect domestic workers' labor rights, including Argentina, Brazil, and Peru.[17] Even more have signed the ILO Convention 189 on the rights of domestic workers.[18]

In the Global North, people often conflate the categories of domestic worker and international migrant worker. However, in most Latin American countries, where domestic work is a major source of employment for poor women, most of these women are not immigrants from other countries. In Latin American countries that do have substantial proportions of foreign domestic workers, they are usually from neighboring rather than distant countries. These workers usually do not have the language barriers that exist for migrant domestic workers in other parts of the world, and they may be able to obtain legal status more easily because of trade and migration pacts among countries in the region. Thus, with smaller numbers of transnational migrant women in domestic work, and shared languages, there are perhaps more opportunities for collective organizing or formalization in Latin America than in the Global North.

In the chapters that follow, I shed light on the informal labor market within which domestic workers make decisions, and how factors such as urban geography and family responsibilities shape these decisions. I also consider whether formalization would universally benefit domestic workers, what formalization would entail, and how domestic worker advocates view formalization. What are the chances of formalization for this type of work? Who benefits most from domestic work being arranged informally? How can workers defend their rights and access the benefits to which they are legally entitled? These are empirical questions that look different in the Global South than the Global North, and not only because of the larger relative size of the informal economy. In general, the workers who participated in this study favored formalization, but rather than assuming workers support formalization in every case, we should ask them.

In summary, paid domestic work occupies a unique position in contemporary capitalist economies. As part of social reproduction, it lies outside of the production process and is valued less than productive work. It also differs from other jobs in its location within the private household and its production of use value, not surplus value. As part of the informal economy, and one of the worst-paid jobs for women, domestic employment is difficult to regulate and serves as a means of survival for those whose only alternatives are other informal jobs or informal self-employment. But to understand fully why this type of work remains so exploitative, we must also attend to the local, colonial, and precapitalist histories of the place in which it unfolds: in this case, Ecuador.

The Case of Ecuador: Highlighting Social Class

Ecuador, located in northwest South America and embraced by the Pacific Ocean on the west and the Amazon River in the east, has a population of nearly 16 million people. The country is divided into four geographic regions, which have distinct cultures and demographics. These are the *costa* (coast), *sierra* (Andean mountain region), *oriente* (Amazonian region), and the Galápagos archipelago. The primary site of my research is coastal Guayaquil, whose metropolitan area is home to approximately 3 million people, making it the largest city in Ecuador. It is estimated that 20 percent of Ecuador's domestic workers live in Guayaquil (Wong 2017). In a trend that is widespread throughout Latin America, Ecuador began to urbanize rapidly in the mid-twentieth century. More than 60 percent of Ecuadorians live in cities, and the proportion of urban versus rural population is expected to continue to grow through at least 2050, at which point three-quarters of Ecuadorians will be urban residents.[19] This population shift, along with the shrinking of formal employment in recent decades as employers drive down wages and increase job precarity (Castillo 2000), means that urban informal employment will probably remain steady or expand.[20] Regardless of the overall size of informal employment, the number of full-time domestic workers is dropping, a phenomenon that I aim to explain in this book through an examination of workers' experiences.

My book addresses contemporary domestic employment, but the histories of Ecuador, the Andean region, and the former Spanish and Portuguese colonies in the Americas are relevant to workers' rights and conditions today and the chances for improvement. The colonial roots of domestic work in Latin America distinguish it from other regions, in which domestic work is new or resurgent (some parts of East Asia), embedded in caste systems (India), associated traditionally with only the very elite (Britain), or confined historically to particular regions and types of cities (United States).[21] Spanish and Creole (*criollo*) elite households in colonial Latin America included indigenous, African, and mixed-race servants and slaves, in a variation on the feudal relations in precapitalist Europe. Servants received room and board and clothing rather than wages, and employers were *patrones* (literally, patrons), obligated to care for and "civilize" people over whom they exerted tremendous power. As time went on and domestic servants were hired in middle-class as well as elite homes, the stereotypes of civilized employers and backward domestic workers continued to affect intrahousehold dynamics and laws treating domestic employment. The stigma associated with domestic work today draws on the long tradition of inequality between household employees and their employers, and on images of domestic workers as women who are dirty, dark-skinned, and inferior.[22]

Many if not most domestic employment relationships in Guayaquil, where I focus my research, are not cross-race relationships. Employers' families and workers all tend to fit in the category of mestizo as people of mixed indigenous, European, and possibly African ancestry. Even so, the stigma of what I call "embodied inequality" is strong enough that I would describe domestic worker as a racialized identity regardless of the ethnicity or appearance of the people so employed (see chapter 2). This racialization makes people laugh at the idea of a white domestic worker, as in the sketch I described at the beginning of this chapter. The legacy of colonialism and racial and status categories that have evolved over time in Latin America is distinct (Feliu 2014). The urban domestic workforce in the United States, for example, has been characterized by ethnic change and turnover. European immigrant women and native-born U.S. black women were the prototypical paid domestic workers, and after each group found pathways out of domestic work, they were replaced (after a period of declining domestic employment rates) with immigrant workers who occupied different positions in the racial order than their predecessors. In Ecuador, the same ethnic groups—indigenous, Afro-descendant, and mestizo—have predominated in domestic employment since the colonial period, although there is not much historical scholarship on this case. A large proportion are internal migrants from the countryside to the cities, or from smaller to larger cities (Radcliffe 1999; see also chapter 3, table 3.2).

The particular forms of relationships across lines of social class are an essential piece of the puzzle of domestic worker exploitation in Ecuador, as is the evolution of legal rights for these workers. We cannot draw a straight line from colonial social and economic structures to the contemporary period, as different political and legal systems have left their mark on domestic employment. In South American countries, liberal postcolonial regimes institutionalized labor rights that excluded women domestic workers, thereby cementing the image of male workers as the bearers of these rights (Pérez and Hutchison 2016). The echoes of the past linger, with employers taking on the identity of benevolent civilizers in a peculiar employment relation that incorporates earlier ideas of patronage and servitude.

In previous versions of the Ecuadorian Labor Code, or Código del Trabajo,[23] domestic workers were treated as an exceptional case with inferior protections and labor rights compared to other workers. Until the 2000s, the minimum wage was lower for domestic workers, the maximum number of work hours was not regulated, and domestic employees were not guaranteed vacation or severance pay (Blofield 2012, 34). Article 262, in the section of the Labor Code pertaining to domestic employment, allowed for potential exploitation of domestic workers by stating that any aspect of the work not mentioned in the law or outlined in a contract between employer and employee would be governed by "the local custom" (*la costumbre del lugar*). However, when a new constitution was drafted in 2008, all workers were guaranteed the same rights, bringing the existing Labor Code into conflict with the Constitution.

For several years in the second decade of the 2000s, overlapping with the period of my study, Ecuadorian lawmakers seemed poised to write a new Labor Code. This did not come to pass. Instead, the existing Labor Code underwent a piecemeal reform, including a new article that addressed domestic workers' rights. Article 269 now sits alongside articles that outline a parallel set of inferior rights for domestic workers, and yet guarantees to "domestic employees and workers the same benefits as any other general worker." So the very text of the code contradicts itself. This additional article went into effect in 2012, after declarations in support of domestic workers by President Rafael Correa starting around 2009, and sporadic labor inspections of employers' homes to enforce the minimum wage and decent working conditions. Article 269 mandates a forty-hour work week and entitles workers to minimum wage, vacation, overtime pay, and social security, without specifically mentioning other benefits such as maternity leave. Despite being granted the same rights and benefits as other workers, however, domestic workers are still vulnerable owing to the lack of enforcement of the law and its limited impact on the informal ways domestic employment relations are negotiated, managed, and terminated. The tug-of-war between the still-relevant "local custom" and contemporary labor laws keeps most domestic work informal despite being subject to regulation.

The number of full-time domestic workers, as well as their share of women's employment, has begun falling in Latin America. In 2000, 19 percent of employed women in the region were domestic workers, with about the same percentage of Ecuadorian women workers in this category. In 2010, domestic workers made up 17.4 percent of Latin American women workers, and 14 percent in 2016 (ILO 2013, 2016a, 4). In Ecuador there has been an overall decrease as well, with domestic workers falling from 18 percent of women workers in 2001 to 8.4 percent in 2013 and just under 6 percent in 2015 (Reyes and Camacho 2001; OIT 2018; INEC 2016). In 2001, there were approximately 249,000 domestic workers in the country, and in 2015 there were around 193,000, according to INEC, the Ecuadorian Census Institute (INEC 2016; PAHO 2011). This represents a decrease of about 23 percent in the number of domestic workers over a decade and a half. The reported number of domestic workers hovered around an average of 192,000 during 2007–15. From 2009 to 2011, when President Correa's administration publicly asserted domestic workers' equal labor rights, and even conducted some scattershot labor inspections in private homes in Guayaquil, we see the most volatility in the numbers of domestic workers.

In this period, the official number of workers dropped by 62,000, which suggests that the uncertainty around enforcement of domestic workers' rights created hesitation among employers and workers to enter into these employment arrangements (INEC 2016).

Alternatively, this dip in the domestic worker population numbers could represent an underreporting of domestic work as enforcement of labor rights ramped up. It could also reflect the rise of part-time work for multiple employers, which could cause workers not to identify domestic work as a full-time occupation. Whatever the reason for the official drop around 2010, the domestic worker population recovered its previous size around 2012–13, when the government began paying less attention to the plight of these workers (see figure 1).

There is almost no scholarly research on domestic workers in Ecuador. The literature on domestic work elsewhere features two narratives, one that fits the Global North and one that fits Latin America. The literature on the United States and Europe tells a story of the resurgence of domestic employment in those locations, beginning in about the 1980s, after a period of decline. Scholars argue that the tasks of social reproduction increasingly involve paid workers in the Global North (Bakker 2007; Ehrenreich and Hochschild 2002; Gregson and Lowe 2005; Kofman 2012; Milkman, Reese, and Roth 1998; Sassen 2001). This narrative does not reflect trends in Latin America, where domestic employment, widespread in the colonial and postcolonial periods, has continued over the years, transforming

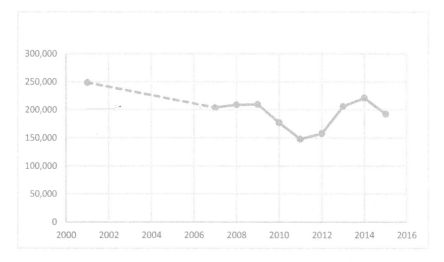

FIGURE 1.   Change in domestic worker population in Ecuador, 2007–15. The dotted line represents the change from 2001 to 2007. Source: Instituto Nacional de Estadística y Censos (INEC).

from unwaged servitude to waged labor (Goldstein 2003). There has not been a resurgence in Latin America; domestic work has been a constant feature of home life for those who can afford it, especially in the cities. Since 2000, however, as the number of domestic employees rose in the Global North,[24] the number of domestic workers in Ecuador and Latin America as a whole dropped.

How can we explain these opposing trends? Paid domestic work in the United States and other developed countries increased because of the increase and intensification of middle- and upper-class women's full-time work, increasing class inequality, and larger numbers of immigrant women willing to do domestic work, especially in larger cities (Milkman, Reese, and Roth 1998; Sassen 2001). Meanwhile, in Latin America, rising education levels and the expansion of the service sector meant that women could hope for jobs that were less stigmatized (if not higher paying) than domestic employment. Women especially looked to avoid live-in domestic work.[25] Occupational inheritance, in which daughters follow their mothers into domestic work, also seems to be less common today, although statistics are not available. In addition, the purchasing power of middle-class households dropped in many countries in recent decades, leading to a steep decline in available full-time domestic work positions, despite overall growth in the population of women workers in the region (ILO 2016a, 4). So a larger proportion of today's domestic workers than in the past are part-time workers, who may not be counted in surveys nor identify with domestic work as an occupation.

Another difference from the Global North is worth repeating. As in the three largest countries in Latin America (Brazil, Mexico, and Colombia), domestic workers in Ecuador and most other Latin American countries are much more likely to be internal rather than international migrants.[26] Literature that conflates domestic worker with immigrant worker cannot simply be applied to these cases without scrutiny. Most studies emerging from the Global North focus on international migrant domestic workers. When viewed in the context of existing research, the case of Ecuador can help us to analytically separate the exploitation inherent in domestic employment from the specific situation of immigrant workers.

Aims of the Book

My book differs from other recent research on domestic work in three main ways. First, I describe social reproduction as the crux of domestic workers' exploitation and potential resistance. Second, I insist on the importance of the urban informal employment context. Third, I focus on social class in addition to—and more than—race and gender, which are more commonly written about. I am not saying that class is the most important aspect of domestic work, but it is the least explored in recent research on the topic. Following the lead of Latin American scholars, I consider cross-class relationships in domestic employment as a labor relation rooted in, yet not identical to, colonial social formations. Combining these three perspectives—returning to social reproduction, bringing informality into the discussion, and foregrounding class—we can uncover how and why Latin American domestic employment subjugates workers and resists change.

While my goal is to uncover general patterns of domestic work and propose solutions to the dilemmas of workers that may apply to other locations, this study is rooted in a specific time and place: in Ecuador (with a focus on the largest city, Guayaquil, though some data from other cities is included), in the years 2010–18. Low-wage labor markets and working conditions, while shaped by globally connected economies at the macro level, are experienced by workers as local phenomena and should be examined with attention to the local. Urban geography, patterns and prevalence of internal migration, unpaid family work, and employment alternatives all influence the decisions of workers and employers. My experience conducting research in and on Ecuador since 1999 allows me to provide an in-depth portrait of domestic work grounded in knowledge of this local context.

It is surprising that Ecuador has been virtually ignored in the existing scholarship on domestic employment, as it has characteristics that make it similar to other Latin American countries. These characteristics include a colonial history of domestic service, a large proportion of the workforce laboring in the informal economy, and high rates of urbanization through internal migration. On the other hand, the left-leaning political regime during the period of the study makes it a theoretically interesting case for examining labor rights. Ultimately, it seems that the socialist rhetoric of the Ecuadorian government did not change the realities for domestic workers, who labored under conditions similar to those in neighboring Colombia and Peru, where conservative politicians ruled. In analyzing this case, I want to bring attention to understudied aspects of domestic work: local labor market supply and demand, body and embodiment, urban space, informal employment, and workers' unpaid labor at home.

Returning to the relationship between reproduction and production, and the political economy of domestic work, I see domestic employment in Latin America as a modified version of a precapitalist form of work, rooted in colonialism, which continues under a capitalist mode of production. According to Peruvian social theorist Aníbal Quijano, the Eurocentric modernity of Latin America is based on persistent colonial categories of "inferior and superior, irrational and rational, primitive and civilized" (2000, 344), distinctions that are crystallized in the domestic work employment relation. Servitude remains a part of Latin American societies, but now under modern capitalism and for a salary (Quijano

2000, 348). Control of labor, along with racial hierarchies, is one of the main forms of power in Latin America, and Quijano dubbed the interlocking systems of domination and classification "the coloniality of power." This coloniality "manifests itself daily for domestic workers in both the private and the public sphere" (Bernardino-Costa 2011, 36).

The major change in this employment relation over time has been the move from in-kind servitude or slavery to wage labor, but this labor still takes place outside of the production process. Domestic employment exemplifies Karl Polanyi's theory that precapitalist social and economic relations are embedded in modern capitalism—both in reproduction and production ([1944] 2001). As Quijano writes, a linear trajectory from precapitalism to capitalism does not fit the experiences of the Third World, and workers who do not belong to the salaried proletariat are often left out of working-class struggles (2000, 363, 372). A focus on social reproduction in Latin America shows how paid domestic labor makes possible the wage labor of employers outside the home—especially women—and thus sustains the capitalist mode of production. Yet domestic work is organized informally despite being dependent on an employer: it is not a typical encounter between capital and labor.

This form of work is wrapped up in stigma, racialization, servitude, false kinship ("she's like one of the family"), and unequal class relations that are rooted in the conquest and colonization by Spain and the subsequent evolution of social, legal, and economic structures. To historicize today's domestic employment relations is not to say that this work exists outside of modernity or is unnecessary in the modern world. But compared to other occupations, domestic work has an unusual relationship to capital, is difficult to regulate due to its informality, and is wrapped up in systems of personalized class domination. These unique aspects of the work may require new theories and new forms of organizing and advocacy for workers' rights. I suggest that we can critique the production/reproduction hierarchy without saying, as some feminist political economists do, that these are essentially the same types of processes (Ferguson 2008).

Research Questions

Informed by this background, and my aim to make an intellectual contribution while also collaborating with domestic worker advocates to produce empirical evidence they can use in their work, two questions guide this book:

1) What is it about the exploitation in domestic work that makes it unique in comparison to other types of work? Put more bluntly, why is this such a bad job?

2) What are some strategies for improving working conditions or creating pathways out of domestic work?

To answer these questions, I use a variety of research methods, attending to aspects of domestic employees' working conditions that have not received much attention. I do not presume to argue that I know best how to pursue justice and dignity for domestic workers. However, evidence from this research—which foregrounds the perspectives of domestic workers themselves—can help suggest new strategies or support existing strategies used by advocates.

Whereas many have proposed one-size-fits-all policies to improve domestic workers' lives, I want to flip the analytical process by beginning with the local. In addition, I draw first on concepts that have emerged in similar rather than disparate cultural environments. In answering my research questions, I emphasize the local context and the utility—the necessity, even—of building on theories and research from Latin America.[27] I've discussed above some of the shortcomings of theories generated from data collected in the United States and Europe when applied to Latin America. I purposely lean more heavily here on the work of scholars theorizing Latin American realities. Much of this work is recent, and only available in Spanish and Portuguese, perhaps explaining why these contributions have not received due recognition and exposure in the English-language literature on domestic work.

My approach involves working with, learning from, and investigating issues suggested by the activists on the front lines of domestic worker organizing in Ecuador. The new knowledge gleaned along the way I owe in large part to them. The data presented in chapter 3 on social security and other benefits and working conditions, and chapter 4 on women's labor market trajectories, were collected using participatory action research (PAR) methodology. In this approach, academic researchers collaborate with community members—in this case, domestic worker activists and advocates—to design studies that address concrete needs (Ampudia 2016; Brydon-Miller 1997; McTaggart 1998; Whyte 1989).

Beginning in 2014, I worked with the members of the Asociación de Trabajadoras Remuneradas del Hogar (ATRH, which translates to Association of Remunerated Household Workers), with input from their major funder. ATRH, based in Guayaquil, is the pioneer organization for domestic workers' rights in Ecuador. Although other local organizations around the country assist domestic workers, there are few with a primary focus on this type of work. (After many years of struggle, ATRH has recently created a national union for domestic workers in Ecuador, which involves many of the protagonists of ATRH.) I had previously conducted research with the organization's members and in its space, but the new projects we embarked on represented a more profound and reciprocal collaboration. Together, we decided on the research questions that would provide them with the data they needed to advocate for domestic workers, and together, we designed the research instruments—surveys and interview guides—and strategies for identifying and recruiting participants. In the process, I learned more about what mattered to the members of the organization and about their outreach style, and they learned more about the principles and techniques of social research. We produced reports in Spanish that were geared at gaining the attention of government agencies and nongovernmental organizations (NGOs), and I could also use the data and analysis in academic publications. The PAR methodology seems well suited to this topic, as domestic worker populations are difficult to reach and organizations need robust data that goes beyond the testimonies and anecdotes that they often present to funders and government officials. Despite this natural fit, most researchers of domestic work do not make use of PAR.

In the chapters that follow, I begin with the abstract ideal of what a domestic worker should be (chapter 1) and then progress in ever-widening circles with real workers at the center: beginning with the role of bodies and embodiment in work in private homes (chapter 2), then conditions for these workers in Guayaquil (chapter 3), then zooming out to labor trajectories of women in different cities (chapter 4) and the workers' collective organizing at the national level (chapter 5). By keeping workers' experiences at the center of this analysis, I highlight the guiding principles behind their behaviors and decisions, which in their own words, are *lucha, trabajo,* and *sacrificio.* These words—struggle, work, and sacrifice—sum up women's commitment to maintaining themselves and their families, and their search for dignity amid the dust.

IN SEARCH OF THE IDEAL WORKER

Word of mouth is the most common way that domestic workers and employ-ers find each other (García López 2012; Pereyra 2015; Toledo González 2013; Moreno Zúñiga 2007). Recommendations move in both directions: employers prefer to have a worker recommended by someone they know, and workers want to get a sense of whether the employer will be a "good" one.

Of course, not every employer or worker has extensive social networks that can facilitate these recommendations. Another possibility lies in the classified sec-tion of the local newspaper, which is now accessible online. Employers can place ads directly, and so can agencies that attempt to match employers and workers, which generally charge employers for this service. Although classified ads are a less-common way of finding domestic employment arrangements, they can tell us something about available positions and what employers say they are looking for in a worker. Classified advertisements "have to be specific enough to save both parties from wasting their time while being terse enough to be affordable . . . so every word needs to tell" (Humez, Humez, and Flynn 2010). These ads have a recognizable style and format, and because of their brevity they condense shared meanings down to their essence. I found that the language ads use to describe the ideal worker corresponds to that used by employers in their word-of-mouth searches as well, as described in research on Latin America (Canevaro 2008).

Who is the ideal worker? I explore this question based on content analysis of more than a thousand classified advertisements from two different years in the last decade. The ads appeared in *El Universo*, which is the major local newspaper for Guayaquil, Ecuador's largest city, and is also the national newspaper with the largest circulation. Using these "help wanted" ads to dissect the image of the ideal worker, this chapter represents the point of view of potential employers and domestic employment agencies acting as intermediaries. The rest of the book centers on domestic workers and their perspectives. But in the hiring process, employers' vision of the ideal worker matters more than the workers' own ideas about what makes a good employee. Here I argue that the ideal worker has a specific set of personal characteristics (age, abilities, etc.; see also García Sainz, Santos Pérez, and Valencia Olivero 2014 on the intangible qualities of the ideal domestic worker, such as being "affectionate" or "quick"). However, the reduced number of advertisements over time is correlated to the shrinking of the domestic labor force, which may mean employers cannot afford to be as picky as they were in the past. While overtly demeaning terms and illegally low salaries have all but disappeared from the ads today, we should not assume that working conditions have improved. In fact, the information I present in subsequent chapters confirms that, while the language used publicly to refer to domestic work may have shifted, the actual behavior of employers in hiring and managing workers has not changed much.

The ideal worker and the ideal domestic employment arrangement, as communicated by the ads, illustrate all three of this book's main themes: social reproduction, informality, and class relations. Paid domestic work, like other forms of social reproduction, invokes stereotypes about gender roles and involves tasks and qualities that connote femininity. Gendered assumptions about social reproduction are embedded in the ads, which nearly always label the desired domestic worker as a woman: *cocinera* (female cook), *niñera* (female nanny/babysitter), *empleada doméstica* (female domestic employee). Work arrangements, including those that begin with an ad in *El Universo*, are usually informal and escape regulation by labor law. The class relations of contemporary domestic employment are also sometimes visible in the text of the help wanted ads. Some ads refer explicitly to the high status of the employers' family (e.g., "an important family") and some indicate status indirectly, for example, mentioning where the family resides, almost always in upper-class or middle-class neighborhoods of Guayaquil, including exclusive gated communities. The class relations of domestic employment, rooted in precapitalist and colonial socioeconomic structures, also appear in references to *trato* (treatment) of the worker by employers. When employers emphasize trato, personal treatment, rather than pay and benefits, they hearken back to patronage relationships based on personal connections rather than labor laws (Pérez and Canevaro 2016). Even today, emotion, care, respect, and honor loom large in domestic employment. Sometimes domestic workers decide not to push for more because "at least the boss is good to me" (Vervecken 2013).

Historical Context

Over the period covered by my research (2010–18), domestic worker advocates and (sometimes) government agencies promoted a vision of formalizing domestic work by guaranteeing the minimum wage and legal benefits such as social security coverage. An analysis of ads from two different points in time allows us to see whether they reflect this push for formalization. As time passes, are more employers promising domestic workers formal work arrangements, as required by law? Are ideas about trato and gender consistent over time? The reality is more complex. We see fewer advertisements in the more recent sample of newspapers, which could indicate that informality has increased, there are fewer workers overall, employers have gone underground in their search for workers, or that newspapers and their websites are not preferred sources of information. Specific mentions of trato decrease, and more neutral terms replace highly gendered ones, indicating (at least on the surface) a break with traditional ideas about domestic service. Another historical trend, toward live-out and part-time arrangements, appears in the ads' texts.[1]

To get a sense of how the content of classified advertisements seeking domestic workers changed over time, I collected ads published in the Guayaquil-based daily newspaper *El Universo* from two years: 2010 and 2016.[2] These years correspond to particular social, economic, and political conjunctures that are worth mentioning. Rafael Correa Delgado became president in 2007, ushering in a new era of political discourse that was populist, inclusive, and tinged with socialist lingo and worldviews. One of his government's slogans, *La patria ya es de todos* (The homeland now belongs to everyone) promoted the idea that previously marginalized groups—people of color, the poor, women—would now be able to participate more actively in the affairs of the nation through a process called "the citizens' revolution." By 2010, the new government had substantially expanded social programs and bureaucracy, mostly based on surging oil revenues.

One of the government's public campaigns aimed to change perceptions of domestic work and improve working conditions in this sector. At that time, I saw on the streets of Guayaquil a government-owned van wrapped in high-quality photos of a woman doing domestic work. The image was garnished with slogans communicating the Correa administration's support for "Dignified Domestic Work" (ILO 2014a). The situation in 2016 was different. President Correa's final term would end after the elections in 2017, and the domestic work campaigns had largely disappeared.[3] Government spending seemed to have expanded beyond capacity, as oil revenues dipped and public employees sometimes went months without being paid.[4] An earthquake of 7.8 magnitude hit the Ecuadorian coast in April 2016, compounding the problems of poor people in the coastal provinces from which most of Guayaquil's domestic workers hail: Esmeraldas,

Los Ríos, Manabí, and Guayas. Looking at ads from this time allows us to assess whether the pro–domestic worker rhetoric, and the somewhat sporadic moves toward formalizing this type of employment, showed up in the ways that employers expressed their hiring preferences.

Classified Advertisements

Publications on domestic work in Latin America almost never mention "help wanted" advertisements.[5] Likewise, studies of other regions tend to overlook these ads. One book on paid domestic work in Britain begins with excerpts of classified ads, but does not analyze them in much depth (Gregson and Lowe 1994). Although the rise of the Internet has reduced the quantity of classified advertisements in newspapers worldwide, and these texts have fallen out of vogue with researchers, there are precedents for studying the ads.

Language in classified ads is highly standardized and characterized by "formulaic repetition" rather than creativity (Bruthiaux 1994, ix). This lack of variation means that observable shifts in the common language of specific types of ads are meaningful rather than just evidence of idiosyncratic ad writing. It is reasonable to ask whether commonly occurring words and phrases are suggested or imposed by staff at the newspaper who receive ad content from customers (in this case, employers or agencies). However, in one experiment in the United States, newspaper staff made no editorial alterations to many ads the researcher purposely wrote in nonstandard ways (Bruthiaux 1994, 184–85), and an *El Universo* manager I interviewed confirmed this was their policy as well.

Whether "classified help wanted ads contain a large percentage of the open jobs in local labor markets" is an empirical question (Walsh, Johnson, and Sugarman 1975, 9) that I do not attempt to answer here.[6] In one study of two U.S. cities, researchers found that "a small number of employers accounted for a disproportionate number of the want ads" (Walsh, Johnson, and Sugarman 1975, 27). While this may seem less likely for domestic work, where each household is an employer, it could be the case if most ads were placed by agencies. And ads placed may not represent all openings these agencies are trying to fill.[7] Thus, rather than analyzing the ads to learn about hiring processes more generally, or the local labor market for domestic employment, I focus on how the ads describe the ideal or desired worker.

I interviewed two employment agency owners in Guayaquil in 2018. They told me that they do not advertise in newspaper classified sections. Their businesses advertised on the Internet, and they worked through word of mouth. They both agreed that most domestic employment arrangements are made without the help of agencies. These agency owners noted that especially attractive ads would mention, for example, foreign employers (thought to pay more), or small family size, and were usually placed by agencies. These agency representatives described the ideal employee in much the same way the ads did, and confirmed that they followed employers' requirements for workers' age, origin, and appearance.[8]

Volume of Advertisements

The most striking finding in comparing the ads from 2010 with those from 2016 is the substantial decrease in the number of ads. The sample from 2010 had 795 ads for domestic employment, and the sample from 2016 had 256, a decrease of 68 percent. There was also a change in who placed the ads. In the more recent group of ads, 19 percent explicitly claimed to represent employment agencies, compared with just a handful from 2010. However, given the repetition of certain carefully crafted, extremely attractive job postings, I suspect that some ads that do not mention agencies directly may indeed be placed by them. It seems unlikely that a nonagency private employer would place the same ad nearly every week throughout an entire year: these repeated ads are likely from agencies. The ads that appear to be from agencies, without explicitly stating so, also increased between the 2010 and 2016 samples.

Why are there so many fewer ads in 2016? A few explanations seem to fit the situation. In Ecuador and Latin America, the number of employed domestic workers for this period also decreased, as I mentioned in the introduction. If there are simply fewer instances of domestic employment, this decreased activity would be reflected in the classified ads. There may also be a connection to the type of employment arrangement. We know that throughout Latin America, live-in domestic work arrangements are generally less common now than in the past (Brites 2013; ILO 2016a). Perhaps employers are more likely to use every means possible to locate a full-time, live-in domestic worker than when they search for a part-time worker. A full-time, live-in worker will become a part of the employers' household, possibly for many years, requiring a more thorough hiring search. Thus, part-time daily or hourly work may have an especially informal hiring process. Since part-time employers are unlikely to enroll workers in social security or pay them the legal minimum wage, they may increasingly shy away from such ads.[9] This informality could thus help explain the declining number of ads for domestic employment.

An executive I spoke with at the newspaper confirmed that classified ads in all categories had decreased during the time period I am studying and surmised that this is due to other, more informal means of advertising on the Internet as well as an actual decrease in available jobs.[10] The domestic employment sector had contracted more dramatically than other occupations, according to this executive. Although *El Universo* has the largest circulation in the country—reportedly printing an average of fifty thousand copies per day—newspapers everywhere are losing readers.

Reduced readership, or a decline in the value placed on newspapers as sources of information with the rise of the Internet and social media, may lead to fewer ads, even when newspapers place their ads on the Internet as well as in the print edition.

What Employers Seek

How do employers and agencies refer to the position for which they are hiring? And why does it matter? Domestic worker organizations and advocates often reject some of the most common ways of referring to the occupation, including "empleada" and "empleada doméstica" (domestic worker or employee). As the members of Guayaquil-based domestic worker organization Asociación de Tra-bajadoras Remuneradas del Hogar (ATRH) like to say, they do not want to be called "domestic" as it implies that they are domesticated, like obedient animals. ATRH has insisted on the long but accurate title of "remunerated household worker" (*trabajadora remunerada del hogar*) and similar efforts to update and dignify terms used for these workers have emerged in countries such as Bolivia and Peru. In everyday talk, a variety of words are used, some of which symboli-cally undermine the status of a domestic worker as a worker.

The job titles used in the advertisements were similar for both time peri-ods. Most of the ads, regardless of year, were seeking a nanny (niñera), cook (cocinera), or general domestic employee (empleada or empleada doméstica). However, I found a greater variety of terms used in the 2010 ads. The terms in 2016 also reflect newer language labeling these employees as workers rather than servants. For example, middle- and upper-class Ecuadorians commonly call domestic workers "girls" (*muchachas*), and the word *muchacha* was used in forty-six ads from 2010. By 2016, only one of the ads referred to a domestic worker as a muchacha. The use in the ads of the more professional-sounding "domestic assistant" (*asistente doméstica*) tripled from 2010 to 2016, now rep-resenting 12 percent of the ads. The eclipsing of the demeaning "muchacha" by terms like "empleada doméstica" or "asistente doméstica" may be related to the consciousness-raising of organizations and government agencies and may indi-cate employers' and employment brokers' knowledge of attempts to formalize the work. Of course, using new, more respectful terminology in help wanted ads may not—and I argue does not—translate into better treatment, pay, or working conditions for employees. Gender is also routinely specified in help wanted ads, for domestic work and other types of employment. This gender discrimination is facilitated by Spanish grammar rules, which require that nouns (such as type of worker) be assigned a gender.[11]

Employers are almost always seeking female domestic workers, but do they prefer younger or older workers? While domestic workers are sometimes younger than the legal minimum working age of fifteen, in the classified ads analyzed, none explicitly sought underage workers. However, they are often quite specific about the age of worker preferred. Ecuador's labor code protects against age discrimination in pay, but not in hiring, so it is perfectly legal to exclude people from jobs based on their age.

In 2010, 14 percent of the ads in my sample mentioned a specific age or age range. In 2016, 41 percent of the ads mentioned age. This is a large increase that shows employers becoming more particular about the age of employee they seek, even as the types of positions did not change much between the earlier and the later periods. In ads mentioning age in 2010, 69 percent gave a maximum age that would be considered, and in 2016, 75 percent of the ads did this. Other ads did not give a maximum age, but implied that employers preferred younger workers, by using the word "young" (*joven*), for example. The proportion of ads that mentioned a minimum age but did not give a maximum (e.g., "25 and up") was 15 percent in 2010, but dropped to 2 percent in 2016. So over time, ads grew more specific about age, and more likely to list a maximum age. Agency owners confirmed in interviews that they and their clients used an ideal age range to recruit for specific positions.

The preferred age range of the ideal worker changed over time, with ads in the 2016 sample more likely to specifically seek younger workers. In 2010, 40 percent of the ads sought a worker who was under thirty years old; six years later a full 65 percent of the ads sought a worker under thirty. The percentage of ads specifying a preference for workers over thirty was relatively stable, at 21 percent in 2010 and 23 percent in 2016. As for age ranges overlapping the under-thirty and over-thirty categories (jobs seeking workers between twenty-five and forty years old), these were three times more prevalent in 2010 than in 2016. The bottom line is that, in 2016, classified ads seeking domestic workers were much more likely to mention a precise age range; and those that did, strongly favored younger workers.[12] This is not the only type of work in which youth is highly valued; in help wanted ads throughout Latin America, the most commonly targeted age group is eighteen to thirty-five (Benavides Passos 2010).

How can we explain the greater proportion of recent ads seeking younger workers? Part of the increase could be related to the changes in terminology discussed above. If "muchacha," which implies youth, is no longer an acceptable way of referring to domestic workers, then an advertiser may choose a more formal term for the position, such as "empleada doméstica," while also mentioning a younger age range. Younger domestic workers may be favored for many reasons: they are seen as physically stronger, more trainable, and less likely to have family entanglements (spouses or children who could interfere with their work schedules). This general preference for younger workers, however, does not explain the increase in younger ages mentioned over time. It could be that employers are becoming more explicit about their preferences: they are now more likely to mention age in the ads. As the labor pool shrinks, however, employers may not be able to behave in strict accordance with these stated preferences. There may be a gap between the ideal workers as described in ads and the real workers who are actually hired.

Domestic worker advocates and former domestic workers I spoke with often said that employers preferred workers from the countryside because they saw them as harder working, more naïve, and more submissive. For this reason, I coded the advertisements for references to the geographic origins of potential workers. I found that a similar proportion of ads mentioned preferences for workers from a specific geographic location (usually, for workers from the countryside, *el campo*) in the 2010 and 2016 ads. However, the 2010 ads were more specific, listing a wider variety of preferences, for example, requesting a cook from the province of Manabí, which neighbors Guayas—the province in which Guayaquil is located—to the north. The stereotype that Manabí's cuisine is flavorful and hearty makes this preference unsurprising.[13] Internal migration has often been a part of the story of domestic employment in Ecuador (Radcliffe 1999), as in other Latin American countries. But the ideal of a worker from el campo, from the more rural *provincias* (provinces) outside of Guayaquil, may be more about demand than supply. In Peru, internal migrants now make up a decreasing percentage of domestic workers (Defensoría del Pueblo 2013), and the same pattern may be unfolding in Ecuador. Of course, these rural-raised workers must exist for employers to hire them, but the reasons that they prefer them stem from stereotypes of rural women as culturally inferior, docile, and uneducated. Such workers would be easier to dominate, or in a charitable yet condescending framework, to "civilize" and "improve" through the employment relation (Cumes 2014).

Employment Arrangements

Paid domestic work generally takes one of three forms: full-time workers live with their employer (an arrangement called *puertas adentro* in Ecuador) or live apart from their employer (*puertas afuera*), or they live apart and work part-time by the day or by the hour (*por días* or *por horas*).[14] Part-time domestic workers may have more than one employer: we don't know how many workers do this, but it is common enough for some social security schemes, including Ecuador's, to accommodate proportional contributions from multiple employers. The trend in Latin America, for the past decade at least, has been toward less live-in work and more live-out and part-time work (Brites 2013; ILO 2016a; Valenzuela and

Sanches 2012). Though we don't have data on the shift in domestic employment arrangements in Ecuador—aside from declining numbers of full-time domestic workers—there are certainly fewer live-in workers than in the past. It is possible that the significant decrease in the number of classified ads seeking domestic workers is connected to this trend. Why go to the trouble to take out an ad if you are only looking for someone to work one day a week? The employee will be spending much less time in your home, so why conduct an exhaustive search? In interviews with employment agencies that place domestic workers, they seemed to confirm this explanation, saying that most of the people who contracted an agency were looking for full-time, live-in workers. Most agencies charge several hundred dollars to place a domestic worker, so agency clients may also have higher incomes than other employers.

Do the classified advertisements reflect changes in the type of domestic employment arrangements in Guayaquil? Yes, there is evidence of a shift, as positions explicitly requiring a worker to live in the employer's home (*puertas adentro*) decreased from 66 percent of the ads in 2010 to 50 percent in 2016. Yet live-in and live-out postings did not simply switch places. The gap created by the decrease in live-in jobs was not filled by live-out positions, which also decreased by half (from 10 percent of ads mentioning *puertas afuera* in 2010 to 5 percent in 2016). The proportion of ads saying that either live-in or live-out arrangements were acceptable held steady at 2 percent for both years, as did the proportion that mentioned other arrangements (e.g., "3 times per week" or "in the afternoons" at 7 percent each year). This consistency in work by the hour or by the day across the six-year gap shows that the shift away from full-time domestic workers and the rise in what the International Labor Organization (ILO) calls "casual" jobs or "mini-jobs" was already happening before 2010, when my earliest set of classified ads appeared (ILO 2016b). But 2016 saw more ads that did not mention the desired employment arrangement, perhaps indicating that employers were willing to negotiate the exact arrangement with the right worker.

Still, the largest proportion of ads in both years are for *puertas adentro* jobs. The subtle preference for workers from outside of Guayaquil may also be at work here. Who would be most likely to be looking for a place to live in a new city, and to pick up a copy of *El Universo* or go onto its website to search for a job on arriving in Guayaquil? A new migrant, perhaps.

One finding stands out: many advertisements from both years do not specify which type of employment arrangement is on offer. In 2010, 20 percent did not include this information, and in 2016, this proportion jumped to 36 percent of the ads. Employers may not mention the mode of employment because they are open to any type of arrangement and want to cast the widest net possible with their advertisement. If this is the case, then employers' flexibility on this point increased over time, as the number of domestic workers decreased. If workers are scarcer, then it makes sense that employers are less choosy about the employment arrangement.

So the shifts reported for Latin America more generally—away from full-time, live-in arrangements and toward greater flexibility in organizing paid domestic work—show up in the classified ads I analyzed. Most ads (80 percent in 2010 and 64 percent in 2016) specify what sort of arrangement employers are seeking, and the largest proportion are seeking live-in workers. Future research should look more at how domestic workers find their jobs, specifically comparing live-in workers with those who live out.[15] Those looking for live-in positions are probably more likely than others to check the classified ads (in print or online) for an employment opportunity.

Salary and Benefits

The most obvious component of working conditions, and one of the main issues that prospective employers and employees must agree on, is the pay. This is another area of change over time. Public campaigns to raise awareness of domestic workers' rights to the minimum wage, overtime pay, vacation time, and social security were gaining steam in 2010. These campaigns were less visible by 2016, yet the increased awareness seems to have remained (see chapter 4). Employers feeling pressured to offer a certain level of salary and benefits will affect employment offers and hiring negotiations. Indeed, in interviews, current and former domestic workers mentioned being fired when employers learned of their legal obligations from information diffused by the government of President Rafael Correa. Knowing this context, we might expect to see better salaries and benefits mentioned in the later ads, or at least fewer mentions of illegally low salaries.

Employment is regulated by Ecuador's constitution, which took effect in 2008, and its Labor Code (Código del Trabajo), which is periodically updated and revised. In addition, Ecuador signed on to the ILO Convention 189 on the rights of domestic workers in 2013, which means the country must bring its laws in line with the convention. However, because of informal arrangements, the contradictions in the documents, and the lack of real enforcement mechanisms for employers who don't comply, the law often conflicts with everyday practice.

How frequently did classified ads mention salary, and did this change over time? The 2010 ads were twice as likely to list a dollar amount for salary (usually monthly, but occasionally weekly), at 36 percent, compared to 18 percent six years later.[16] Just as some ads did not mention whether the position required a worker to live in the employers' home, some did not give a specific salary. A similar proportion of ads from both years claim to offer a fair or good salary, with 11 percent in 2010 and 12 percent in 2016 mentioning salary that is described as "good," "excellent," or in one hyperbolic listing, "the best salary on the market." Many of the ads that used this language appeared to be placed by agencies. Still, most ads did not explicitly address the important issue of salary. Even if a salary is listed in an ad, what a worker actually gets paid may vary, and we know from the narratives of domestic workers that employers sometimes reduce salaries or pile on additional tasks after employment begins. In our survey (chapter 4), some employed domestic workers reported earning as little as eighty dollars per month for full-time work, which is far below the minimum wage. We found wide ranges in reported salary, with median monthly wages just below minimum wage.

In 2010, the monthly minimum wage for full-time work was $240, and in 2016 it was $366. Did any ads offer jobs that paid less than the legal minimum wage? Yes: in 2010, 8 percent of the ads listed salaries below the legal minimum wage (*sueldo básico*). Yet no ad from 2016 did this.[17] This suggests that, even if employers knew they could not or would not pay the minimum wage, they did not advertise this information. Awareness campaigns about domestic workers' right to minimum wage, as well as the controls that the newspaper claims to have in place, could explain why ads stopped mentioning salaries below this standard. In both years studied, the average wage offered in the ads was higher than the minimum wage at the time: $150 higher than minimum wage in 2010, and $60 higher in 2016.[18] Perhaps the dip in the mentions of salary is due to employers' growing awareness of their obligations and their hesitance to outwardly flout the law.

Increased awareness among employers of their legal obligation to enroll domestic workers in the social security system, and contribute on their behalf, also may have affected the content of ads. Benefits were mentioned more often in later ads. The proportion of ads in 2010 referring to legal benefits (e.g., vacation time) was 4 percent, and this proportion went up to 8 percent in 2016. Social security was mentioned twice as frequently in the 2016 ads, but still in a dismally small percentage of the ads, at just 2 percent. In both samples, live-ins are likely to be guaranteed permission to leave the home every two weeks (the legal minimum) rather than every week. In both the earlier and the later samples, nonsalary benefits are nearly absent.

Wages seem to be a straightforward indicator that an employment relation is in place, and that the domestic worker is indeed a worker. However, language in the ads I studied hearkens back to the precapitalist and colonial-era roots of domestic work in Ecuador. The mention of trato, or treatment of the worker by the employer, highlights the informality of paid domestic work. There are no strict policies or rules to tell employers how to act, which means that they may fall back on the culturally acceptable roles of patron, benefactor, and "civilizing" force in their relations with domestic workers, particularly those who live in the household (Cumes 2014; García López 2012). As we know, the discourse of treating domestic workers as "part of the family" can be used to obscure the labor relation and to exploit workers (Blackett 1998; Canevaro 2008; Rollins 1985). The culture of servitude is not explicitly part of the salary negotiation, but it is a meaningful part of working conditions. In fact, an attorney I interviewed said that in his experience, about 70 percent of domestic workers filing legal claims against their employers do so because of maltreatment (including physical or verbal abuse), and only 30 percent because of issues related to pay or employment benefits.[19]

There were many more references to trato in the earlier group of advertisements. A total of 110 of the 795 ads from 2010 augment or replace claims about salaries with reference to the treatment that workers will receive, describing it as "good," "like family," "friendly," or "respectful." Only 3 of the 256 ads from 2016 do this. Why the virtual disappearance of references to trato in the more recent ads? Perhaps the awareness campaigns, and the sometimes-successful denunciations of employers by former workers, have made an impact. Rather than viewing it as an extension of family structure or a personal relationship, more employers may have begun seeing domestic work as a labor relation. But based on the accounts of domestic workers in this research, it seems unlikely that a sea change has occurred in employer attitudes. I suspect that the decline in mentions of trato is connected to the reduction of live-in and full-time work. Some experts suggest that part-time work leads to less face-to-face contact between employer and worker and reduces the importance of their affective bonds, making employers see it as an employment relation rather than a familial relation (Pereyra 2015). It is somehow easier for employers who hire someone to do a particular amount of work (measured in hours or tasks) to perceive that person as a worker. If they are perceived as a worker, the negotiation becomes more about concrete issues like pay than about the nebulous ideas of treatment and respect.

Another aspect of the classified ads worth mentioning is the loaded phrase *buena presencia*, which requires that a worker present a "good" appearance. This term mostly refers to physical appearance, although it could include intangibles such as language and manners. More important, it excludes darker-skinned, indigenous, or black job applicants or those whose bodies show the effects of poverty (e.g., missing teeth, worn clothing). In the 2010 sample of ads, a total of eleven mentioned buena presencia, and in 2016, only one used this phrase. Employment agency owners I interviewed in 2018 mentioned this characteristic of ideal workers, so I think it is still part of decision making in hiring. It is difficult to pin down the meaning of this reduced number of mentions (which is also a reduction in the proportion of ads using this term), as it could reflect a shrinking labor pool that makes employers less picky, or a new sense of political correctness that leads them to use less discriminatory language.

Specific Household Tasks

Which tasks or duties do classified ads for domestic work mention? Some positions imply what the worker's duty will be: nanny or cook, for example. Aside from the job title, however, specific tasks were mentioned in many advertisements. In both samples, the most frequently mentioned task was cleaning, followed by cooking. Other tasks mentioned specifically in both years included caring for children and (less commonly) the elderly or disabled, washing, and ironing. The proportion of ads saying that the domestic worker would be responsible for all of the household work (*todos los quehaceres*) or several different tasks (*oficios varios*) increased slightly from 5 percent in 2010 to 7 percent in 2016. There were also proportionally more ads in 2016 that mentioned "quehaceres domésticos," which could mean cleaning and a variety of household tasks. New terms also emerged in the 2016 sample that imply this catchall category of domestic work, such as "polifuncional" and "multifuncional" (multifunctional). This development fits with research showing that paid domestic work is becoming less specialized as workers are increasingly called on to perform multiple functions or even what would previously have been considered multiple job roles. If a middle-class household in Latin America has paid domestic help today, it is most likely provided by just one worker. In addition to the shift toward part-time work, which had already begun before the first set of ads I am analyzing here, this decrease in specialized domestic work positions can increase workloads or worsen conditions for domestic workers. The worker is now expected to do everything during her working hours, whatever they may be.

How do the tasks specified in these classified advertisements match up with the accounts of domestic workers I collected with the help of my research collaborators in Ecuador? In general, the two sources seem to provide similar information about what domestic workers do. Our survey of four hundred current and former domestic workers in Guayaquil (chapter 4) asked what tasks they performed in their current or most recent job. The most common answers were cooking (77 percent reported cooking) and cleaning (74 percent), the two most frequently mentioned tasks in the ads. Yet only a third of survey respondents reported caring for children in their current or last job, despite "babysitter/nanny" being one of the most sought-after job titles in the classified ads. Tasks that were not mentioned specifically in most ads—washing and ironing clothes—were reported by 62 percent of our survey respondents as part of their most recent domestic employment. So if we compare the content of the ads to the tasks reported by actual domestic workers, we find fewer workers caring for children than we might expect, but more workers doing laundry than we might expect. Of course, since most domestic employment is not arranged through classified ads, and ads don't perfectly reflect what employers will require workers to do, we cannot compare supply and demand. But it is probable, from the accounts of domestic workers, that employers demand more or different tasks from workers once they are employed, compared to what they specified at the moment of hiring.

What can we learn about the ideal domestic worker by analyzing classified ads? We know that she is a woman, as are most people who dedicate paid or unpaid time to the tasks of social reproduction. We know that she is young, under thirty, and that younger workers are increasingly preferred in more recent advertisements. Whereas older ads emphasized a rural/urban divide in which workers from the countryside were preferred, today internal migrants seem to make up a decreasing percentage of workers, and these preferences are more muted. While I have focused on the main newspaper in Guayaquil, I would expect to see similar criteria in other Ecuadorian outlets.

Other information in the ads reflects shifts in domestic employment arrangements. The number of ads looking for live-in domestic workers has shrunk, but this employment arrangement is still the most commonly mentioned in the ads. Now that employers know more about domestic workers' right to the minimum wage, exact salaries are increasingly absent from the ads. This absence shows the resistance of domestic employment to legal formalization. There were many fewer ads in 2016 than in 2010, which may reflect the increase in part-time domestic work, arranged in informal ways between employers and employees, as well as the decline in newspaper usage in print and online. The tasks mentioned as part of the job remained largely the same over time, although they seem to be consolidated, with more workers performing multiple roles (i.e., cook and nanny rather than one or the other).

The idea of *buen trato*, or a paternalistic beneficence toward domestic workers, is less frequently mentioned in the more recent ads, indirectly showing increased awareness among employers of domestic workers' rights and status as workers rather than servants. This awareness may lead only to the superficial appearance of compliance with the law and the new rights discourse from domestic worker organizations and government. Employers have all but ceased to advertise the position as "muchacha" or to publish salaries below the minimum wage, for example. The class relations in domestic work have not changed so much as the language used to refer to them has become less acceptable, driving more offensive terms—but not feelings or interactions—deeper underground. As the next chapter shows, these deep-seated ideas about class manifest within the private space of the home-as-workplace in ways that they do not in the help wanted section, setting up a dichotomy of superior and inferior bodies.

2

EMBODIED INEQUALITY

> I was cooking and I felt like I was suffocating. I wanted to lie down, because I felt sick. . . . I took [spread out] some newspapers and lay on the kitchen floor. I felt like I was dying, that I couldn't get air, that I was suffocating. And the employer gets home and the other employee tells her, "The *empleada* [domestic worker] is sick." "Oh, no," she says, "what's my daughter going to eat now, who will cook for her?"
>
> —Cristina, domestic worker, age forty

Cristina has spent much of her life cooking and cleaning in private homes in Guayaquil, Ecuador. Her anecdote highlights domestic work's physical demands and employers' privileging of their corporeal needs over those of their employees. Based on interviews with domestic workers and employers, I argue in this chapter that bodies matter for how domestic employees experience their work (beyond often-discussed issues of sexual harassment or abuse). Domestic workers' accounts emphasized physical labor and the embodied inequality between employer and employee. Domestic work assumes particular forms in coastal Ecuador, where workers and employers often have similar racial backgrounds and middle-class people see their social and economic position as precarious.

Domestic employment entails a unique physical proximity of bodies from different class groups, a boundary-threatening situation that must be managed by workers and employers (Gorbán and Tizziani 2018). In this private sphere, bodies can reproduce or challenge class inequality. Although "domestic work constitutes bodily subjectivity in a particular way" (Bahnisch 2000, 59, referencing Gatens 1996, 69), research tends not to place the social meanings of workers' bodies at the center of the analysis. This is true despite the "decisive" role of bodies in relations of power (Quijano 2000, 380). Ecuador, with its long history of paid domestic work and its rigid class system (Miles 1998; Roberts 2012)—in which even lower-middle-class families have traditionally employed domestic workers—is an ideal site for exploring the intersection of class, work, and body. Like many low-prestige jobs, domestic work draws on and propagates social constructions of poor people's bodies as deviant and worthless.

35

Research on working bodies "progress[es] only by adopting the vantage point of the embodied worker and listening to their accounts of workplace experience 'from the inside'" (Wolkowitz 2006, 183). I take domestic workers' accounts concerning health, food, and appearance as a starting point, asking: How do bodies matter in domestic work? How does this employment arrangement relate to broader ideas about differently classed bodies in Ecuador?

Reports about domestic work from international agencies tasked with defending workers' rights, such as the International Labor Organization (ILO), often mention cultural factors in explaining the poor working conditions and exploitation in this employment sector. Yet culture remains a black box, rather than a site of exploration, perhaps because of the comparative, cross-national character of many of these documents. One purpose of this chapter is to delve into culture as a set of habitual, embodied practices that reinforce the unequal positions of employers and workers. Cultural norms regulate domestic employment relationships more strongly than legal rules, so while legislation and its enforcement are important, we must also understand cultural assumptions in order to change them and thus improve workers' status.

Because domestic workers engage in the tasks of social reproduction, they do not produce permanent or exchangeable goods. They provide instead an embodied service. Their work, and thus their very person, is devalued in part because of the intangibility of the services they provide, services associated almost exclusively with women, who have lower social status than men. They embody deference not only to men but also to women of higher class standing. Because they are not protected by formal contracts and their work is invisible, they are not spared physical exhaustion or guaranteed respectful treatment. So social reproduction, informality, and class once again come together in the embodied inequality that prevails in domestic employment.

Theoretical Perspectives on Working Bodies

Two complementary theoretical and empirical approaches apply to working bodies. The first, rooted in Marxian theory, views the body as a limited resource, damaged and deformed in exploitative production processes (Quijano 2000, 380). Marx described factory work's destructive effects on workers' bodies and psyches ([1844] 1978, 74) as the collateral damage of capitalist expansion. Indeed, "labor power, the power of the body, is central to the reproduction and accumulation of capital" (Bahnisch 2000, 64). In today's service economies, the "human body continues to be deeply involved in every aspect of paid work" (Wolkowitz 2006, 55). The "body as resource" perspective is often used to describe the types of physical labor identified with men. However, feminist theorists have described women's bodies as resources used or used up by others (Beauvoir [1949] 2011; Grosz 1994; Young 2005). These theorists focused more on maternal bodies' unpaid work, but there is some affinity between their ideas and Marx's view of workers' bodies.

The second approach, drawing on Bourdieu's (1990) concept of *habitus* and on symbolic interactionism (e.g., Goffman 1959), views the body as symbol. The symbolic body does not communicate unequivocal messages, comprehended similarly by everyone we encounter.[1] However, habitus is observed and interpreted by others according to the "dominant symbolic" (Skeggs 2004b, 87), even if we are unconscious of how social structures produce particular behaviors and bodily dispositions. For Bourdieu, habitus "causes an individual agent's practices, without either explicit reason or signifying intent, to be. . . 'sensible' and 'reasonable' to members of the same society" (1977, 79). Bodily aspects of habitus make sense to those able to recognize and classify them. Others' reactions to our bodies are shaped by cultural meanings, and these reactions can affect how we feel about ourselves and how we move through the world (Fanon 1967). Thus the symbolic body goes beyond surface appearance.

Dress, appearance, and movement communicate bodies' positions in hierarchies of race, class, gender, and occupation. Embodied habitus is "a statement of social entitlement" (Skeggs 2004a, 22), reproducing class inequalities in, on, and through bodies, and becoming a source of conflict or approbation in interactions between people of different classes. Workplaces can be agents of socialization, building or reinforcing habitus, especially when workers begin at young ages, as in domestic employment. Expanding on Bourdieu, Wolkowitz (2006) elaborated the idea of *occupational habitus* related to people's work identities. Domestic work is one setting for the construction of occupational habitus.

The "body as symbol" perspective often focuses empirically on gendered appearance. Research shows how workplaces value certain forms of gender performance (Casanova 2015a; Freeman 2000; Hall, Hockey, and Robinson 2007; McDowell 1997; Nencel 2008; Salzinger 2003). Yet there is scant research on embodied work outside of organizations, except for sex work. Building on the "body as resource" approach, research shows how emotions, signaled through physical cues, are harnessed in gender-segregated service occupations (Hochschild 1983; Kang 2010). Yet Wolkowitz laments the "relative invisibility of the corporeal in the employment-oriented literature on emotion" (2006, 79), and the sociology of the body is just beginning to examine the large portion of an employed person's life that is spent at work.

The term *body work* (Shilling [1993] 2003; Kang 2010) synthesizes the material and symbolic aspects of bodies. Here, drawing on Gimlin, I consider body work "the management of embodied emotional experience and display, and . . . the production or modification of bodies through work" (2007, 353). Consistent with a "body as symbol" frame, employers expect domestic workers to present a certain appearance. As in "body as resource" theories, domestic workers' bodies are produced and transformed through the work.

Drawing on domestic workers' narratives, I propose a more holistic, micro-level approach, "embodied inequality." A theoretical framework of embodied inequality bridges the "body as resource" and "body as symbol" approaches and their conceptual offshoots, body work and occupational habitus. Domestic workers' bodies are used as tools, and suffer the physical consequences; yet they must also have an appearance acceptable to their employers and indicative of their socioeconomic position. Unlike academic narratives that privilege only the material or the symbolic dimensions of working bodies, the workers' accounts combine these perspectives for a broader view of embodied inequality.

Paid Domestic Work and Embodiment

Several researchers have addressed domestic workers' *embodiment*, which I define as the experience of being and having a particular type of body in a particular time and place. More than three decades ago, Rollins discussed the physical demands of domestic work (1985, chapter 3), workers' assertions that employers do not see them as human (1985, 132), the symbolic importance of food practices, and tensions around gifts (e.g., of clothing) (ibid., 69, 132–34). Rollins's study was based in the United States, with some domestic workers' anecdotes dating back to the 1960s; yet many of these issues remain relevant for the participants in my research and in studies of domestic work elsewhere.

There has been much more attention to workers' embodiment in studies of the Global South, including work by Anderson (2000), Arnado (2003), Brites (2014), Chatterjee and Schluter (2018), Cumes (2014), Durin (2014), Gill (1990), Goldstein (2003), and Maich (2014a). Some scholars portray domestic workers' bodies as spatially marginalized: live-ins given poorly located or cramped quarters or workers not allowed to sit on furniture or spend time in certain rooms of the home (Ceballos 2014; Gill 1990; Goldstein 2003; Maich 2014a; Ray and Qayum 2009). Ray and Qayum state that domestic workers in India "are expected to do work that requires them to be strong, healthy, and clean" (2009, 153) and Chatterjee and Schluter (2018) discuss the ways that Indian employers try to mold workers' appearance, behavior, and language. King argues that in South Africa, "employees' manner, dress, and deference are integral parts of the employer and servant relationship" (2007, 1). Gill's (1990) examination of domestic work in Bolivia explores the stereotype of domestic workers as "ugly." Research sites in the Global South encourage attention to the body; class operates differently in these locations than in the Global North. In Latin America, for example, class can be read off of physical appearance or embodied acts such as speech or even handwriting (Goldstein 2003).

Bodies are always implicated in domestic food practices. Food plays a symbolic role in distinguishing people of different social status (Bourdieu [1984] 2007; Lupton 1994; Ward, Coveney, and Henderson 2010; Warde and Hetherington 1994). The home is an important site in the sociology of food and eating (DeVault 1994) because the "preparation and eating of food is central to household organization" (Warde and Hetherington 1994, 759). Valentine urges scholars to examine "how patterns of eating are negotiated and contested within households" (1999, 491). While much recent scholarship about food centers on the family, domestic workers are often overlooked in literature on food from the Global North. Ray and Qayum mention Indian domestic workers eating foods different from their employers', attributing it to Hindu caste distinctions (2009, 153). Yet in Latin America, without caste systems, domestic workers have told researchers stories of going hungry, eating alone, and only being allowed certain, less-desirable foods (Goldstein 2003; Gorbán 2013; Maich 2014a; Toledo González 2013). In this context, "food distinctions work to reproduce colonial stratifications of *us* and *them*" (Saldaña-Tejeda 2012, 127).

This chapter investigates embodied aspects of domestic work in an unexplored site, urban coastal Ecuador. Taking my cue from workers' interview accounts, I set the body at the center of my inquiry. Zooming in on the body, we see how crucial embodiment is to women's understanding and experience of this type of work. Domestic workers described how class relations become embodied and personalized when acted out between individuals in the private sphere. Distinctions between employers' and employees' bodies are not simply symptoms of larger inequalities, played out in rote ways; the very distinctions themselves are created through sometimes hurtful everyday interactions. Although bodily aspects of habitus build up over time so that people are not always conscious of the reasons for their actions (Bourdieu 1977), the domestic workers interviewed pointed to specific moments when they felt degraded as classed, gendered, and sometimes racialized bodies. We can better understand domestic workers' experience of their work by listening to how they talk about their working bodies.

Local Structures of Class, Race, and Labor

The introductory chapter provided some background information about domestic work in Latin America and Ecuador. Rather than restate these figures, I will focus here on the class relations and labor markets that shape domestic work in Guayaquil specifically. The female labor market is bifurcated, with a limited set of "good" jobs available to college-educated women, and a set of less desirable jobs, or informal self-employment, available to less-educated women (Arango Gaviria 2001; Casanova 2011a). Women with low education levels living in poverty often see domestic work as the least appealing employment option because of low pay and potential exploitation by unregulated employers (Goldstein 2003; Tizziani 2011); many prefer other informal work (e.g., selling; Casanova 2011a, 164–65). This is increasingly true for younger women, who reject the servile demeanor that employers expect of domestic workers, opting for low-paid self-employment, service work, or factory work (Valenzuela and Sanches 2012). This rejection of domestic work as a bad job that requires undue deference to a middle- or upper-class employer is part of the reason for the decline in the number of live-in and full-time domestic workers in Latin America (Brites 2013; Goldstein 2003).

In Guayaquil, middle-class as well as upper-class families commonly employ domestic workers. Employment arrangements vary, from elite households employing entire live-in staffs to lower-middle-class households having someone work a few hours per week. Many families' most visible claim to middle-class status is the presence of a domestic worker in their household. Long an informal, under-the-table, contract-free type of employment, domestic work has become the object of increased government scrutiny and public consciousness-raising by worker organizations, giving workers and employers the sense that the sands are shifting.

The timing of this study was ideal, as the left-leaning government of President Rafael Correa began enforcing labor laws protecting domestic workers—though not systematically or continuously—around 2009. For a period of about two years, domestic workers' issues frequently appeared in news media, and workers' organizations ramped up advocacy and outreach to leverage state support and improve working conditions. It had always been difficult for domestic workers to negotiate living wages and bearable workloads because of the unequal positions of employer and employee and the lack of regulation (Tizziani 2011a). Public attention around domestic workers' legal rights in this period made such discussions even more uncomfortable. In 2010, when I began fieldwork, the Ministry of Labor was conducting house-by-house inspections in some wealthy neighborhoods of Guayaquil to determine the presence of domestic workers in the home and whether they were receiving the government-mandated minimum wage and benefits (e.g., social security). According to the domestic worker advo-cates I knew, employers hearing of the inspectors' presence in their neighbor-hood often erased a domestic worker's body by giving her the day off, hiding her in another part of the house, or presenting her as a cousin visiting from the countryside. Inspections ended just as abruptly as they began, and were never pursued systematically, though the middle and upper classes still felt threat-ened by the populist, socialist-identified rhetoric of the Correa administration. They needn't have worried too much, as the government's labor legislation and antagonism toward labor movements belied its progressive, pro-worker dis-course (Gaussens 2016).

Many studies discuss the complex racial dynamics of contemporary Ecuador, with most citizens identifying as mestizo (of mixed indigenous and European ancestry) and sizable indigenous and Afro-Ecuadorian minorities (de la Torre and Striffler 2008; Rahier 1998; Roberts 2012). Throughout Latin America, the high degree of social and economic inequality is often literally written on the body (Bank Muñoz 2008; Casanova 2011a; Edmonds 2010; Roberts 2012). Nonwhite appearance and darker skin are generally associated with low class status, and domestic workers are stereotyped as having these characteristics. In Guayaquil, few people self-identify as indigenous or wear traditional indigenous dress. Coastal mestizos/as have much less contact with indigenous people than do mestizos in the Andean region (*sierra*); it is rare to find indigenous domestic workers in *guayaquileños'* homes. In fact, in nearly two decades of conducting research in Guayaquil, I have never encountered a woman who self-identified (or was identified by others) as indigenous laboring in a private home. Guayas Province, where Guayaquil is located, has the country's largest population of self-identified Afro-Ecuadorians (INEC 2012). While it is more common to find Afro-Ecuadorian than indigenous women among Guayaquil's domestic workers, there is widespread discrimination against black people (as seen in classified ads requiring "buena presencia").[2] My sense from speaking informally with employ-ers is that they prefer mestiza domestic workers; I have also observed many more mestiza than black workers in middle-class homes.

Thus, unlike locales where employers and employees are always separated by caste (Ray and Qayum 2009) or race (Gill 1990, 1994; Parreñas 2001; Rollins 1985), in Guayaquil it is common for domestic employment arrangements to link women whose official racial classification would be mestiza and who may have similar phenotypes. As in the Philippines (Arnado 2003), this employment relationship is not usually a cross-racial one, meaning that class differences—especially embodied ones—can be more fruitfully explored, as they are not con-flated with racial differences. However, identifications of race and class in Ecua-dor are somewhat fluid and mutually constituting: mestizos with higher class status are perceived (and see themselves) as whiter than poorer mestizos, regardless of phenotype. Whereas popular conceptions of race in the United States rest on ideas about immutable biological differences, in Andean societies, including Ecuador, race is "experienced as alterable, through changes in body and comportment . . . [rather than] genetically determined" (Roberts 2012, 120). People who are mestizo/a can become white(r) by complying with middle-class norms of bodily self-presentation, education, and employment—by successfully embodying middle-class habitus. Thus the "fabrication" of race is not "theoretical" or a priori, but rather "race is enacted and . . . reenacted through a wider range of characteristics than physical appearance as transmuted through genes" (Roberts 2012, 114; see also Casanova 2018).

This racial mutability makes creating embodied differences a priority for employers, who want to visually distinguish themselves from the help. Compounding the racial uncertainty and jockeying for whiteness is the precarious status of the middle class. During the Correa years, middle-class people's generally low salaries and their (mostly overblown) sense that they were targeted or neglected by government policies that favored the poor became an important factor in this group's self-identification. Under these conditions, it is unsurprising to see lines drawn in the home-as-workplace to remind domestic workers of their (racialized) class position. The most obvious means for marking the bodies of employees is the uniform. The more frequent use of uniforms in Latin America (compared to the United States, for example) underlines the different and perhaps more acute embodied experience of these workers.[3] Strategies of corporeal distance, degradation, and differentiation are ways of shoring up tenuous claims to privileged statuses such as whiteness, decency (*decencia*), and middle-classness in this local race/class/gender context.

Meanwhile, the daily life of domestic workers—as described by participants and as I have observed—remains much the same as in decades past. Most families eat their largest meal (*almuerzo*) at midday, which (in households that can afford it) includes a first course of soup, followed by a protein with rice and vegetables. Cooking can be laborious, often requiring tedious and physically demanding tasks such as grating green plantains by hand or peeling and straining fruits for juice. Most middle-class homes have washing machines; however, employers sometimes require special clothing (like children's school uniforms) to be washed by hand, usually at special stone sinks with washboard-like ridges. Even in homes with automatic dryers, clothing is usually hung outside to dry and then ironed, which is more physically taxing. It is common for employers to prohibit domestic workers from using labor-saving household appliances,[4] or require them to use inferior or older equipment than that which they (the employers) use when they perform household chores (French-Fuller 2006; Silva 2010). Other considerations include the dust that accumulates in this urban environment (even in enclosed structures) and the caustic contents of common cleaning products (domestic workers tend not to bring their own products or request specific products). Most live-out domestic workers have long workdays and live in areas distant from public transportation, making for long commutes (see figure 2).

This chapter draws on interviews with fourteen current and former domestic workers (all women) and three employers (two women and one man) conducted in Guayaquil, Ecuador, from June through August 2010.[5]

Embodied Narratives of Domestic Work

Common body-related themes in interview accounts were (1) the role of the body in domestic workers' physically demanding tasks (the body as a limited resource that suffers because of the work); and (2) the embodiment of class inequality (the body as a symbol of social/economic position). The second theme encompasses two subthemes: (a) the construction of employers' bodies as more valuable than workers' bodies through health and food; and (b) perspectives on appearance and the use of the "maid" uniform.[6]

Physical Labor in Domestic Work (Body as Resource)

Nearly every worker interviewed emphasized the physical demands of housework and child care, "the production or modification of bodies through work" (Gimlin 2007, 353). Cecilia, middle-aged and unemployed, complained that "physical exhaustion" set in over time:

> In the first month, we're wonderful, but in two or three months we're feeling a physical exhaustion [*agotamiento físico*] that leads to us feeling more and more tired, and we end up getting an illness . . . related to the tiredness, the stress . . . and then the employer begins to complain. . . "What's going on with you? You started off working hard, but now you don't clean here, you don't clean over here"—but she doesn't recognize that I am human, too.

Most of the domestic workers interviewed began work at a young age, some at ten or twelve (among our survey respondents, the median age of entry to paid domestic work was seventeen, with 43 percent of workers beginning before the age of sixteen; see chapter 3). The toll on the body over time, and the difficulty of getting hired and danger of being fired as an older worker because of perceived or actual physical limitations, were common concerns.

Some domestic tasks are more physically demanding than others. Longtime domestic worker Patty recounted: "I have been doing laundry for twenty-two years, and my hands began to swell up on me . . . there was a horrible pain that grabbed me in my [lower] back . . . and my whole hands were full of fungus, and they bled every time I washed [by hand], they were so irritated . . . it was a rash . . . from the detergent, the soap . . . and the bleach." After spending a day washing clothes for her employers, Patty would return home and wash her own family's clothes. She consulted a doctor, who recommended she stop hand-washing clothes: "If you keep washing, you are going to die," Patty remembers the doctor saying, because the exposure to bleach could cause cancer. Despite the tremendous pain, Patty "went on for some time more for [her] children," whom she helped support. She said, "I was not the same person you see today"—strong, energetic, with a physically commanding presence—because of her overwork. Despite the fact that she no longer washes clothes for a living, I could see the effects of this toil on her hands. For Patty, one of the most troubling aspects of domestic work is that "physically a person gets worn out, deteriorates, doesn't care for herself."

As with much manual labor, domestic work's detrimental physical effects are not well compensated.[7] In interviews, workers listed negative physical consequences: back pain, exposure to hazardous chemicals without protective masks or gloves, and injuries. Former worker Ximena recounted cleaning marble stairs during the final weeks of her pregnancy, when she slipped and fell. The pain she felt afterward, she soon realized, was the beginning of labor. (Perhaps Ximena was fortunate to be working, as two other domestic workers reported being fired when employers learned of their pregnancies.) Patty affirmed, "The work in the home [of employers] is hard . . . and one arrives home dead, pulverized." Since asking for time off is often not an option, several workers noted that they would simply quit a job when they needed rest, taking a month or two off before returning to work, usually for a new employer.[8]

Workers used embodied metaphors to describe their toil. Belén, employed in one of Guayaquil's wealthiest neighborhoods, referred to her job as earning money "with the sweat of your brow," and Cristina claimed to have "given up even my lungs" to the work; these powerful images signify the bodily sacrifice of domestic work. Such statements recall a tradition of body-as-resource theories inspired by Marx, who saw the body destroyed by the capitalist mode of production. Stories of sacrifice exemplify one of Gimlin's (2007) definitions of body work: "the production or modification of bodies through work." These bodies are modified negatively, and (re)produced as lower-class bodies, through physically demanding tasks.

Embodied Inequality: Employers' Bodies as More Valuable (Body as Symbol)

Workers often discussed distinctions made by employers between employers' and workers' bodies as related to health and health care, food, and clothing. These accounts recall the body-as-symbol perspective, as bodies are seen as carrying different amounts of social worth. In health issues, we can clearly see the overlap between the two views of bodies. Health concerns, discussed here as examples of the symbolism of bodies, also result from the physicality of the work and show that the body is an exhaustible resource. Workers' bodies are so devalued by differential treatment that Cecilia asserted, "The family dog is treated better than the household worker."

Nearly all the workers described myriad health problems, some leaving them temporarily unable to work. Ailments may stem from a variety of causes, including physically demanding work, poor women's already-precarious health status, and lack of health-care access.[9] As former worker Ana María put it, "A [domestic] worker has little time to go to the doctor." Rather than seeing a doctor, she said domestic workers "go to the pharmacy to self-medicate,"[10] or consult neighbors and friends rather than medical professionals. Because most of these women depend on subsidized health services or low-cost clinics, a doctor visit can involve waiting an entire day or more to be seen.[11] Paola, a full-time student and former domestic worker, discussed employers' inflexibility with regard to workers' schedules: "We don't have any right to get sick." Paola and other interviewees connected health disparities to class inequality: "We are also human, just like them [employers], except the difference is that they have money, and we don't." When employers get sick, they visit the doctor and take time off from work to recuperate; when domestic employees get sick, they are often unable to do either. When Fátima asked her last employer to help pay for her prescription, she was berated by his adult son, and felt that skin color and class prejudice were at play: "They let me know that because a person is ugly, [and] black ... and they [the employers] are white, they can give you a kick in the rear ... But why, if we are all human and have feelings?" She compared this employer to a previous one, who, when she fell ill, took her to an expensive private hospital and paid the bill.[12] Workers see the body as a resource, while also seeing the employers' denial of their health needs as a material and symbolic devaluation of their bodies.

Food was another site for drawing lines between upper- and lower-class bodies. Based on my interviews and observations, deep-rooted practices, such as having domestic workers eat separately and offering them different (or less) food, are still common in urban Ecuador. These practices continue to exist throughout

Latin America (Maich 2014a; Toledo González 2013), and indeed, employers who don't engage in them see themselves as exceptionally generous (Goldstein 2003). Recent Bolivian legislation granting labor rights to domestic workers specifically requires that they be provided access to the same food as their employers, which indicates that equal food is not always provided (ILO 2010; see also Gorbán 2013). Several women complained that employers denied them food during the workday. Fátima said, "They didn't even give me a piece of warm bread." Others recounted having to eat reheated leftovers when there was plenty of fresh food available, or watching employers throw out food the worker had requested. Domestic workers, said Cecilia, often do not get "decent food."

More offensive to Belén was being forced to use dishes that were just for the help: "From the teacups to the spoons, everything . . . all the utensils were different from theirs." This humiliating experience made her feel insignificant. The symbolism of objects that touch only a worker's body, but never an employer's body, communicates a powerful message of inferiority to the worker. This message is that domestic workers' bodies are polluting elements, out of place in the home of a well-off family (Cumes 2014; Durin 2014b; Maich 2014a; Saldaña-Tejeda 2012). Another worker recalled having to eat outdoors while the employer's family ate inside; typically, domestic workers eat in the kitchen or an adjoining room.

Legitimating the study of food as a social and cultural object, Bourdieu ([1984] 2007) focused on divergent eating habits due to class-based tastes; yet here different eating practices are based not on taste, but on the exclusion of lower-class bodies from nourishment and desirable foods. By refusing to share eating utensils and eating space with domestic workers, employers shore up embodied class boundaries and prevent even indirect bodily contact.[13] In describing "good" employers, workers (as well as employers and employment agency representatives) often pointed to eating the same food, or eating together at the table, as evidence of kindness. Alternatively, we could see this egalitarian gesture as a distraction from the inherent economic inequality in the employment situation, a way of providing good trato but not guaranteeing salary or benefits.[14] Given the incorporation of food-related routines into domestic workers' occupational habitus, it is likely that many workers, unlike those interviewed, do not resist or complain about these practices.

Cristina recalled taking her young daughter to work, so she could "see what I do." Her daughter asked, "*Mami*, why do you make such delicious food here?" Cristina replied, "At home we don't have the same money as they do here." Her daughter complimented Cristina's cooking, saying she wished she could cook such rich foods at home. Cristina responded, "*M'ija* [My daughter], that is why I am working here, because some time we want to eat well too."

Employers I spoke with connected food and bodies in ways that alternately reaffirmed or obscured class boundaries. Clara, a thirty-something woman, claimed to have fired a previous employee in part because of her cooking style, saying the food "had a bad flavor [because] her hands were dirty, and her whole appearance was . . . messy." With their current worker, Clara and her husband Alfredo emphasized, they all ate together. They looked down on those who made domestic workers eat separately, since "we are the same, [we're] human beings."[15] The new employee's ability to present a neat appearance made her presence at the dinner table palatable to her employers. Though I did not probe into the racial dynamics of this story, I would not be surprised if the "messy" domestic worker differed more from these mestizo employers in her phenotype and embodiment of middle-class dress and appearance norms than the new worker. Employers commonly claim that domestic workers are "like family,"[16] and these discussions of eating together bring out the embodied dimension of what it means to be treated like family. But, as sociologist Débora Gorbán writes in the case of Argentina, "Why clarify where and what [domestic workers] eat? These clarifications indicate what they hide: the processes of differentiation at play in the relation between employers and employees" (2013, 72).

Interviewees also discussed embodied inequality in dress and physical appearance. Domestic workers admitted that there were clothes or other items that they enjoyed or aspired to purchase. As Cristina put it, "Although I don't have money, I like to go to stores, to look and to fantasize." Fátima referred to the popular Ecuadorian saying, "They treat you according to how you look [a uno como lo ven, lo tratan]." She used this social practice of judging appearance (Casanova 2011a, chapter 4), which connotes a particular—often racialized—class status, as a justification for always wanting to look good in public. With such statements, workers like Fátima reaffirmed the symbolic importance of physical appearance for women of all class backgrounds. Her employers took notice, and when she requested their help in buying her prescription medicine, they criticized her for having money to do her hair and nails and buy perfume, but not to provide for her health, implying that lower-class bodies did not deserve to be made attractive. Her attempt to make a claim on middle-class bodily habitus was thus delegitimized.[17]

Workers often criticized employers' "vanity" or "fashion," referring to the value employers placed on presenting a socially acceptable middle-class appearance. Elsa had recently left her job over issues of back pay and vacation time. Her employers claimed they couldn't pay her the salary she was owed, yet Elsa noted that any time the mother and daughter were invited to "half a party [medio reunión]," they would rush out to get their hair or nails done. Other workers said money that could have been used to pay domestic workers (whose presence in the home is a key symbol of middle-class status) was spent on what they perceived as superficial, temporary, bodily markers of class. Irma, an experienced domestic worker, was overwhelmed by the quantity of clothing, makeup, and accessories in her employer's home, confiding, "I'd go crazy with so much clothing, it's amazing. . . . Miss, there were suitcases full of purses, full of every kind of makeup." It is harder for low-income women, including domestic workers, to access and use these symbolic props for middle-class respectability, and if they do, they are sanctioned. Gorbán and Tizziani relate an anecdote from an Argentinian employer who catches the domestic worker wearing her employer's clothing. She is surprised by how good the worker looks, and angry because the worker's attractive appearance "challenges the superior position in which the employer has placed herself and reveals the constructed nature of the differentiation between the two [women]" (Gorbán and Tizziani 2014, 61).

Women employers sometimes loan clothing to workers, or give them used clothing (this practice has been noted: Cumes 2014; Rollins 1985). Some workers viewed this as a benefit of their job. At Christmas, Patty's employer gave her money to buy clothes and loaned her clothes to attend social events in her rural hometown.[18] Yet she maintained the class line distinguishing worker from employer, telling Patty never to wear the borrowed clothing "in the [employer's] neighborhood," only out of town, and Patty complied. Marina, whose daughter had also worked in private homes, told me that she accepted used clothes from her former employer because she did not want to waste them. Instead of wearing the clothes, she distributed them among poorer family and friends. Not all workers appreciate hand-me-down clothing. Marina's daughter Francisca frowned on those "who give you the blouse they don't want any more. . . . No, that's not a good employer. A good employer says, 'Come on and I'll buy you a new blouse.'" Cast-off clothing, especially if it's worn-out or ill-fitting, marks the lower-class body (Adair 2001), whereas new clothing adds value to the worker's appearance.[19]

The Uniform as Embodiment of Inequality

In popular culture portrayals, it is easy to pick out the domestic worker in a privileged space: she's the one wearing the maid uniform. Uniforms are sold in Guayaquil's department stores and grocery stores, where uniformed domestic workers can be spotted pushing employers' shopping carts or tending to their children. These garments tend to be loose-fitting housecoats, or resemble medical scrubs: the stereotypical, black-and-white version seen on TV and in movies is rare. Uniforms are different enough from everyday street clothing to visually distinguish women as domestic workers at a glance. Many employers pay for or provide uniforms, while others (to the chagrin of workers) take the cost out of the employee's pay.

I asked both workers and employers about uniforms.[20] These employers did not require uniforms, describing them as unnecessary and old-fashioned. They mentioned wanting the worker to feel comfortable, especially when caring for young children. Employer Clara, who wore a uniform in her job as a hotel manager, said she had denied her domestic worker's request for a uniform. Perhaps because of her own embodied experience of wearing a uniform as a professional, she saw uniforms not as indicative of low social status, but the opposite: "I personally see the uniform as a differentiation of social strata, so here you see people wearing uniforms who are . . . from a higher socioeconomic level." For Clara, the uniform symbolized middle-class, professional, rather than low, status. It was part of her occupational habitus as a college-educated manager.

Of the workers who expressed opinions about uniforms, seven viewed them negatively and one positively.[21] Plain-spoken Paola, who had to wear a uniform a few times at a previous job, declared it "a humiliation" and "a piece of trash [una porquería]." When a uniformed domestic worker goes out in public with her employer, Paola said, "a person can distinguish who is the employee and who is the boss." This is especially relevant when both the employer and employee are mestiza. Paola questioned a society that would create such an embodied class division, saying, "Where are we? Where are we headed?" Patty, who had never worn a uniform, described domestic workers' uniforms as "sad dresses." She said that simply because a woman was a domestic worker she shouldn't have to be "all scruffy . . . with ugly sandals." (In Guayaquil, "ugly" sandals or flip-flops signal lower-class status—middle-class habitus generally reserves flip-flops for beachwear or housewear.) The point of such a display, Patty said, was for an employer to demonstrate that "that person is their employee." When the lady of the house goes shopping with her daughter, no one mistakes the daughter for a domestic worker, Patty remarked. Domestic workers generally felt that when they wore uniforms in public, people thought, "Look, there's an empleada, a nanny."[22] The uniform clarifies and amplifies the message of the symbolic body.

Francisca, otherwise calm and soft-spoken as we chatted, spoke excitedly when the talk turned to uniforms: "It's like they [uniforms] make you feel like a cachifa [derogatory term for maid], like you're less than." While working for a downtown family, she had to wear a uniform only when she went shopping. When asked how she felt, she replied, "Ooooh, like the lowest, because, imagine, in the middle of downtown and dressed like that . . . I felt really very bad [me sentí recontra que mal]." Francisca eventually told her employer that she didn't like going shopping, so that she would not have to wear her uniform on the crowded street. Surprisingly, the employer did not push back and agreed not to send her shopping again.[23] Francisca forfeited an opportunity to escape the confines of the home due to the embarrassment the uniform entailed, which shows how important this issue can be for some workers.

While workers expressed concerns about public perceptions, they also discussed how these stigmatizing clothes looked and felt on the body. Several bemoaned the poor quality of the uniforms required by employers. Francisca described feeling physically uncomfortable in the uniform, which was "like, too hot, different, [when] one is used to wearing her own little clothes." Paola said vehemently: "Aside from everything else, it's a poorly made uniform. . . . If it were a uniform, a little pantsuit with a little T-shirt, great, fine. Or, why can't I wear pants and a T-shirt like they do in offices? . . . But instead they have to buy the worst fabric . . . because that's how they've treated us, like the lowest of the low [*la última rueda del coche*]." More egregious than bad fabric was bad fit. Patricia, who was about to return to domestic work after having a baby, complained about having to use worn-out uniforms left behind by previous employees. Women's bodies are all different, she explained, "one is fat and the other is thin . . . there should be a uniform that fits one's body." When Belén protested the poor fit of her uniform, her employer replied, "I bought it for your body." Belén disagreed, telling me, "I look like a potato sack with no potatoes, because it fits me so big, and I don't like that." So she wore it around the house, but changed into her own clothes to go out, because the uniform "fit me so ugly." Ugliness is thus associated with both domestic work and lower-class status (Cumes 2014; Durin 2014; Gill 1990). And in the context of domestic work, as we see, ugliness is imposed.

Several workers described households as having just one uniform for whoever was working in the home. References to a one-size-fits-all, used uniform evoke the image of a garment hanging on a hook in the kitchen, waiting for a domestic worker to literally put on or embody the role of the help. The uniform stays on the hook and the individual worker (with her unique size, shape, and preferences) changes. This represents the ultimate deindividualization of the worker, in which any body can be stuffed into or swim around in a generic uniform not chosen for her needs, but to symbolize a social and occupational role. Irma, who generally liked uniforms and whom I often saw wearing medical scrub-type garments, decided to get her own well-fitting uniforms in order to avoid those provided by employers, which she described as "mistreated" and "badly washed."

Some interviewees interpreted the employers' choice of ill-fitting (usually too-large) and unattractive uniforms not just as a demarcation of workers' low status but as an effort to desexualize their bodies, to prevent them from being viewed or targeted sexually by male employers.[24] Patricia commented, "The important thing is that it fits you big, because they don't like it small"; yet for workers, such a large garment felt like "a nightgown." When Cristina was searching for words to describe the physical encumbrance posed by overly large uniforms, I offered:

> ERYNN: You have to be able to move to do things. . .
>
> CRISTINA: Yes, of course, right? So sometimes they give you a long dress, but I say, what's the reason for the long dress? What's it for? They must be thinking that you're going to steal their husband or something, right?

Cumbersome clothes limit the ability to use the body as a resource, but also have a symbolic dimension: Cristina viewed these modesty requirements as a way of managing the sexual threat posed by the presence of an unrelated woman in the home of a married couple. Paola was explicitly instructed by a female employer to "be careful around the son and the husband," and to "wear a bigger pair of shorts, so that you couldn't see my. . . ." While we might applaud the employer for wanting to protect her, it is worth noting that she put the onus on Paola to discourage harassment, rather than expecting her male relatives to behave appropriately. Paola agreed with the employers' suggestion, saying "it was obvious" that she should dress more modestly. Domestic workers thus adjust their appearance as employers require, whether or not they internalize stereotypes that characterize them as hypersexual.

The questions driving this chapter were (1) How do bodies matter in domestic work? and (2) How does this employment arrangement relate to broader social ideas about bodies of different class status? In the accounts presented here, workers described their embodied employment experience in ways that fit both "body as resource" and "body as symbol" theoretical frameworks, pointing to the usefulness of a more comprehensive, holistic approach to embodied inequality.

Bodies matter in all jobs: Even the most cerebral, intellectual tasks are performed by humans who have/are bodies. In discussing their work, domestic workers emphasized the physicality of the tasks and the deleterious effects on their bodies. They described their work as exhausting, accelerating the deterioration of their bodies, and potentially dangerous. These accounts conceive of the body as a limited resource that women draw on to do their work, a resource that can be used up or damaged in the process.

Bodies also matter because of the symbolic distinctions drawn between "good," middle-class/elite bodies and "bad," lower-class/deviant bodies—between employers' and workers' bodies. Workers face clear boundaries between themselves and employers in relation to health, food consumption, and appearance. Even employers who buck tradition by pursuing more egalitarian relations (e.g., dining with their workers) are aware of the differential values typically placed on differently classed bodies in Ecuador. The uniform, an iconic symbol of domestic service throughout the Americas, was viewed by most of the workers and by the young employers I interviewed as a superfluous relic of a more oppressive class order. Yet, 70 percent of the domestic workers I interviewed had been asked by employers to wear uniforms at some point, so the practice is still alive. Most workers hated being made to wear ill-fitting, cheaply made uniforms, and several described feeling embarrassed for other women they saw visibly marked as domestic workers in public spaces. Many who referred to the physical challenges of domestic work also drew on the idea of the body as a malleable symbol of status in describing the embodied aspects of their relations with employers.

Although habitus, and the newer idea of occupational habitus, implies behaviors and physical orientations that are automatic rather than intentional, interview accounts point to moments in which workers resist what is seen as the appropriate corporeality for their station. While they generally enact the physical labor and appearance-related elements of domestic worker habitus, they sometimes resist the symbolic degradation of their bodies. However, when the workers aspire to or attempt to embody elements of gendered middle-class habitus in Guayaquil (e.g., getting their hair professionally styled), employers criticize them.

These accounts highlight "the management of embodied emotional experience and display" (Gimlin 2007, 353) seen in domestic workers' acquiescence to the bodily regimes of employers in a context of limited employment alternatives. The successful embodiment of modesty (in dress and manner) required by employers is one example of domestic workers managing their bodies and emotions. Workers' stories of the physical damage and health hazards of the job exemplify "the production or modification of bodies through work" (Gimlin 2007, 353). Bodies are often changed for the worse by engaging in domestic work, and lower-class women's bodies are (re)produced as "less than" or "the lowest of the low," to use the workers' terms. The products of this bodily labor are invisible and fleeting, and they must be repeated again and again; this is the essence of social reproduction and part of the reason employers do not see it as real work.

Based on the enforcement of bodily distinctions and the negative stereotypes about domestic workers' appearance, I agree with other researchers who argue that domestic work is a racialized occupation. Santiago Bastos wrote: "Domestic service is labor that ethnicizes, racializes" (2014, 349; see also Baptista Canedo 2010; Goldstein 2003; Gorbán and Tizziani 2014; Lautier 2003). People, and social roles, become racialized "insofar as they are *associated* (by skin color, cultural identity, language, or accent) with *other* socio-geographic spaces" (Ferguson 2008, 52). The otherness of domestic workers is wrapped up with ideas about race, and "domestic worker" acts like a racial category that is applied to the person that does the work. As one Brazilian domestic worker interviewed by Louisa Acciari said: "Domestic [employee] is a race that is discarded [*desclassificada*]," that is, domestic is its own racial category that society does not value (2016, 8). And this category is divorced from whiteness. Even when performed by a lighter-skinned person, domestic work is a job that symbolically excludes you from whiteness.

Once, while I was visiting Ecuador in the early 2000s, I refused to open the door to someone on the street who said he needed to deliver some papers to my husband's aunt, with whom I was staying. I was home alone and did not know the man, so I thought this the wisest choice. He later complained about me to the aunt, telling her "your empleada is very rude." She and her daughters treated this mistaken identification as a hilarious joke, because they could not conceive of someone with my appearance as a domestic worker. "Imagínate, ¡una empleada con ojos azules!" they chuckled. Imagine, a maid with blue eyes! The same "joke" is behind the TV sketch I recounted at the beginning of this book. The way working bodies are produced and represented in Latin America means that, though there may be domestic workers with blue eyes, they will always be viewed as an anomaly.

These distinctions make up embodied inequality, which emerges out of Latin America's colonial and postcolonial legacies of racial classification and ordering of bodies from whitest and hence highest-status to darkest and lowest-status. According to Peruvian social theorist Aníbal Quijano, the "universal social classification of the capitalist world," which began in colonial Latin America and spread globally, places the dominant groups in the "white race" category, and the subjugated groups as "races of color" (2000, 374). Regardless of people's skin color and features, domination and high status are coded as white and low status is coded as nonwhite. People seen to be in the "wrong" category based on their looks are viewed with hostility and suspicion. In this way, the body is "a site of incorporated history," as Donna M. Goldstein argues for Brazil (2003, 81). She traces the degradation of domestic workers, and the expectations for their deference and servility, to slavery. However, even in countries like Ecuador, without a history of widespread plantation slavery tied to the trans-Atlantic trade, we see similar racialized meanings and abject positions projected onto domestic workers' bodies.

My work in this chapter can help further theoretical understandings of bodies, work, and class in Latin America and beyond, following the lead of the domestic workers as lay social theorists who combine the "body as resource" and "body as symbol" perspectives in a comprehensive view of embodied inequality. These workers see and describe "the contradictions of an occupation that seems to require, at once, high levels of intimacy and distance" (Saldaña-Tejeda

2012, 130). Examining one case in depth demonstrates how class-based occupational habitus is created or resisted in jobs, especially those that begin early in life, like domestic employment. Domestic workers in Guayaquil come from lower-class (sometimes rural) backgrounds, and their bodies are marked as poor and undesirable prior to entering the workforce—in a sense, the lower-class body is already a sort of uniform. Workers become further accustomed to the material and symbolic devaluation of their bodies as they are fed inferior food with separate dishes in separate areas of the home, not permitted to attend to their health problems (some of which emerge from the repetitive physical damage of domestic labor), and denied the objects associated with an acceptable or attractive middle-class feminine appearance.[25]

The informality of the employment arrangement and lack of contracts allow for the physical and psychological maltreatment of domestic workers. Workers exercise the most resistance in the area of appearance, subverting employers' dress codes or compensating for the symbolic degradation of their bodies at work by investing in a feminine appearance outside of work.[26] Workers—in individual accounts and in organizations such as the one I collaborate with—often frame their complaints about embodied inequality as an appeal for dignity and recognition of their humanity ("I am human too"). Dignified work is available for others, but dignity is often denied these workers. "The need to make reference to dignity lets us glimpse the historically-rooted conceptions that situate this work as marginal and degraded," writes Francisca Pereyra (2015, 96).

In a local context characterized by racial and class anxiety, and (perceived or actual) political challenges to middle-class status and elite privileges, employers were and are invested in holding the line that separates them from employees, and employees are acutely aware of this.

INFORMED BUT INSECURE

(Written in Collaboration with Leila Rodríguez)

In Guayaquil in 2014, while I was pondering the next direction my research on domestic work should take, my collaborators in the Asociación de Trabajadoras Remuneradas del Hogar (ATRH) and their major funder approached me with an opportunity.[1] They wanted to conduct a large-scale survey of domestic workers in Guayaquil, where ATRH is based, and where I had been conducting social research since 1999. They were tired of talking to politicians and government agencies about poor working conditions and being told that these were simply anecdotes, not evidence of systemic problems. They also needed information to evaluate whether campaigns to increase social security coverage of domestic employees had been successful, and to help design new campaigns and advocacy tools. These questions corresponded with my own: which rights and benefits were Ecuadorian domestic workers receiving, and which were they still being illegally denied?

Collected from four hundred current and former domestic workers in the summer and fall of 2014, the survey data in this chapter help fill a gap in the existing literature on paid domestic work. Few empirical studies report on Ecuadorian domestic workers' conditions, with most information coming from the International Labor Organization (ILO) or the government. These reports usually take the nation as the unit of analysis, so we know little about local conditions. Focusing on one city my collaborators and I know well, we privileged the perspective of the workers by meeting them where they live and having current and former domestic workers administer the surveys. Recognizing the circuitous and interrupted work trajectories of domestic workers (which I discuss further in chapter 4), we included (1) former workers who did not plan to return to domestic work, (2) workers who were currently unemployed but planned to return to domestic work, and (3) those who were employed as domestic workers at the time of our survey. This broad base of women with experience in domestic work provides a more complete picture of working conditions than would a snapshot of only employed domestic workers.

We expected that most of our survey participants had not received the legal rights and benefits to which they were entitled, including coverage by the national social security system administered through the Instituto Ecuatoriano de Seguridad Social (IESS). Indeed, participants reported a lack of social security membership and low compliance among employers with laws requiring them to enroll workers. We wanted to get a sense of why workers were not enrolled in social security. Did they know about their right to social security? Most did. Had they discussed with their employers the possibility of enrolling? Most had not. Analyzing the survey results helps pinpoint possible places for intervention, as well as determine which workers are most vulnerable.

The survey results provide evidence for the three dimensions of exploitation on which this book focuses: social reproduction, informality, and class. It matters that domestic workers perform tasks of social reproduction rather than production. Employers can deny them their rights because they are not seen as real workers. The poor working conditions and lack of benefits that survey participants reported are enabled by informal, contract-free domestic employment arrangements. And the class dynamics of domestic work echo traditional relations between patrons and servants. These parties hold unequal power in the employment relationship, with the expectation that workers will remain submissive rather than demand their rights. Many workers embody docility and passivity as a strategy for remaining employed. They have decided, at least for the moment, that a bad job is better than no job.

Nongovernmental organizations (NGOs) and the ILO argue that formalization is the best way to ensure good working conditions and social protections. A key component of formalization is social security, yet there is not much local-level data on domestic workers' social security coverage, as most of the data are national level and used for cross-national comparisons (ILO 2016a; Razavi and Staab 2010). Knowing more about the working conditions of domestic workers, and their access to and views on social security, we can think critically about formalization as a policy solution. We found that most domestic workers know about their rights to social security, want to be enrolled, and do use the benefits of social security when they are enrolled. The resistance they encounter from employers is the main reason that most remain outside the social security system.

Around the world, the increase in informal and precarious work throughout the economy means that domestic workers are demanding rights and benefits that are being stripped from other workers, even those in formal employment. The expansion of social security in Ecuador in recent years, including the incorporation of previously ineligible people, is an exception to this trend. Under Correa's government, Ecuador included new types of workers, and unpaid caregivers, as eligible, while extending benefits to dependent children and spouses and increasing loan programs. The population eligible for social security benefits more than doubled from 2007 to 2013. Whether this ever-expanding social security system is economically sustainable is another question, one which I think scholars should take up.

Despite Ecuador's much-discussed "turn to the left" and the state portraying itself as a friend to workers, domestic employees' poor working conditions, lack of social security coverage, and informal employment arrangements persist.[2] It is not only these most vulnerable workers who suffer under regimes that claim to be socialist or post-neoliberal, however. Because informalization (of employment arrangements) and formalization (via legal measures or enforcement) are both happening at the same time, my findings on domestic workers may be relevant for other workers in Ecuador and other parts of Latin America.

Social Security, Working Conditions, and Benefits

Social security systems aim to guarantee people's economic and physical well-being. Like informal workers generally, in most countries, most domestic workers lack social security coverage. A full 90 percent of domestic workers worldwide are legally excluded from social security systems (ILO 2016a, ix), and de facto exclusion because of complicated bureaucracies, employer noncompliance, and other hurdles is also common. Most Latin American countries (58 percent) allow domestic workers to participate in a national social security system, with such coverage mandatory in some places and voluntary in others. Mandatory systems usually have higher coverage rates than voluntary ones. Ecuador mandates social security coverage for all workers, yet coverage rates are especially low for women workers, including domestic workers. In 2003, 23 percent of women domestic workers in Latin America were enrolled in social security, and the rate was 11 percent among domestic workers in Ecuador (ILO 2010, 57). This rate has risen over time, with Ecuador having the second-biggest increase in domestic worker coverage in Latin America between 2005 and 2015 (OIT 2018, 131). Overall, in Andean countries, domestic workers' social security coverage rose by about 8 percent during that period (OIT 2018, 19). Still, mandatory systems, despite their name, do not directly translate into full coverage of eligible workers.

Latin American social security programs are modeled on their European predecessors (German and British, specifically; Tamez González and Moreno Salazar 2014). These programs focus most strongly on access to and provision of health care. In the region, social security is more of a philosophy or ideological commitment than a practical reality, leading scholars to call these social security systems "incomplete" (Tamez González and Moreno Salazar 2000, 474). The systems generally provide for illness, work accidents, disability, and pensions. Social security is funded jointly through contributions from employers, workers, and government, and how much each of these contributors pays varies from country to country. In Ecuador, the contributions are calculated as a percentage of workers' salaries, with employers responsible for paying 11.15 percent of the workers' salary to social security. Employees contribute 9.45 percent of their salary (Orozco 2016).[3]

Social security represents a state intervention into social reproduction processes. Helping to sustain the capitalist workforce (wage workers and their families), social security facilitates reproduction and, indirectly, production. In Latin America, social security was initially available only to urban workers formally employed by industry or government. As these workforces increased in the period of economic growth and urbanization through the 1960s, the social security rolls swelled. In recent years, many countries have looked to extend coverage to agricultural, informal, and self-employed workers as well (Tamez González and Moreno Salazar 2000). Social security is one type of antipoverty measure, and when health care is part of the system, as in Ecuador, covering more people is also a boon to public health.

The first social security system in Ecuador, focused primarily on pensions, emerged in 1928. The government-run pension scheme and health-care administration were merged in 1963, and in 1970, this autonomous agency was named the Instituto Ecuatoriano de Seguridad Social (IESS). In 2013, there were about 2.9 million IESS-covered workers, representing approximately 16 percent of the population (IESS, n.d.); this is not counting family members, dependents, or self-employed voluntary enrollees. Today the number of people covered by IESS is 8.4 million, including 2.8 million employees, more than 1 million independent farmers, and 374,000 pensioners, plus family members of workers (IESS, n.d.). Increasingly precarious jobs, imperiling even formal workers' benefits, can lower the number of social security members. Yet under the government of Rafael Correa, social security eligibility expanded to include unpaid household workers (stay-at-home caregivers, housewives), farmers, and the self-employed. Being eligible does not guarantee someone will enroll, and enrollment is necessary for, but doesn't guarantee access to, the benefits of social security (e.g., if workers can't get time off or have difficulty traveling to service providers). During this period, enrollment in social security grew along with other social programs to combat inequality. Overall, social security coverage of Ecuadorian workers nearly doubled between 2005 and 2015, to 43 percent of the employed population (OIT 2018, 84).

In addition to health care, social security provides unemployment benefits, disability coverage, pensions, and funeral benefits. There is also a savings bank where IESS-enrolled workers can apply for personal loans and mortgages (IESS, n.d.). Ecuador is similar to the most typical model of Latin American social security and health-care provision, which has (1) a dual public health system, with social security for working people and a public option run by the ministry of health (Ministerio de Salud) for the poor, plus a myriad of private providers; (2) fragmentation in the system, with some workers able to bargain for dedicated services (e.g., hospitals just for the police); (3) inefficiency and varying quality of services; and (4) generally low coverage rates (Tamez González and Moreno Salazar 2000, 477–78). In this context, health services available through the social security system can be of poor quality and often involve long waits and visits to multiple providers across the city (Miles 2013). But people enrolled in IESS can access higher-quality and more comprehensive care than if they were not enrolled, which is why domestic worker advocates have pushed to increase coverage among this vulnerable population.

The government has worked sporadically to increase domestic workers' inclusion in social security, for example, through an informational campaign featuring 260 mobile sites that reached out to both employees and employers about domestic workers' labor rights (FORLAC 2015). Many employers of domestic workers, perhaps because they don't think of themselves as employers, do not know that there is a criminal penalty for not enrolling their domestic employee within a month of the first day of work.[4] Whether domestic workers themselves want to enroll is an empirical question: simply assuming they do, few researchers actually ask them.

In Ecuador, domestic workers are eligible for the same social security coverage as other workers, at the same contribution rates. In theory, domestic workers who work part-time for multiple employers should be covered, with employers contributing according the amount of time the employee works for them per month.[5] In practice, it is usually full-time workers with a single employer who get enrolled in social security (Pereyra and Tizziani 2014). The ILO recommends that contribution rates be lower for domestic workers and their employers than for larger employers with more employees, but many Latin American countries do not follow this suggestion, instead requiring the same contribution proportions for all employers and workers, as in Ecuador.

In addition to our interest in the social security situation of domestic workers in Guayaquil (home to at least one fifth of Ecuador's domestic workers), my collaborators and I used the survey to find out if these workers were receiving other benefits the law entitled them to, including overtime pay, vacation days, and yearly bonuses. There are other legal rights to which domestic workers are entitled, such as paid maternity leave, but we opted to keep the survey as simple as possible to maximize the number of participants that could be surveyed in each trip to the field. The survey also provides an idea of the tasks that domestic workers are asked to do. This is the most recent and largest empirical study conducted to date on working conditions among domestic workers in Ecuador.[6]

Demographics of the Domestic Workers Surveyed

Age

Survey respondents ranged in age from sixteen to ninety-three, with an average age of forty-three. Many had begun to work in private homes at young ages. Two women said they began domestic work at age seven, 12 percent said that they started working at age twelve or younger, and a full 43 percent said they began before age sixteen. The median age at which they began domestic work was seventeen.

Family Situation

Nearly all the women surveyed (94 percent) were mothers. This means that in addition to engaging in paid social reproduction in employers' homes, they were responsible at some point for the unpaid work of social reproduction in their own families. Of mothers, 62 percent had children under eighteen. The average number of children was 2.2 per participant. More than half of our participants were coupled: 19 percent were married and 40 percent were *unidas*, meaning that rather than a legal marriage, their relationship was an *unión libre* (civil union or cohabitation). Unión libre is quite common in the working class. More than a third of the survey respondents, 35 percent, were single, and most of these were mothers. If we add up all the mothers who were unpartnered (single, divorced, separated, and widowed), they compose 37 percent of the sample.[7] So the stereotype that many domestic workers are single mothers was borne out. Of course, mothers who are unidas are also legally single, and they compose another 39 percent of the sample; however, the statistical analysis found more similarities than differences between married and unida women.

Education Level

More than half (55 percent) of the participants had completed no more than primary school (elementary school). Twelve of the research participants (3 percent) reported never having attended school. Those who completed secondary school (high school) made up 18 percent of the sample, and only two of the women had graduated from college. Details are provided in table 3.1. Given previous research documenting low levels of schooling among domestic workers, and informal workers more generally, this profile is not surprising and corresponds well to the figures at the national level for domestic workers (Wong 2017, 25).

Place of Birth

Much of the academic research on paid domestic work refers to the large proportion of workers who are transnational migrants. This is true for studies in the United States and Europe and for some Latin American countries, such as Argentina, Chile, and Costa Rica. Ecuador has not typically been a receiving country for immigrants, although this has changed in recent years.[8] Only one survey respondent was born outside the country (in neighboring Colombia). There were also fewer internal migrants than might be expected, given that research on Latin America describes domestic workers as mostly internal migrants (e.g., Cumes 2014; Durin 2014; Maich 2014b). A full 35.5 percent were born right in Guayaquil (located in Guayas Province), the most common city of birth in the survey.

TABLE 3.1. Education level (n = 398)

	NUMBER	PERCENTAGE
No schooling	12	3.02
Did not finish primary school	83	20.85
Finished primary school	124	31.16
Finished primary school, but not secondary	104	26.13
Finished secondary school	70	17.59
Some college	3	0.75
Finished college	2	0.50
TOTAL	**398**	**100%**

TABLE 3.2. Place of birth for domestic workers surveyed

PLACE OF BIRTH	PERCENTAGE OF SAMPLE
Guayas Province (including Guayaquil)	47.8
Esmeraldas Province	20.9
Manabí Province	16.6
Los Ríos Province	6.8
Other province in Ecuador	7.6
Foreign-born (Colombia)	0.25

A total of 21 percent of participants were born in the northernmost province of the coastal region, Esmeraldas. Another 17 percent were born in the coastal province located northwest of Guayas, Manabí. Many other participants were born in the outskirts of Guayaquil, in small towns and rural areas, so that the participants from Guayas Province, including those born in Guayaquil, made up 48 percent of the sample. Those born in another province northeast of Guayas, Los Ríos, made up nearly 7 percent of participants. The two most common birthplaces of participants, Guayas and Esmeraldas provinces, have large concentrations of Afro-Ecuadorian residents.[9] Table 3.2 shows the birthplaces of survey respondents. Internal migrants did not dominate the sample, and international migrants were nearly completely absent.

Neighborhood

Members of the research team used their networks of friends, relatives, and acquaintances to help expand the geographic areas represented beyond the four neighborhoods where survey teams went door-to-door. The sample includes women living in more than twenty-four different neighborhoods, most of which are considered low-income or marginal areas. We also collected data on the neighborhoods in which participants worked, which helped with mapping their commutes across the city from home to work (figure 2).[10]

Getting to Work: Domestic Worker Commutes

Commutes into or across urban spaces are an often overlooked aspect of working conditions. Most Latin American domestic workers live in neighborhoods that are marginal, "both in terms of location and in popular conceptions," parts of the city that lack transportation infrastructure and are far from the comfortable neighborhoods of employers (Fleischer and Marín 2019, 42). What good is an employer respecting the eight-hour workday, if you must spend two hours to get to work, and they don't subsidize your transportation costs? Workers may live in areas that public transportation does not reach, or where bus service is sporadic or infrequent; because they must leave so early in the morning to get to their faraway workplaces, they are also vulnerable to robbery or assault (Fleischer and Marín 2019). These

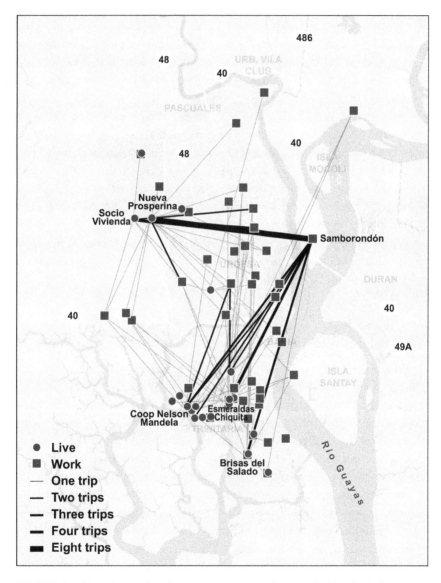

FIGURE 2. Mapping workers' commutes across Guayaquil. Map by Juliana Sarmento da Silveira.

urban journeys are necessary because of the spatial segregation of cities, in which people who can afford to do so insulate themselves from the urban poor in "richer, socially homogeneous" neighborhoods (Fleischer and Marín 2019, 28).

To get a sense of where domestic work jobs are concentrated geographically and the distances that workers must travel to get to those jobs, we collected information from 405 current and former domestic workers on their neighborhood of residence and the location of their most recent domestic employment. In a typical example, a worker living in La Isla Trinitaria and working in a gated community in Vía a Samborondón would have a commute of approximately 3.5 hours round trip. As I discuss in chapters 4 and 5, domestic workers feel that they have limited time with their own families, and the difficult treks between work and home cut into this time even more.

Urban planner Juliana Sarmento da Silveira created the preceding diagram based on our survey data, using the computer program Esri on publicly available maps. The starting points of domestic workers' commutes—that is, their home neighborhoods—are marked with circles. Their destinations—the neighborhoods in which they currently work or most recently worked—are marked with squares. The thicker lines represent more workers making that trip across the city. When considering that the areas in which most live-out domestic workers reside are often the most underserved by public transportation, and that the routes are never going to be straight lines as shown in this diagram, we can appreciate the true significance of their journeys to work.

Working Conditions

As discussed above, we included not only currently employed domestic workers, but also former domestic workers who were unemployed or working in other occupations. These women may have been planning to reenter domestic employment, and were thus temporarily inactive (a reserve army for social reproduction). Or they may have retired from domestic work and could thus provide information on working conditions in previous periods. When researchers include only current domestic employees, they get a static snapshot of an unstable and shifting workforce. Since women move in and out of domestic employment and other informal jobs, it makes sense to include those who are not working in this occupation but have in the past or may in the future. Forty-three percent of respondents were employed as domestic workers at the time of the survey, and 57 percent were previously employed, many of whom had plans to return to domestic work. Of the respondents employed at the time of the survey, 59 percent worked full-time versus 41 percent part-time.

Employed Workers

A total of 173 women, or 43 percent of the sample, were actively employed in private homes at the time of the survey. Of these women, 91 percent were working *puertas afuera* (living outside of homes they worked in) and only 9 percent *puertas adentro* (living in the employer's home at least during the week).[11] Though we don't have statistics for live-in and live-out domestic work in Ecuador, research on Latin America shows that live-in work has been decreasing (ILO 2016a). Still, it is possible that the sample underrepresents the percentage of domestic workers in Guayaquil living in employers' homes. We reached out to workers in the low-income neighborhoods where they resided, and many live-in workers may not visit these neighborhoods, spending most of their time in employers' neighborhoods. Still, we made an effort to recruit those who worked puertas adentro, who the research shows are more vulnerable and more exploited.[12] Whatever the working conditions reported by our respondents, then, it is reasonable to suppose that they are more favorable than those experienced by most live-in workers.

How much were these domestic workers doing? Those who worked full-time (and as one participant memorably put it, "Tiempo completo, ¡y más!")[13] made up 59 percent of the employed survey respondents. The other 41 percent work part-time, some in more than one home.[14] Part-time work for multiple employers is growing relative to full-time work throughout Latin America (ILO 2016a), so this result fits with larger trends. While studies of domestic workers often show that they work long hours, on average the workers we surveyed reported working eight hours per day, a standard work day in line with labor laws. Research shows that those who work puertas adentro have longer hours (ILO 2010), and this probably would be reflected in the aggregate data if more of these workers had participated in the survey.

What tasks were current workers doing on the job? They most commonly reported cooking and cleaning. More than three-quarters (77 percent) reported cooking as part of their job, and 74 percent reported cleaning employers' homes. One-third of these respondents cared for children, and 9 percent cared for elderly or disabled adults. Washing and ironing clothes, some of the most physically exhausting domestic tasks, were performed by 62 percent of the participants. Most workers named two or three tasks. This finding fits with the research on the evolution of paid domestic work, in which hiring several workers, each specializing in one task (e.g., laundry, cooking, child care), has given way to hiring one worker who does "a lot of everything" (Moreno Zúñiga 2013, 96). These findings also echo the classified advertisements discussed in chapter 1, which often sought a "polyfunctional" domestic worker to fill multiple roles.

On average, the participants had been at their current job for 4.5 years; however, there were several participants who had been employed in the same home for decades, which skews this figure higher. The median time at the current job was two years. The average salary that participants reported receiving was $256 per month,[15] which is significantly less than the government-mandated monthly minimum wage at the time we collected data, $340. The minimum wage has since risen to $375 in 2017, $386 in 2018, and then $394 in 2019.

Domestic workers are legally guaranteed the same benefits as other Ecuadorian workers, such as overtime pay, vacation time, the payment of annual bonuses known as the *décimo tercero* and *décimo cuarto*,[16] and social security, which I will discuss separately. Among employed workers, only 14 percent received overtime pay. Less than a third (28 percent) received vacation time, and some of those who did said that they were obligated to take vacation when their employers took their own vacation; they could not decide the dates of their vacation. Slightly more workers (29 percent) reported receiving annual bonuses, although some of them said that they only received partial payments rather than the full amount to which they were entitled. The most striking finding: nearly two-thirds of employed domestic workers (62 percent) told us that they *did not receive any of these benefits*.

Unemployed Workers

Unemployed women, all of whom had been previously employed as domestic workers, represent 57 percent of the sample (n = 227). The median amount of time they had been unemployed was two years. More than half of them, 53 percent, were actively looking for work, and those who were not seeking work had withdrawn from the paid labor force (because of age, health, or family concerns) or given up on finding work. The survey asked unemployed former domestic workers about their previous working conditions. Including in our sample workers who were employed in past decades can give a sense of how working conditions have changed over time, though this analysis is not longitudinal or historical. Like current workers, some of these women had worked in several houses, in different parts of Guayaquil, and thus had a long trajectory of comparative experiences in the occupation.

When asked which benefits they had received in their previous domestic employment job, only 6 percent of these women reported receiving overtime pay, with 7 percent saying they had gotten vacation time, and 7 percent saying they had received bonuses. A full 89 percent of the one-time domestic workers who were not employed at the time of the survey reported having received none of the benefits to which domestic workers are legally entitled. It is possible that

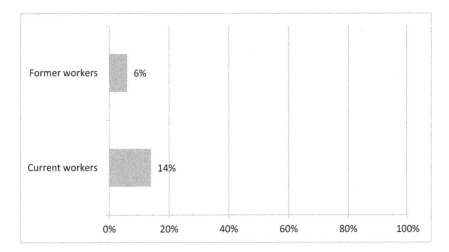

FIGURE 3.   Percent receiving overtime pay

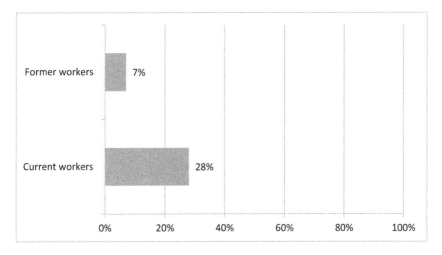

FIGURE 4.   Percent receiving vacation time

these workers' conditions were poorer than those of other workers. Low pay and lack of benefits are some of the main reasons domestic workers are dissatisfied with, and decide to leave, domestic employment, and this may be the case with this group. Because employers are now more aware of their obligations, more of them are providing these mandated benefits as time goes by. Still, the proportion of previously employed workers reporting that they received none of these benefits is significantly higher than the proportion among the currently employed workers (89 percent compared to 62 percent).[17]

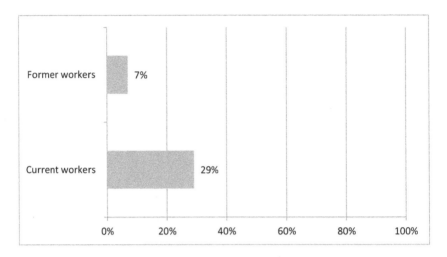

FIGURE 5.   Percent receiving annual bonuses (at least partial payments)

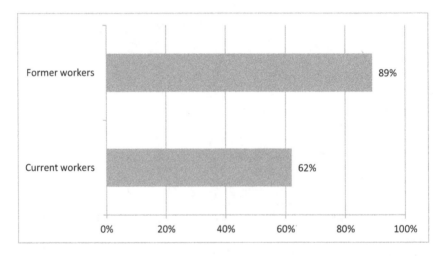

FIGURE 6.   Percent receiving no benefits

Social Security

Domestic workers have the right to enroll in (*afiliarse* in Spanish) the national social security system, IESS. Employers are legally mandated to enroll domestic workers in IESS and contribute on their behalf, with further contributions from the state and the worker herself. Following public campaigns to raise awareness about domestic workers' rights and employers' obligations regarding social security, the research assessed workers' knowledge of their right to enroll. There is almost no published academic research on social security enrollment among

TABLE 3.3. Social security knowledge, enrollment, and use

	YES (%)	NO (%)
Knows that domestic workers have the right to social security	88	12
Is enrolled in social security	19.8	79.2
If enrolled, has used benefits or services	73	27
If not enrolled, has spoken with employers about social security	43	57
If not enrolled, wishes to be enrolled	90	10

Ecuadorian domestic workers, or on their knowledge about it (except for Casanova, Rodríguez, and Bueno Roldán 2018 and Wong 2017). In this survey, several specific questions addressed social security, as shown in table 3.3.

Did Research Participants Know That Domestic Workers Have the Right to Social Security?

Workers' awareness of their labor rights matters for two reasons. The level of awareness helps measure indirectly the success of popular education campaigns, for example, those that ATRH and the government had undertaken beginning around 2009. Gauging awareness also lets us see how much remains to be done in this area. If many people still don't know about domestic workers' rights, then more awareness-raising efforts are needed.

Across education levels, most of the employed and previously employed domestic workers had at least basic knowledge about social security. The vast majority, a full 88 percent, knew that domestic workers have the right to enroll in social security and thus access the benefits that come with enrollment (such as health care), while only 12 percent said they were not aware. This finding shows that there is a high level of knowledge or at least familiarity with this topic. Both former and current workers generally know that their domestic employment makes them eligible for social security. This is good news, though of course the goal is for 100 percent to know their rights.[18]

Were Research Participants Enrolled in Social Security?

Domestic workers' awareness of their rights is important, but the goal of organizers and advocates is for people to exercise their rights. They want all domestic workers to not only know that they can join social security, but also to enroll and start to pay in to the system, along with mandated contributions from employers. Most of these workers were not enrolled in the social security system, however. Only 19.8 percent of the participants, or 79 out of 400 women, said they were enrolled; 79.2 percent said they were not, and 1 percent of participants were not sure whether they were enrolled or not. So while most of the domestic workers surveyed knew about this right, they were not exercising it, and a few were even unsure of their status. This is why I argue that, despite being covered by labor law, domestic work is still informal. The gap between awareness and enrollment shows that there is still much more work to be done to enforce the rights of these workers and confirms just how difficult it is to formalize informal jobs.[19]

Were Those Enrolled Making Use of the Benefits of Social Security?

Social security coverage is only symbolic until beneficiaries start using programs such as health care, pensions, or home loans. So while domestic worker advocates need to investigate levels of awareness and enrollment, they should also show that if these workers join social security, they will use the services to improve their lives. Our data show that the survey participants who are enrolled in social security are making good use of the benefits. Of the participants who said they belonged to IESS, 73 percent said that they had used social security benefits and services. Of the twenty-one participants who were enrolled and had not used their benefits, five said they had not yet needed to use them (three of these women said they had just recently joined). Another five participants who were enrolled said they had not used the services because of lack of time.[20] One of these women commented, "I don't have time, I have to work" (*no tengo tiempo, tengo que trabajar*). This finding confirms previous research that discusses employers' reluctance to give domestic workers time off for medical appointments (Casanova 2013). Another woman who was enrolled said that she had not used the services because "I haven't been taking care of myself" (*me he descuidado*). Domestic workers often do not have time to take good care of themselves, focusing more on their roles in paid and unpaid social reproduction.

Why Were Some Not Enrolled?

Any serious effort to enroll all domestic workers in social security should be based on an understanding of why workers aren't already enrolled. What is impeding their access to their social security entitlement? Among the 316 unenrolled workers we surveyed, the most common reason for not having social security was that their employers did not want to enroll them or to make contributions on their behalf; 30.5 percent of unenrolled participants gave this as the reason they were not enrolled.

Traditional class relations block workers' rights. Employers benefit from the informal arrangements of domestic employment, made possible by poor women's need to work. Employers may see themselves not as employers, but as patrons who help women in need. They see domestic workers not as part of the labor force, but as people who help out around the house and are "like family." The second most common reason, given by 18.8 percent of unenrolled respondents, was they did not know about their right to enroll. Some past domestic workers have since learned of their right to enroll, but did not know about it when employed. The top reasons participants gave for not being enrolled include:

- Employer does not want to enroll me (30.5 percent)
- I didn't know about my right to social security (18.8 percent)
- I am not working right now (6.8 percent)
- I don't want to enroll (5.5 percent)[21]
- They didn't do it back then; when I worked they didn't enroll domestic workers (4.8 percent)
- I don't work anymore (permanently out of the labor force; 1.3 percent)
- I only work part-time (1.3 percent)
- My employer promised to enroll me, but hasn't yet (0.8 percent)
- I just started working (0.3 percent)
- My employer tricked me (0.3 percent)
- I am under eighteen (the legal age to sign up for social security; 0.3 percent)

Though most workers want to be covered, a small percentage do not, perhaps "perceiving the benefits of social security coverage . . . to be of marginal value, while the amount of money lost to taxation is more tangible" (Tomei 2011, 202). We can see from these results some gaps in workers' knowledge about the social security system and how enrollment works. For example, unemployed workers can continue their coverage "voluntarily" until they begin working again (if they can afford it). People who work part-time are eligible, with each employer paying a proportion of the contribution.

Although there are a variety of responses to this question, the most obvious points for possible intervention are the resistance of employers to the idea of enrolling domestic workers, and some workers' lack of awareness about their rights.

Have Unenrolled Respondents Ever Spoken with Their Employers about Social Security?

Workers' knowledge and employers' attitudes are consequential, but even the most willing employer and the most informed worker need to communicate about enrollment and make a joint decision. Is such communication taking place, or does silence surround the topic of social security? The survey asked participants who were not enrolled in social security whether they had ever discussed it with their employers. Less than half, 43 percent, said they had ever had this discussion. Obviously, an employer agreeing to contribute to a domestic worker's social security starts with a conversation. If employers and workers are not talking about it, it will be difficult to increase the percentage of domestic workers enjoying labor rights such as social security benefits. Even so, these are risky conversations for individual workers to have, because there is no real protection against them being fired. In fact, five participants said they had lost previous jobs because employers didn't want to enroll them, and a couple of these women said they were fired for simply bringing up this possibility in conversation. In a survey done in Guayaquil around the same time, 95 percent of domestic workers surveyed agreed that enforcing the social security mandate would decrease employment of domestic workers (Wong 2017, 31). Employers' greater power in the labor relation, and their preference for docile workers who will settle for less, shape these conversations. Rather than experiencing class domination in a collective way alongside other workers, domestic employees experience it as an intense one-on-one relationship. This personalized oppression is difficult to resist as a single, isolated worker.

How Many Unenrolled Respondents Wanted to Enroll?

A skeptical person could look at the low rates of social security enrollment among the domestic workers surveyed and conclude that maybe these women just don't want to participate in social security, that it doesn't matter to them. It is true that twenty-two women gave not wanting social security as their main reason for not being enrolled. Rather than assuming whether uncovered workers wanted or didn't want to be part of IESS, the survey asked them whether they wanted to enroll. The response was overwhelmingly affirmative: 90 percent of the unenrolled domestic workers said they would like to be part of the social security system. Only 10 percent, 32 of the 321 unenrolled women, said they were not interested.

Which Domestic Workers Are Most Vulnerable?

Statistical analysis helped clarify the relationships between social and demographic categories and three dependent variables: (1) whether a worker knew about her right to social security; (2) whether a worker had spoken with her employers (most recent or present) about social security; and (3) whether a worker was enrolled in social security. The sample size of four hundred allowed us to bring to light causal relationships using logistic regression. We ran regressions with several independent variables to see how they affected the main dependent variables. Here I focus on the relationships that were strongest, particularly those that were statistically significant.

Which Workers Are Most Likely to Know Their Rights?

We used logistic regression to find out who is most likely to know that domestic workers have the right to social security. Table 3.4 shows the results of this analysis.

Age and education are both related to this dependent variable. The older a worker is, the less likely she is to know her rights, or at least the right to social security. The effect of age is statistically significant but not very large. We were curious at what age the knowledge of rights drops off. Where is the dividing line between younger women more likely to know and older women less likely to know about social security for domestic workers? Figure 7 shows these results. The percentage of workers who know about this right drops precipitously between the age 50–59 category and the 60–69 category, and then again when we move to the oldest age category. Domestic workers under age sixty are more likely to know their rights.

The respondent's education level is much more likely than their age to affect their awareness of this right. There are two significant variables: primary education (the respondent had some primary schooling or completed primary school/ elementary school) and secondary education (the respondent had some secondary schooling or completed secondary school/high school). College education was not statistically significant in this regression. The effects of primary and secondary education are large and positive, suggesting that workers with these levels

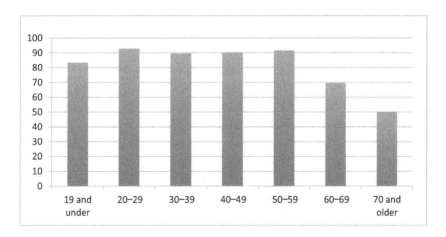

FIGURE 7. Percentage of respondents who know about right to social security, by age category (n = 400)

TABLE 3.4. What factors make workers more likely to know about the right to social security?

| | | | CONFIDENCE INTERVAL | | |
| | | | | | |
VARIABLE	COEFFICIENT β	SIG.	LOWER LIMIT	UPPER LIMIT	EXP (B$_i$) ODDS RATIO
Age	−0.026*	0.054	−0.0526	0.0004	0.974
Primary school education (Ref. = no schooling)	1.352*	0.038	0.0716	2.633	3.866
Secondary school education (Ref. = no schooling)	1.667*	0.020	0.2664	3.0680	5.297
College education (Ref. = no schooling)	0.682	0.596	−1.8406	3.2053	1.978

Prob > chi2 = 0.0067
*Significant at the p ≤.05 level

of education are much more likely to know about their right to social security than those who never attended school.[22] The impact of secondary education is stronger than the impact of primary education. Workers with primary school educations are four times more likely than those who never went to school to know about this right, and workers with secondary school educations are five times more likely.

Which Workers Are Most Likely to Have Spoken with Employers about Social Security?

We used logistic regression to find out who was most likely to have had a conversation with their employer about social security. Table 3.5 shows the results of this analysis.

The most significant variable for explaining whether a domestic worker had spoken with her employer was marital status. Being single or having "other" as her marital status—divorced, separated, or widowed—rather than being married makes a woman significantly more likely to have spoken with her employer about social security. There was no statistically significant difference between legal marriage or cohabitation/civil union, which is logical, as this is a similar relationship status and both types of couples would commonly be considered "married" in the low-income neighborhoods where most participants lived.[23] The result here is robust: being in the nonmarried category increases the likelihood that a woman has spoken with her employer about social security. In fact, single women are more than twice as likely as married women to have had this conversation, and women who are separated, divorced, or widowed are more than three times as likely as married women to have discussed this topic with their employers.

TABLE 3.5. What factors increase the probability that workers have talked to their employers about social security?

| | COEFFICIENT | | CONFIDENCE INTERVAL | | EXP (B₁) |
VARIABLE	β	SIG.	LOWER LIMIT	UPPER LIMIT	ODDS RATIO
Age	−0.009	0.334	−0.0269	0.0991	0.9912
Civil union / Unión libre	0.388	0.279	−0.3150	1.0920	1.4747
Ref. = married					
Single	0.835*	0.022	0.1200	1.5502	2.3051
Ref. = married					
Other marital status	1.275*	0.028	0.1408	2.4085	3.5776
Ref. = married					

Prob > chi2 = 0.0694
* Significant at the p < .05 level

This result is important because many domestic workers, in this sample and around the world, are single mothers. It could be that single or otherwise unpartnered women are more independent and subscribe less to traditional gendered behaviors (i.e., they are more assertive), so they stand up for themselves more in their workplace. Or it could be that because they are the main source of economic support for their families, the unpartnered women are more motivated to get the maximum benefit out of their paid work. These explanations are compatible, so both cultural and economic dynamics could play a role.

Although the effect is small, the older a worker gets, the lower the probability that she reports having spoken with her employer about social security. Perhaps because of greater public attention to domestic workers' rights in recent years, about half of the workers in the youngest age category (nineteen and under) said they had had this conversation with their employer.

Which Workers Are Most Likely to Be Enrolled in Social Security?

We used logistic regression to find out which workers were more likely to enroll in IESS. Table 3.6 shows the results of this analysis.

Age has a statistically significant, but rather small, effect. Being older makes a participant slightly more likely to be covered by social security. Women in the 40–49 age range made up the largest proportion of those who were enrolled. There were no enrolled workers in the youngest and oldest age categories, which identifies two groups that could be targeted for enrollment. Working full-time rather than part-time has a very large effect. Domestic workers in our survey who worked full-time were four times more likely to be enrolled in social security than part-time workers. Since the trend in Ecuador and other parts of Latin America is toward more part-time, sporadic work, all of which is arranged informally,

TABLE 3.6.   What factors make workers more likely to be enrolled in social security?

| | | | CONFIDENCE INTERVAL | | |
| | COEFFICIENT | | LOWER | UPPER | EXP (B₍) |
VARIABLE	β	SIG.	LIMIT	LIMIT	ODDS RATIO
Age	0.031*	0.014	0.0076	0.0686	1.0389
Works full time	1.404**	0.000	0.6904	2.1176	4.0714
(Ref. = Works part time)					

Prob > chi2 = 0.0003
*Significant at the p ≤ .01 level
**Significant at the p < .001 level

this data point raises a concern. If the full-time workforce is shrinking and part-timers are less likely to be enrolled in social security, we may expect coverage rates to grow slowly despite efforts to formalize.

This chapter analyzed the most extensive survey to date of domestic workers in Ecuador, with four hundred women sharing information about their working conditions, benefits, and social security. The survey was administered by ATRH members, who have similar experiences and backgrounds to the survey respondents, in the neighborhoods in which workers tend to live. Most useful for informing policy and organizing strategies are the insights about *which workers* are most likely to know and demand their rights and the evidence that working conditions of current workers are better than those of former workers, which could indicate change over time. Efforts to inform workers of their right to social security seem to have been successful: 88 percent of the survey participants knew that domestic workers are entitled to join IESS. The main barrier to coverage is the reluctance of employers to enroll workers and contribute on their behalf: nearly a third of survey respondents who were not enrolled reported that their employers' opposition was the reason why. Employers' stance on social security is linked to other working conditions as well. A survey conducted with 349 domestic workers in Guayaquil a few months before ours found that enrollment in social security was correlated with higher wages and compliance with other benefits such as vacation time and overtime and bonus pay (Wong 2017). So employers complying with social security mandates are also likely to comply with other labor laws. This fits workers' narratives in interviews, which distinguish between "good" and "bad" employers.

While domestic workers are often thought of as a homogeneous group, statistical analysis of the survey data pinpointed the most important demographic variables. Who was more likely to know about domestic workers' rights? Who was more likely to speak with employers about social security? Who was more likely to be covered by social security? Age was a significant predictor of all three dependent variables. Older workers were less likely to know they were entitled as domestic workers to social security, with knowledge dropping substantially after age fifty-nine. Older workers were slightly less likely to have spoken with their employers about social security, yet slightly more likely to be covered. This may seem contradictory, yet older workers have a longer work history, which means they have had more chances than younger workers to get social security through their job or jobs. Still, older workers are vulnerable if they do not know their rights and are hesitant to discuss them with their employers. Because previous generations held even more rigid ideas about class hierarchy than younger ones, it makes sense that older workers would be more reluctant to confront employers about their rights.

Education also mattered for the knowledge of rights, which seems logical. The differences between those who had not had formal schooling and those who had were quite stark. Workers with an elementary-school education were four times more likely to know about the social security entitlement than those who had not gone to school, and workers who had attended high school were even more likely to know. Lower-educated workers, including informal workers like these women, are more vulnerable to being denied their legal rights as they are less likely to be informed about them. It is possible that some of the women with lower education levels were illiterate as well, which would limit the ways they could gather information.

The numbers tell a story of vulnerable workers, but they also tell a story of those who are brave. Among younger women, under age nineteen, half said that they had spoken to their employer about social security coverage. These young domestic workers, whom we might expect to be timid or lack experience in navigating this labor relation, report having these conversations as much as their fifty-year-old colleagues, and more than some other age groups. Are class relations shifting slightly in these new employment arrangements? We need more research to specifically investigate how younger workers think about class, domination, the obligations of employers and employees, and how they interact with employers.

We also found that single mothers are boldly entering the social security conversation. Nearly all participants were mothers, but their marital and relationship status varied, and this status affected behavior. Single women were more than twice as likely as their married counterparts to speak to employers about social security. Those who were uncoupled due to some major life event—separation, divorce, or death—were three times more likely to have the social security conversation with employers. Either these uncoupled mothers were less beholden to traditional expectations of submissive behavior from domestic workers, or their status as the breadwinner for the family spurred them to obtain the maximum benefit from their employment . . . or both. These women are used to *la lucha*, the daily struggle to support their families and claim respect in a society that judges them harshly for being on their own. Their sole responsibility for unpaid social reproduction *and* economically supporting their household affected how they approached their paid work of social reproduction.

Confirming research findings from around Latin America, working conditions reported by our participants are not good. But they seem to be improving somewhat over time. More than twice as many current workers reported receiving overtime pay when compared with former workers. For vacation time and bonuses, more than four times as many current workers reported receiving these benefits. We do not have details about when exactly former workers left the domestic labor force, nor longitudinal data, but these figures indicate that today's workers are receiving more benefits than their predecessors. Among current workers, a full 62 percent receive *none* of the benefits the survey mentioned. Former workers overwhelmingly reported no benefits, at 89 percent. Despite this considerable improvement, there's still a long way to go for today's domestic workers.

The survey results highlight some possible points for intervention by domestic worker advocates and organizers. The conversation with employers is a critical moment, in which the worker can try to ensure her full legal rights, including that of social security coverage. Yet many workers are avoiding this conversation, and with good reason; some workers in our survey said that they were fired for simply bringing it up. There is not much previous research on these negotiations between employers and domestic workers regarding social security. One study in Argentina showed that employers often gave pretexts for not enrolling their worker that amounted to saying the worker did not want or need social security. When granted, enrollment was usually a unilateral decision by employers rather than something that workers requested. Workers' negotiation efforts were aimed at obtaining good salaries or raises, rather than the more long-term goal of social security membership (Pereyra 2015).

Perhaps there are ways to make this conversation less risky for workers, and more of a routine practice at the time of hiring. If there were a script for employers and workers, a small paper that they could use to guide these conversations, maybe they would be easier. Yet pressuring workers to talk to employers is probably not a good strategy. Domestic workers, especially those who have been on the job for some time, know their employers' temperaments and to some extent, their social and political attitudes. The worker must decide for herself how to handle the situation. But if she does want to talk it over with the employer, advocates could give her a sort of cheat sheet to help her communicate effectively. One key moment for intervening and encouraging this conversation is the very beginning of the domestic employment relation: hiring. Though power relations play out differently in different homes, some employers respect domestic workers who come in knowing their legal rights and expecting them to be honored (Canevaro 2008). Others identify with a more rigid class boundary and expect workers to do their job and not speak up.

Along with strategies for workers and greater awareness and commitment from employers, enforcement of existing laws is needed. Workers should not bear all the burden, because they hold much less power than the employer in this labor relation, and as the sole employee in most homes, they do not have the option of collective action in the workplace. The penalties for employers' non-compliance are rarely implemented in Ecuador, and even so, are not substantial enough to act as a deterrent. Better enforcement would require sustained investment from the government, which so far has not happened. In addition to systematic labor inspections and punishments for employers who are not following the law, one Ecuadorian economist has suggested that government subsidies for middle-income employers could increase social security enrollment rates (Wong 2017). Such a policy recognizes that some employers are being truthful when they say they cannot afford to provide workers the legally mandated wages and benefits.

Another possible point for intervention is education. The survey results show that the more educated a domestic worker is, the more likely she is to know her rights, which is the first step toward defending them. Higher levels of education may keep women out of domestic work altogether. In the next chapter, women's accounts of their work histories show how family and economic pressures can force young women out of school and into low-paid and exploitative work, including domestic work. Interventions designed to keep young girls in school, by providing school fees or other assistance, can increase education levels among women from poor and working-class backgrounds. We know more education can help them get better jobs, but this survey also shows that even in less desirable jobs, being better-educated can help them know their rights. Efforts to keep young women in school will benefit those eventually employed in domestic work, and members of this vulnerable population more generally.

Most of the women in our survey, and most domestic workers, are mothers. Many are single mothers. We found that the boldest workers in bringing up conversations about the right to social security were those who were the primary provider for their household. Domestic work organizers could target these single mothers—already pushing for more respect in their workplaces—in recruiting activists and representatives. Single mothers may be the most likely to respond to organizers' calls for collective action to improve domestic workers' lives because of the independence forged in fighting for their families and battling negative stereotypes. The absence of a male partner who might discourage them from activism may also help (Magliano, Perissinotti, and Zenklusen 2017).

Drawing on the commonalities of single mothers may also be a way to get some employers to support a domestic workers' rights platform. While all women tend to be responsible for unpaid social reproduction, many single mothers are doing this unpaid social reproduction while also engaging in paid work as the primary or sole breadwinner for their households. Today, 29 percent of all Ecuadorian households, across class levels, are headed by women. Among women heads of household, 13.4 percent are domestic workers, 27.3 percent work in the private sector, 13.5 percent work for the government, and 35.4 percent are self-employed (INEC 2012). These statistics mean that today's domestic workers are more likely than their predecessors to work for a woman employer who is single, separated, or divorced.[24] Could there be a space for solidarity between single mother employers and single mother domestic workers? It is impossible to know this in the abstract, but perhaps some pilot programs in this area could answer this question. Women employers and domestic workers sometimes bond over shared experiences of separation or loss of a partner (Canevaro 2008). There may be a way to harness these intimate exchanges and similar—though certainly unequal—experiences of single motherhood to improve the labor relation and working conditions.

Formalization can entail passing specific laws regarding domestic employment, or enforcing existing laws consistently. The survey results provide evidence that can be applied to the debate over formalizing domestic work: whether to formalize, and how and why. My research takes the worker's perspective as a starting point and privileges this subjective experience and expertise. It makes sense to evaluate the idea of formalization by asking whether workers want to formalize, rather than assuming that they do. In our survey we did not ask about formalization directly, but we did focus on social security coverage, a major component of formalization efforts in Latin America. We asked women whether they wanted to enroll in social security, to ascertain whether they saw enrollment as advantageous. We also asked those who were not enrolled about their reasons for not joining IESS, which provided another opportunity for them to voice resistance to the idea of social security. The women's voices support formalization, at least in social security coverage. Of those who were not enrolled in the social security system, 90 percent said they wanted to be enrolled. Only 5.5 percent of the participants who were not enrolled said it was because they did not want to be, and some of these women claimed that they would change their mind if they could keep other government benefits, such as welfare payments, along with getting social security coverage. We also know from the survey results that, once they are in the social security system, domestic workers use the services. So most workers support the idea of formalization, but they need to feel that they are not giving too much up to gain access to social security.

We learned indirectly from these workers about employers' resistance to for-malization, which is the most serious barrier to overcome. Because of the class relations embedded in contemporary domestic employment, which are partially rooted in precapitalist and colonial social structures, it is difficult to get employ-ers to see themselves as employers rather than patrons doing a good deed by employing a domestic worker. Paid domestic work, since it is part of social repro-duction rather than production, is not seen as real work by employers, who feel their denial of domestic workers' rights is justified.

In the next chapter, on women's work histories and trajectories, we once again see these three aspects of domestic worker exploitation: social reproduction, informality, and class. Women tend to move in and out of domestic work and unpaid social reproduction or informal employment in the service sector, rather than into the production process or formal employment where they might have better working conditions. Their class-based networks and low levels of educa-tion make it difficult to break out of this cycle of low-paid employment, unem-ployment, and informal income-earning activities aimed at survival. Often, cruel or domineering employers push them out of work in private homes, yet domestic workers continue seeking dignity.

PATHWAYS THROUGH POVERTY

¿Qué le ha impedido salir de este trabajo?
Porque no hay otro.
¿En qué trabajaría si saliera del trabajo del hogar?
En lo que sea.

What has kept you from leaving this work?
Because there is no other work.
What work would you do if you left domestic work?
Anything, whatever there was.

—Excerpt from domestic worker interview

Ahorita no hay trabajo, el país está muy—es muy difícil conseguir trabajo. Las personas ahorita no dan trabajo así nomás. Gracias a Dios conseguí el trabajo que tengo. [Right now there is no work, the country is very—it is very difficult to get work. People right now aren't just giving jobs easily. Thank God I found the job I have.]

—Domestic worker interviewee who works fifty-six hours per week for
$60 weekly salary

People often assume that domestic work is a transitional occupation. In the Latin American version of this narrative, young women move to urban areas from the countryside, join the informal workforce as domestic workers, and then move on to other types of employment once they establish themselves in the city. Yet the research shows that this is a myth: domestic employment is not really a stepping stone to other, better work. There are few avenues for mobility in domestic employment (Hondagneu-Sotelo 1994; Lautier 2003; Tizziani 2011a), and the story of the maid rising up to become the lady of the house, with her own domestic employees, is usually a *telenovela* fabrication. Rigid class boundaries and low levels of education limit upward mobility for domestic workers and other informal workers.

Researchers sometimes tell another slanted story, making it seem that "domestic worker" is a static occupational role and identity (e.g., García López 2012). In this view, domestic work is not something you do, but rather something you are. This perspective makes intuitive sense, since paid domestic work is what sociologist

Erving Goffman (1963) might have called a discredited identity. The stigma of dirty work stubbornly clings to those who do it, as I showed in chapter 2. But employment patterns of past eras—in which a domestic worker stayed with the same employer from youth through old age—have changed. Multiple employers and part-time work are more common than ever before. Whether women identify as domestic workers, whether it is a lifelong occupation, or whether they use domestic employment as their main source of income are all empirical questions. Does the image of domestic work as a static category and a dead-end job match up with the stories that women who have done domestic work tell about their lives? We interviewed fifty-two women in four Ecuadorian cities about their work histories, which all include stints of paid domestic work, periods of unemployment, and usually other jobs. The goal was to find out what sorts of labor trajectories were the most common among this population, whether women who left domestic work were doing so for better jobs, and what factors weighed most heavily in their decisions about paid work.

The women's accounts explode common assumptions. Domestic employment has not been a stepping stone to more desirable jobs, but neither has it been the only job that these women have done. Their employment in private homes has been disrupted, temporary, sporadic, and anything but stable. Rather than mobility, I found circularity: women cycling in and out of the informal labor market over the course of their lives, making employment decisions that are shaped by economic, health, and family crises. Their engagement in unpaid social reproduction affected both their choice to do paid social reproduction in the first place, and the way they managed that reproductive labor over time.

Upward mobility is largely out of reach. Life consists of *la lucha*, struggle: a metaphor but also a daily routine. La lucha is collective and individual. It involves both reacting to uncontrollable events—especially tough economic conditions that the women euphemistically referred to as *la situación*—and also strategically planning and aspiring to better circumstances. When we begin to see domestic workers not as an isolated group, but as informal laborers and members of the working class, new possibilities emerge for solidarity among broader swaths of workers. While domestic worker organizing is crucial for progress and has borne fruit in many Latin American countries, the realization that women are not only or always domestic workers can lay the groundwork for more far-reaching alliances.

This chapter traces the labor trajectories of Ecuadorian women who have done domestic work: some are currently employed in private homes, and some are not. By including both employed and unemployed domestic workers, I recognize and incorporate, rather than avoid, the messiness of poor women's work histories. Without formal contracts, their jobs are precarious and unstable, as are many other aspects of their lives. Most research, fixated on current employment in domestic work as the sole criterion for selecting study participants, reproduces "domestic worker" as a fixed occupational identity. Yet these women juggle many roles and identities in their daily luchas: mother, daughter, wife, self-employed, domestic worker, caregiver, student, and more. The stories they told contradicted even the assumptions of the research team that designed the interview guide. Rather than leaving domestic work for better employment opportunities, more often than not women left the occupation to protest poor working conditions, or in response to life events outside of work. The question of whether they were better off in domestic work or out of it was moot: they seemed to struggle regardless. Rather than moving into formal employment, they told us about past and present jobs that were nearly all located in the informal economy.[1] These stories help us to better understand not just women who do domestic work, but also the employment decisions of poor women more generally.

Previous Research on Domestic Workers' Trajectories

Conventional wisdom—as seen in media portrayals, academic research, and advocacy discourse—is that women *are* domestic workers, that the occupational identity, if not each individual job, is stable. Some Latin American research has shown that women do domestic work intermittently, and combine domestic employment with other work (e.g., Tizziani 2011a), but we still need to know more about women's nondomestic employment and the labor trajectories of ex-domestic workers to get a fuller picture of low-income women's work lives. There is little room for upward socioeconomic mobility through domestic employment, but women workers without formal education do move frequently between different types of domestic work and other work, between paid work and unemployment, and from one employer to another (Lautier 2003; Tizziani 2011a). Rather than remaining in one job, or staying unemployed once they leave a job, people use their social networks to find employment, just as employers use their networks to find workers (Toledo González 2013; see Undurraga 2011 for a description of social networks and women's employment in Chile). Domestic workers' labor trajectories are "not linear but full of pendular movements and searches" (Tizziani 2011a, 323–24). We might describe this as horizontal rather than vertical mobility. Yet the illusory potential for upward mobility serves a purpose, as hope becomes a survival strategy that helps workers to endure poor working conditions (Lautier 2003). When this hope breaks down, domestic workers can internalize a sense of inferiority and become fatalistic, doubting their ability to shape or change their lives (León 2013, 202). Both hope and fatalism were evident in our interview data.

The other work that women do in between or in addition to domestic work is also usually "poorly paid and without social protections" (Toledo González 2013, 52), but it is unclear how women decide to move in and out of domestic work, and what they think of their different jobs. In research focusing on domestic employment, we often do not get enough information on how women make these decisions, or how they experience the other types of work that they do over the life course. Knowing more about the "universe of labor possibilities" (Tizziani 2011a, 315) open to women can also inform strategies for improving their working and living conditions.

Women stay at domestic work jobs for different lengths of time. Among the interviewees for this chapter, one woman quit after two weeks, and another worked for the same family for six years. Most dipped in and out of the domestic labor market over the course of their lives, working less than two years at each place on average. Some research has shown that working in the occupation over many years is a source of strength and resistance for domestic workers (Thornton Dill 1988).[2] We also know that relational skills matter more for working conditions than technical skills (Tizziani 2011a, 322). Thus this pattern of shorter stints of domestic employment could reduce workers' bargaining power and capacity to resist employers' exploitation. Yet according to our data, older workers—those with more time in the occupation—seem to resist the personalized domination of domestic employment less than their younger counterparts. They often accept the common belief in the moral correctness of a class hierarchy in which some women are born to be *patronas* (employers) and some to be *empleadas* (domestic workers; Ávila 2008). As seen in chapter 3, younger workers we surveyed are more likely to know their rights and to talk to their employers about social security. They may be more willing to negotiate or actively resist rather than simply quitting a bad job.

This part of the research was spurred by an interest in women's pathways into and out of domestic work, which I shared with my collaborators from the Asociación de Trabajadoras Remuneradas del Hogar (ATRH) and FOS, their funder. What resources did women draw on when trying to leave domestic work, in hopes of finding better pay and better treatment in other jobs? What kept women in domestic work when they would prefer to be doing some other type of work? And how did women fare after leaving domestic work? In our initial discussions of work trajectories and individual labor histories, some members of ATRH questioned the purpose of our proposed research. If we were able to find out information that illuminated pathways out of domestic work, wouldn't we be reducing the population of domestic workers and thus shrinking the association's constituency? Would ATRH be putting itself out of a job? Thinking out loud together, we reaffirmed the exploratory aim of this research project and the probability that domestic work would continue in some form in Ecuador regardless of our actions. We agreed that we wanted women to have positive work experiences and educational or training opportunities, whether or not they were domestic workers. This settled, we got to work designing the research project. In total, fifty-two participants—current and former domestic workers—were interviewed in four Ecuadorian cities.[3] Despite slight differences in participants' average education levels in the four cities, interview accounts revealed similarities in women's work lives across the cities.

Entering the Workforce

The average age at which interviewees began paid work was eighteen. But of the fifty women who told us when they started working, twenty-two reported being under age sixteen, with some as young as eight when they first entered the labor force. Why did women first enter the workforce, some of them leaving school to begin paid work? Those who began working young, before the current legal age of fifteen, often said that their family needed money for food or for their studies or those of their siblings. Many mentioned living with a single mother. Those who grew up in the countryside saw agricultural work, paid or unpaid, as a natural part of childhood: as one woman said, in farming families you work "from the time you are born." Often there simply were not enough resources without all possible earners being in the paid labor force (García López 2012 discusses similar pressures driving rural Colombian women into domestic work). Life in their families of origin involved a constant lucha. Some of those whose first job was domestic work reported their entry into this employment: "My mother was very poor, and had no way to support us. My father always had work but never cared about us. . . . [I started to work] from almost eight years old. . . . We didn't have opportunities and were suffering from hunger. My mother gave me to some people [unos señores] in Quito to work [in their home]." Some women who began domestic employment as children said their employers did not allow them to go to school. We know from previous research by ATRH and throughout Latin America that child labor is still a serious problem in domestic employment (ILO 2016a, 2010; Romo 2013), and that some underage domestic workers are paid only in room and board.

Another reason that women left school, often to begin paid work, was that they entered into a serious relationship with a man (me comprometí, as they put it). One interviewee told us that her male partner insisted that she leave school:

"There are husbands [*maridos*] that don't want the woman to progress, [and] my husband is . . . one of those *manabas celosos* [jealous men from the province of Manabí]." These new partnerships that women mentioned might not be a legal marriage, but involved them leaving their parents' home and building a life with their partner. Often, pregnancy precipitated a young woman's decision to leave school or move in with a partner. When one interviewee was asked, "Why did you stop going to school?" she answered with a laugh, "Because I got pregnant, why else?" Others said, "because I fell in love" or "because I entered a committed relationship" (me comprometí). When it came to paid work, some women said that they started working because they were pregnant (though others quit working for the same reason). Sometimes unpaid carework other than motherhood was their reason for quitting school. As one woman told us, "My mother was ill and I was the one who had to care for her during the illness; if not, I would have kept studying." Social reproduction is seen as women's work, and even at young ages these reproductive tasks may shape decisions. A small minority of women said they left school because they did not like it or were not good at it. Only one interviewee told us she left school to pursue vocational training.

Women who entered the paid workforce at older ages—in their twenties and beyond—often did so in response to a change in their relationship status or family income. Either they had separated from their partner, or he had lost his job. A typical response of a woman (who began working at twenty-two) to the question of why she entered the labor force: "Because I separated from my children's father and I needed money [*la necesidad*]." This group of women had previously been doing unpaid household work and found themselves obligated to work for pay, with little education or training and thus few employment options.

How do women find that first job, and the job after that? Nearly always, they rely on friends and family to both recommend them to potential employers and to vouch for those employers. Although one woman said she found her first job by going door to door, it was much more common to learn about work opportunities through sisters, mothers, or in-laws. Friends can help, too: "Sometimes you need to work and your friends say to you, 'You know, there's a job,' so then [I say] 'look, take me there to find out how it is.'" Employers may also use their networks to help former employees find new work. An interviewee described this process: "From the previous job I left, they recommended me and I started the next job, and from there I also left and they recommended me and I went to work somewhere else." These kinds of recommendations usually only happen when employer and worker part on good terms, which, as we know from workers' narratives and existing research, is often not the case.

Why Domestic Work?

We already know that women often see domestic employment as a last resort, even those from poor backgrounds (Casanova 2011a; Goldstein 2003). Some research participants exemplified what social scientists call occupational inheritance: their mothers were also domestic workers. This was the case for 29 percent of our sample. The pattern of multiple generations of domestic workers is well documented in the academic literature, although the recent aging of the domestic worker population means that it is becoming less common (Brites 2013; Tizziani 2011a; Valenzuela and Mora 2009). Some participants had other relatives in domestic employment, including sisters and grandmothers. Perhaps these women were socialized to see paid domestic work as something that they could and would do when the time came.

Some women claimed that they engaged in paid work only because they needed to, whereas others valued being able to work: "Being stuck in the house and not doing something active and useful makes me feel bad," said one interviewee. When we asked women why they started domestic work, many indicated that they lacked other skills, saying, "It's all I know how to do." They had been doing housework and carework as children without being paid, socialized as girls in a society with stereotypes about women's natural abilities that classified social reproduction as a feminine role. Yet responsibility for social reproduction does not always keep women out of paid work. In fact, they often mentioned entering the labor force *because* they had added social reproduction responsibilities at home. One said she quit school and started working because "I got married, had kids, and had to work."

But many women pointed to another reason why they initially entered domestic employment, why they continued in it and returned to it after periods of interruption, and why they might return to it. They complained about the lack of employment alternatives, saying that it was nearly impossible to find other or better work. A common explanation was, "There was no other work, I was looking and no, they don't want to give you work right now." When asked what job she would like to do in the future, one woman replied, "Whatever job I can get, basically." Another said, "No, I don't want to leave [domestic work] because it is difficult to get other work." Though it may be challenging to find domestic work, requiring that women activate their social networks and subject themselves to employers' scrutiny, there are no formal barriers to entering this occupation.

These reasons for working in private homes explain women's first jobs, but also why they keep coming back to domestic work after periods of unemployment (voluntary or involuntary) or other types of work, almost exclusively informal. They want to work, but would prefer a job "where they don't exploit me and don't pay me too little." I will discuss these movements in and out of different types of jobs later in the chapter.

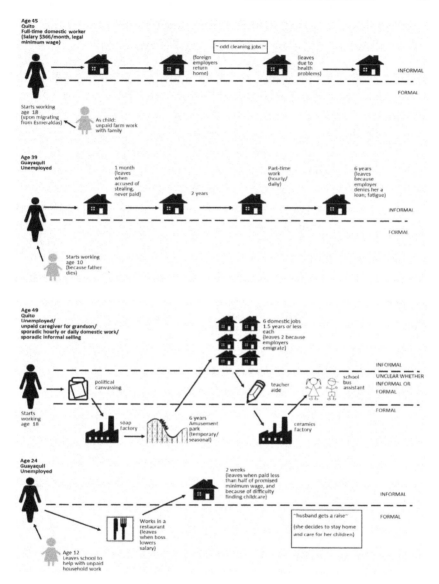

FIGURE 8. Mapping interviewees' work histories

Paths to Unemployment

There are three ways of understanding unemployment among this population of low-wage urban informal workers. First, the domestic work sector is shrinking and there are not many options outside of domestic work, especially for older and less-educated women. Second, domestic workers decide to leave specific jobs because of poor working conditions; a moment arrives when they decide that not having a job is better than having this particular bad job. Third, women pull back from paid work altogether periodically throughout their lives because of individual, familial, and social factors.

Most of the women interviewed had worked in several houses. They kept coming back to domestic work, despite nearly all agreeing that they wanted out of this occupation. Learning why employment relationships break up gives us a view into working conditions and workers' limited negotiating capacity (which also leads to their lack of social security coverage: see chapter 3). If women had fewer than four domestic work jobs in their work history, we asked them why they left each one. If they had more than four, we asked about the reasons for leaving the last few jobs. Several answers recurred within and across individual work histories.

Domestic workers often left jobs because of the pay. Specific complaints include low pay (for example, a daily wage of ten dollars for eleven hours of work), and several workers said that their salaries actually went down over time, which is the opposite of what we might expect in formal employment. One woman told us, "In a few homes they paid me $180 per month [less than minimum wage] and then they kept paying me less and less"; another said, "instead of raising my salary, they lowered it." Because written contracts are rarely part of domestic employment arrangements, workers felt they had no recourse. Another common issue was irregular payments (*pagos impuntuales*). Employers would often fall behind on paying the domestic worker, and she would not know when to expect payment despite verbal agreements on pay periods when the work relationship began. Unpaid back wages and underpayment are forms of wage theft, a frequent problem in informal work that depends on an employer (and also an issue in low-paying formal jobs). One worker said she left because her employer only paid her every two months and owed her a month's salary when she decided to quit. Workers have little power to negotiate these issues, especially in the absence of a written contract or a formal employment relation. As one worker put it, "I have had bad luck with those jobs. I don't know, it's like they see my face and they don't want to pay me." In salary disputes, the worker usually leaves without ever receiving restitution from the employer. But job opportunities are so scarce that some workers end up returning not only to domestic work but to the same irresponsible employers. This worker's story shows such a return:

> Correa became president [and started talking about domestic workers' rights] and the lady [employer] didn't have enough to pay for my social security and the minimum wage. So I left and I filed a complaint against

her, but then I ran out of money to keep going with the process. And
then I returned to the same job. . . . I don't have resources, nor savings,
and little skills or knowledge.

Several women also said that they quit their job because their employers refused
to enroll them in social security. In one extreme case, a woman told us her
employers had lied about her being enrolled, which she only learned when she
went to get medical care and was informed by the clinic staff that she was not
covered. After that humiliating experience, she left her job.

Written contracts lay out payment terms and describe the workload. Almost
always working without written contracts, interviewees recounted being required to do more work once they were hired than what they originally agreed to.
This could mean the addition of new tasks: for example, she was hired to care
for children and then the employer asked her to clean also. Or it could mean that
agreed-upon tasks were especially onerous: for example, when the employer said
to clean the house, they also meant to wash the windows, which the worker had
not expected. One interviewee said that she was asked to attend to more people
than she had originally been told.

Workers often complained that they were asked to do the job of more than one
person: "I did everything: cooked, cleaned, ironed, and they paid me whatever
they wanted." This reflects a shift in the patterns of domestic work in Ecuador
and elsewhere in Latin America, as households that could previously hire multiple employees—say, a general worker and one who only did laundry—now hire
just one, who has to do everything. This trend is correlated with issues of space
(houses are smaller in increasingly crowded cities) and money (as employers
expand their consumption, they do not want to increase their budget for domestic work). The classified advertisements I analyzed in chapter 1 clearly show that
multiple roles and disparate tasks are included in most "domestic worker" positions today. This exploitation and overwork were other reasons that women gave
for voluntarily leaving a job. Some women did not think that they were asked to
do an unfair amount, but still described the work as "tiring" (*cansado, agotador*),
"heavy" (*pesado*), "physical" (*forzoso* or *forzado*), or involving a risk of injury.
One interviewee said, "The going up and down stairs is too much." Or they had
trouble reconciling long hours of domestic employment with unpaid domestic
responsibilities, as one woman said: "I didn't even last a month. I quit because
my schedule was from eight in the morning to eight at night, and my son was
little." In an employment arrangement without legally mandated breaks or vacation time, and with long commutes, the only way some workers can rest is to quit
their job.

Workers we interviewed discussed suffering from health problems: diabetes, high or low blood pressure, poor eyesight, and joint pain. These health problems were sometimes acute enough for a worker to quit her job. It is impossible to know whether some of the women's health troubles were caused directly by their working conditions, or their generally low socioeconomic status. But poor health is exacerbated by, if not caused by, their domestic employment. They certainly lack access to medical care. A few workers specifically mentioned leaving a job because of their advancing age, which inhibited their ability to do physically tax-ing work and meant their health deteriorated more rapidly.

The issue of trato (treatment) in domestic work is a major point of con-tention for workers and employers, who may have different ideas about how they should relate to each other. Power dynamics vary across households, but trato implies the management of emotions, distance, and respect by employers. Trato is one marker of the boundaries between the family and the domestic worker, as employers can use a more brutal form of class domination or a softer form of paternalism or condescension (Canevaro 2008, 17; Durin 2017). The idea that good treatment can make up for low salaries or other material disadvantages is rooted in colonial and neocolonial patronage and master-servant relations (Brites 2014; García Lopez 2012). These relations are stronger with live-in work, which (not coincidentally) has poorer working conditions. As one woman described it, "They would be bossing me around, like if I was already in bed, they'd get me out of bed to make tea for so-and-so." Another said she quit a job because she had to sleep on the floor in the room of the child she cared for. A third said she quit because she was left alone for long stretches of time locked in the house, something I had heard in other workers' accounts. Some women explicitly linked their dream of having their own business or being their own boss to these negative experiences with "authoritarian bosses." A former domestic worker explained that she left the occupation (she hoped for good) because "employers [los patrones] are bad, they treat people bad: they want to humiliate them." A few women reported being passed to or shared among different family members' households as if they were property.

Some interviewees expected a more traditional patronage-type relation-ship, and appreciated the personalized nature of domestic employment when compared with other types of work (see similar findings from Argentina in Tiz-ziani 2011a, and Brazil in Brites 2014). One woman who began domestic work very young expressed appreciation for employers who "didn't see me as a maid [empleada] but as a girl that they should help. . . . They didn't exploit me, if they went shopping, they bought something for me too." Another thought that her employers, who paid her eighty dollars for working twenty-five hours per week—substantially less than the minimum wage—"have me work there to help me out." An excerpt from another interview shows how particular forms of trato can obscure the labor relationship and impede workers' rights:

> INTERVIEWER: Did your employers give you severance pay [*liquidación*] when you left that job?
>
> INTERVIEWEE: No, because they were like my parents, they were my godparents for my wedding. I helped out working with them, and my husband worked there. . . . When I was first married, I kept working there. . . . I liked earlier times better [*me gustaba más los tiempos de antes*].

Such employees sometimes left jobs when they felt that employers were not living up to the ideals of helping the worker or including her in family activities. One worker mentioned loans, which could be seen as a normal part of a patronage relationship: "I had been talking to them about needing a loan for two months . . . and they pretended to be deaf, mute, and blind and then that made me angry [*me dio coraje*] and I left on my own." Others felt that their work entitled them to dignified treatment just as any other worker would expect, and they left jobs because of poor trato. One full-time domestic worker said she quit a previous job because "the lady mistreated me, but verbally, I mean, she had a really strong character [*tenía un carácter muy fuerte*]." In Ecuador, "strong character" is a euphemism used to refer to people who are abusive, mean, or domineering.

Research participants also described pulling out of the workforce entirely, rather than leaving one job with the goal of finding another immediately. Similar rationales applied to these decisions: their health problems demanded rest and attention, or they felt that they were getting too old (age discrimination is a part of this calculation, not just their self-assessments).[4] Those under sixty years old usually planned to reenter paid work after their situation changed.

The most common reason for leaving the paid workforce was a major change in family life or family structure. Pregnant domestic workers often quit their jobs before they are fired, since they know they cannot expect maternity leave; many also intend to stay home to care for young children for a while. Leaving paid work is a decision mothers often justify by saying that their children need them. Getting married or moving in with a romantic partner is another reason women pull back from paid work; on the other hand, these life changes can sometimes propel them into the labor market. Just as entering a committed relationship can disrupt young women's schooling, it can disrupt their employment at any age. Another family-related reason for leaving paid work, as with leaving school, has to do with women's unpaid social reproduction. The interviewees described having to stop working to care for parents or other relatives who were sick or disabled. In the tug-of-war between paid and unpaid social reproduction, the unpaid work won out because of women's dedication to their family members and the expectation that they would be the ones to prioritize family over employment. Shifts in family life might also mean that women suddenly find themselves with no children to care for, and at least one woman quit her job for this reason: "My daughters both left home to live with their partners, and I was left alone, and I didn't really feel any motivation to work anymore." This may be a goal for some women, as one interviewee said that rather than paid work to support others, she would prefer "to live alone without having to worry about this one or that one, but just have to take care of myself."

So far I have focused on voluntary, or at least self-initiated, unemployment. But workers may find themselves out of a job for reasons beyond their control. Employers may fire them, for example: "I left after a month, because the *señora* [employer] claimed that I had supposedly stolen a wedding ring and her husband's chain. But that was a move by her so she didn't have to pay me." Or employers die, especially if they are elderly, and their surviving family members often feel no obligation to a domestic worker whom they did not hire. In a now-familiar scenario, employers' families may decide to migrate to other countries, leaving the worker without a job. This sometimes happened to the same worker repeatedly, as with the participant who told us that some of her employers "had gone to live abroad, some went to Spain, others went to Italy, and then . . . I didn't have anywhere to work." While such employers may refer workers to other potential employers, there is no guarantee that they will do this or that it will result in a new job. And since they rarely give severance pay, workers may be left scrambling.

There are many causes of unemployment among women who are poor and live in marginal urban areas. In the case of domestic work, however, particular narratives reappear as workers make sense of their own work decisions, untimely firings, or breaks from paid labor. Most say that they want to leave this occupation, but they are more likely to leave particular jobs—to protest with their feet—and take periodic time-outs from domestic work, returning to work in a new house, than to move on to better types of paid work.

Other Employment

What other kinds of work were women doing in between (and in a few cases, along with) stints of domestic employment? Nearly all these jobs were located in the informal sector and generated low earnings, which questions the assumption that moving out of domestic work means moving up into a better job. Self-employed informal workers earn on average $90 less than the monthly minimum wage, and agricultural or other day laborers may earn $200 less than the minimum wage (*Revista Líderes* 2015; *América Economía* 2015). Leaving domestic employment does not equal upward mobility.

Most of the other work that women described fell into the category of informal self-employment such as the selling of food or small consumer goods (e.g., clothing), and a handful of women did informal service work (nursing, flower arranging, or beauty work such as doing nails). This work could be sporadic and provisional: as one interviewee put it, "I sell whatever I can [*cualquier cosa*] to try to get ahead." Some of the items that women sold included: meat, sweet or green cooked plantains, *bolones* (a fried snack or breakfast food made from green plantains and stuffed with cheese or pork rinds), sausages, fish pies (*corviches*), hominy (*mote*), corn, underwear, birds, and ice cream. The common thread here is that these are products that require only a small amount of capital to acquire or make, and at least in the case of food, the profit margins are also quite small. One woman told us that she earned twenty dollars every two weeks with her selling, for example. Informal sales fill a gap not only in urban employment but also in urban consumption. Informal sellers often sell to their neighbors in high-poverty areas of the city that are marginal both in their geographic location and their relation to the city's commercial networks. These neighborhoods are poorly connected by public transportation to the city's commercial districts and are overlooked by retailers. But when customers can't buy, sellers don't make money. One participant summed this up: "There are times when you don't sell anything either, because the [economic] situation is screwed up [*jodida*] for everybody. So sometimes you sell, sometimes you don't sell, and when you don't sell, there's no money." This small-scale, own-account selling is more of a survival strategy than a career, as the women recognized: "Since there is no money to start a bigger business, well, people help themselves however they can," said one woman who sold food. In most cases, they claimed not to be earning more from this selling than from their domestic work jobs.

Several women said they were involved in another, similar income-earning activity: direct selling. Direct sellers sell branded products directly to customers, usually under the auspices of a multinational company that produces the items and creates catalogs to help sell them. Direct selling straddles the formal and informal economies: the companies are formal enterprises that pay taxes, yet the members of the sales force are not formal employees. Direct sales is a form of reselling in which the women buy goods—perfumes, makeup, costume jewelry, herbal supplements—at a discount and then resell them at a retail price set by the direct selling organization (DSO). In these interviews, women specifically mentioned working with Avon and Omnilife, and the two people who had left domestic work for direct sales said that they made more money selling than they had working in private homes. Direct selling can sometimes require a bit more capital to get started than, say, informal food selling, and if sellers become involved in the DSO, they will probably invest more time and money attending trainings or other events.[5]

Sales, whether of food, clothing, or Avon products, appeal to the women we spoke with because these types of work allow them to spend time at home with their children. They enjoy the symbolic status of stay-at-home mothers while also generating income. As one told us, "I sell and sell, and buy [more things to sell] . . . and that way I can dedicate more time to my children; I stay here in the house." Women who participated in home businesses (usually with their husband or male partner) also described this as an advantage. One interviewee who raised pigs said that she decided to do this type of work "to be close enough to care for my daughter." Some cared for other relatives, like the woman who told us "I have my dad here, and I care for him and for my sister . . . two disabled people." Women see selling as a strategy for keeping up with unpaid social reproduction while contributing economically to their household.

The attractiveness of working at home highlights the dilemmas domestic workers face in managing paid household work in the employers' home and unpaid household work in their own home. In helping employers accomplish the tasks of social reproduction, they often feel that they must neglect the social reproduction work in their own home. The stigma of domestic employment also helps us understand women's expressed preference for home-based work. The image of the degraded and exploited domestic worker is less desirable than that of the respectable and respected housewife or mother. Since many women in this population are single mothers, a social role that is already seen as deviant, they may have even more incentive to be seen as dedicated mothers who are home with their children. In my conversations with domestic workers in Guayaquil since 2010, they frequently described the anguish of having to prioritize paid social reproduction that benefits employers and the feeling of neglecting their own families because of economic necessity. Informal selling and direct selling seem to help resolve this tension, although the assumption that it is easy to combine child care, housework, and paid work is overly optimistic (Casanova 2011b).

Two more questions emerge when analyzing women's discussions of their work histories and particularly their jobs outside of domestic employment: (1) What counts as work? and (2) Are all jobs the same? Going through the interviews, I was perplexed when women said they were unemployed, but then listed their current income-earning activities. The following exchange exemplifies this puzzle; in the interview recording, the woman's grandkids—whom she watched for free—can be heard playing noisily in the background.

INTERVIEWER: How many hours of paid work do you do each week? Right now, paid.

INTERVIEWEE: Right now? None.

INTERVIEWER: How many jobs or forms of income do you have? What are they?

INTERVIEWEE: Oh, well, I sell a little Yanbal [cosmetics/direct sales], sometimes I make tamales, *quimbolitos* [a type of sweet tamales], and sell them in the neighborhood.

This tendency of women to underestimate their income-earning activities raises the question of what counts as work for them: an excellent topic for further research. Possibly, knowing our interest in domestic work, women called themselves unemployed if they were not working for pay in a private household. But it is also plausible that they might not consider small-scale, informal, part-time, sporadic, or self-employed work to be work in the sense of a job.

The other idea that many women shared, and sometimes worded identically, was: "All jobs are the same." In the words of one interviewee, "All jobs are the same, all of them are hard." When we asked them about their work histories, it was often difficult for them to say which jobs they liked and which they didn't. Likewise, when we asked them to imagine whether leaving domestic work would mean finding a better job, they were pessimistic. I think this is a realistic assessment of the employment opportunities open to them. They may leave domestic work, but in most cases they would not be earning more. Sometimes removing themselves from a toxic work environment and escaping the personalized domination of a "bad" employer felt like progress. One woman who had left domestic work for a worse-paying informal job said that there "aren't better jobs where you can earn well. . . . There's no such thing as being treated well and paid well." These women are under no illusions about the types of jobs that are available for women with low levels of education, single mothers, and residents of high-poverty areas. Typically, they see all these jobs as equally undesirable or as equally necessary to try to keep the family afloat. Their ideal situation would be "a stable job where you can earn well, with a good salary, with good treatment [*un trabajo seguro donde vaya a ganar bien, con un buen sueldo, un buen trato*]." Yet their experience tells them this is a pipe dream; the ideal job does not exist.

Searching for Real Upward Mobility

One purpose of these interviews was to learn more about women's chances of achieving upward mobility by leaving domestic work. We found little evidence of such mobility. Perhaps women who have left domestic work for better jobs are no longer in the neighborhoods and social circles where ATRH usually goes to find domestic workers. But the stories we heard were of women trapped in a cycle of domestic employment, underemployment, unemployment, and low-wage informal employment. One interviewee described her work history:

> It was always a little work here, a little work there, because of the reason and the issue that I got married very young, I had kids, and obviously I have never had a stable job. So I worked by the hour, worked temporary jobs, because of my kids . . . sporadic jobs. [Uy, puros pique aquí, pique allá, por razones y cuestiones de que me casé muy temprano, tuve hijos y obviamente nunca he tenido un trabajo seguro. Entonces yo trabajaba por horas, por temporadas, por los hijos . . . trabajos esporádicos.]

Despite this common narrative, we found a handful of stories of women who left domestic work (seemingly for good) and went on to earn more in other lines of work. Only one of these women joined the formal workforce, after pursuing further studies. The others started their own businesses. We don't know whether these businesses are located in the formal or informal sector, though the latter is more probable given the location and circumstances of the women and their families. The woman who left domestic work to raise pigs said she earned the same amount as before, while working for herself at home. Another woman raised pigs and also worked with her spouse in a carpentry business, and she claimed to earn more and like her work more than her previous domestic employment. A third interviewee with a home-based business—repairing shoes—had less success, saying that she earned less than minimum wage, and "since the [economic] situation is really tough, whatever money I happen to get goes to feed my family."

It is worth noting that these businesses are not in sectors that are seen as traditionally feminine, meaning that women may need to break with gender norms to secure a better livelihood. In all of these cases, women were partners in business with their husbands or took over businesses their husbands had started. These partnerships may give them access to social capital or credit that would be more difficult to obtain on their own. When we asked these former domestic workers about their aspirations for the future, they had very specific goals. All wanted to increase their business and have more access to credit. As the woman who repaired shoes said, "I want to grow my workshop, have more machines to help me . . . and I would like the government to help people, to make it easier to get credit." Those who didn't have their own business wanted one, and those who did have a business wanted it to be bigger and more sustainable. Part of the reason women want to be entrepreneurs has to do with the trato they have experienced in domestic employment. They seek "my own business where I can be independent, where nobody tells me what to do," in the words of one participant, who dreamed of owning a beauty salon, or to escape "being the slave I was before," as another told us. Personal domination, born of class-based power relations, makes domestic work a bad job.

In contrast to the small business owners we interviewed, most women leave domestic work for other informal work, or more rarely, enter the formal workforce and then return to informal work. This cycle is full of instability and stress, which is reflected in their aspirations for themselves and their children. Some women told us that they were too old to have goals and aspirations for their own lives; when asked whether she wanted to go back to school, one forty-five-year-old woman said, "At this late stage of my life, I don't know." But they all had hope that their children's lives would be easier than their own. As one sixty-year-old woman said, "I no longer think about my future. I think about my children's futures. . . . I want them to study because the situation is difficult." Regardless of their children's ages, they wanted them to study, to become professionals, to own a home. One interviewee said she wanted her children to "have a good job, a stable job," and many others specified that they wanted their children to have their own businesses, so they didn't have to work under someone else.

The phrase that many women used to sum up their aspirations for the next generation of their family—and to contrast that hoped-for future with their own experience—was that they wanted them to "be someone in life" (*ser alguien en la vida*). As one put it, "I want them to be someone in life. . . . If I had had that opportunity . . . I would be a good professional now." Being poor, being a woman, and being a domestic worker were all obstacles to people seeing these women as "someone." Many of the interviewees' mothers—nearly a third of our sample—had been domestic workers. Yet the women we spoke to clearly did not want their daughters to enter this occupation. These individual narratives reflect the trend across the region: the domestic worker population is aging and shrinking at least in part because the younger generations are seeking other types of employment. One interviewee told us that although domestic work was difficult and complicated, she was proud of using it to help her daughter finish college. In general, though, it seemed that women felt they had little control over their children's lives and outcomes. Several women admitted that some of their children finished school and others dropped out.

While many participants claimed to be too old to continue with formal schooling, most expressed interest in vocational training.[6] Out of fifty-one women who answered questions about nonschool training, thirty-three said they had participated in this type of skills development. The trainings the women mentioned were almost equally likely to be free or to have some cost, and they were offered by a variety of providers, from government agencies to churches to for-profit academies. Most often the trainings participants had taken were for jobs usually done by women in both the formal and informal sectors: nursing, sewing (clothing), and beauty work. Crafts were also a common topic. A full 85 percent of those who had taken trainings said they'd had a chance to use what they learned, but we do not know how many earned money by using these skills. All but three of the fifty-one women who answered questions about training opportunities were able to name some specific trainings or courses they would like to take in the future. The most common area of desired training was beauty work, followed by cooking (especially specific skills such as cake-baking) and crafts, sewing, and nursing. But given that most women had a goal—however vague—of owning their own business so they "would no longer have to depend on anyone," they also talked about needing access to loans or capital to jump-start their entrepreneurial activities. Among the business-oriented trainings women desired were those on computers, accounting, and entrepreneurship. Some specifically mentioned microcredit groups as a possible means for starting a business. There is apparently a need for more professional development opportunities, and when women are thinking about such opportunities, it is clear that they are basing their desires on types of work that women in their communities are already doing.

Social Reproduction

Recalling theoretical discussions of social reproduction as I analyzed the interview transcripts, I was struck by the unique perspective of these interviewees. Rather than dividing social reproduction that is paid (domestic employment) from that which is unpaid, these women underlined the strong connections between the two. They saw paid and unpaid domestic work as "all they know how to do," and also as activities along a continuum rather than a rigid dichotomy. When they go to work for pay in a private home, and then come home to do similar tasks for free, it feels not like two workdays (jornadas) but like one long one: "I work Monday to Saturday and I have pretty long days [jornadas], because I leave one job and then I go to work in my house." One participant summed up this endless cycle of paid and unpaid work: "All the time that you aren't working outside the house, you're working inside the house." When asked how many hours of unpaid work she did at home each week, one currently employed full-time domestic worker answered, "Uy, hijita, es todo el fin de semana que saca la madre," which roughly translates in English to "Oh, sweetie, it's the whole weekend and wipes me out." Another said, "[It's] all day . . . but every day." Paid or unpaid, the tasks of social reproduction are never ending. They get done and then have to be redone again and again.

When they were unemployed, women would say that they worked "in my house, as employee of the kids [*en mi casa, pues, empleada de los muchachos*]" or as an unsalaried domestic worker (*empleada sin sueldo*). Another woman said, "I work as a babysitter, as a cook, I do all of that at home." Several women cared for their grandchildren, and multigenerational and extended family households were common. Those who were out of the paid workforce said they preferred domestic employment to unpaid domestic work because at least they got paid. According to one interviewee, "I'm not doing it for free . . . getting paid brings satisfaction." One woman who had left paid domestic work and was now caring for her grandchildren without pay said, "I don't like it, but I have to adjust to it [*lo que toca es acostumbrarse*]." Other women expressed a different point of view, saying that spending time with their children was its own reward.

> INTERVIEWER: Are you earning more now than when you were work-
> ing for pay in a home? [¿Está ganando más que cuando trabajaba en
> casa?]
> INTERVIEWEE: I win because I am with my children. [Gano porque estoy
> con mis hijos.]

Women who cared for grandchildren sometimes expressed similar sentiments: "I'm happy spending time with them," said one.

As we can see from the women's work trajectories and the rationales for their decisions to enter and exit the paid (informal) workforce, their lives revolve around social reproduction. Most are single mothers, forming the backbone of not only their own families but their low-income communities. Most also strongly identify with their role of caregiver and anchor of home life (Gammage 2012). They care for others, sometimes for pay, sometimes not, and these caring responsibilities structure both their daily lives and their life course. The stage of family life can influence work decisions: for example, women with small children may make different choices from those whose children are grown.

The pressures that force them to begin working, to keep working at low-paying and undesirable jobs, and sometimes to leave paid work are important factors for understanding the women's work histories. Those who wanted to leave domestic employment often gave reasons related to their family responsibilities for why they could not. Aside from the research on transnational mothering (Arriagada and Todaro 2012; Hondagneu-Sotelo and Ávila 1997; Parreñas 2001), some studies take into account the work-family dilemmas of women in domestic employment (Ally 2009; Brites 2014; Durin 2017; Saldaña-Tejeda 2012; Rojas-García and Toledo-González 2018). The majority of live-out domestic workers in the world are similar to these Ecuadorian research participants: they are not international migrants and often not even internal migrants,[7] their families and children live with them in the same city where they work, and their commutes across the city may be very long and cut into their nonwork time (figure 2 in chapter 3; Fleischer and Marín 2019). These women's decisions about jobs related to social reproduction are shaped by their unpaid social reproduction. If "female participation in the workforce can be better understood by knowing the place that women assign to their own domestic work in their daily routines," we would expect to see more research on how they manage paid and unpaid work (Rojas-García and Toledo-González 2018; Casanova 2011b; Gammage 2012; Lobato 1997). Yet the work-family tensions of this population of workers are often not part of global conversations on work and family or those on informal employment. These women do similar tasks in radically different locations and settings, yet they insist that we consider the continuity rather than the differences in these forms of paid and unpaid work.

Another common theme in the women's narratives was unplanned pregnancy, which often led young women to abandon formal schooling or to take or leave particularly exploitative jobs. The social and religious conservatism of many Ecuadorian politicians, even under an economically progressive government, has watered down or blocked efforts at sexual education and birth control interventions. Teaching young people about the advantages of delaying childbearing, and empowering them to prevent unwanted pregnancy, are ways to prolong women's schooling and give them a sense of control over their destinies that is often lacking when they see pregnancy as something that just happens to them and determines the course of their family and work lives.[8]

Lucha, Trabajo, Sacrificio

When talking about the future, some women we interviewed were quite pessimistic, but most of them had loosely defined hopes and dreams for their children and grandchildren. When we asked those who talked about specific goals, such as buying a house or helping their children graduate, how they thought they might accomplish these goals, the same language emerged again and again. They expected life to be a struggle—lucha—and they recognized the sacrifices (sacrificios) they had already made for their families. When faced with a choice, they prioritized their children, for example, leaving school "because I had my children and we could no longer afford it, and I prefer to sacrifice myself so that they can continue studying." They planned to keep working, whether in paid domestic employment or other informal activities, or unpaid household and carework. As one woman told us, she had to "keep working, keep helping myself so that they [my children] can move ahead. I need a job so that I can help my children."

Another woman said she could reach her goals by "working, working, struggling, and saving [*trabajo, trabajo, luchar y ahorrar*]." Regardless of the specific work histories and trajectories they recounted, the participants emphasized the ubiquity of these three elements of poor women's lives: struggle, work, and sacrifice. Since no one was looking out for them, they had to do for themselves while also making a life for their loved ones. While there were ways out of particular work situations, they didn't see a way out of their position at the economic margins of society. Some had a fatalistic view of their lives, saying that all they could do was ask God to make things work out.

The experiences of women in and out of domestic employment, and their opinions on these experiences, should be essential to our thinking about ways to improve working conditions and organize domestic and other low-wage workers. La lucha could be individual or local, but there have to be ways to connect these small-scale struggles to the collective struggles of oppressed people and exploited workers. Since women see unpaid and paid domestic work as two sides of the same coin, valuing unpaid social reproduction needs to happen simultaneously with valuing paid social reproduction. One interviewee mused that there should be salaries for unpaid household work: "I tell my husband that they should give an incentive to those of us who are [working] at home from Monday to Sunday, however we don't receive that, and should earn at least something."

Because of their low levels of education, it may be unrealistic to expect women to graduate out of domestic work and into formal employment. What other types of work, then, make sense in parts of cities that are sites of informal economic activity? Simply escaping the personal domination of domestic employment—a legacy of colonial relations between masters and servants—feels like progress for many women. But it is often temporary, and they return to paid domestic work because of limited options.

The importance of formal education also comes through in these women's accounts. Truly free education would be a game changer, since most of the women said they quit school because they could not afford the expenses of books, fees, and uniforms, and also because their families needed more income earners. Today, having missed out on those additional years of schooling, they feel stuck in jobs that are physically taxing, risky, or unstable, and have no possibilities for advancement. Rather than moving out of these jobs into better ones, they often leave paid work in a private home for unpaid work in their own home, or for informal self-employment that means just scraping by . . . or worse. With more education, they may have a better chance at low-level formal employment in the service sector, which would be a modest step up from the current possibilities. Yet even governments that claim to be sympathetic to the plight of the poor, like the Ecuadorian government under President Correa, have difficulty creating decent jobs for these most vulnerable workers. Informal employment, often more of a survival strategy than a reliable income, continues to be the only option for many people, including the women whose stories I presented here.

Domestic work is neither a ladder nor a dead end. Its instability means that women do not just remain trapped in this work but instead cycle in and out of it, alternating with periods of unemployment and other income-earning activities.[9] Structural barriers, including women's social reproduction responsibilities in their families, low levels of education, and lack of employment alternatives and job training, all perpetuate this cycle. The pathways described are common throughout Latin America, where internal migration is just one part of the story of how poor women try to make ends meet. The women see their paid and unpaid social reproduction work as similar, calling to mind the phrase used by Spanish feminists: "¡Queremos empleo, trabajo nos sobra! [We want *employment*, we have more than enough *work*!]" (Seoane Vázquez 2011).

Because currently employed domestic workers are a portion of the larger potential domestic workforce, we need to include and yet look beyond them. Collecting data from the pool of past, current, and potential domestic workers yielded powerful insights. A holistic view of poor women and their ingenious and diverse survival strategies shows us the limits of seemingly solid categories such as "domestic worker" and the myopia of focusing on individual workers rather than their collective identities as members of families and communities. I see a spark of hope in using this more comprehensive view. Perhaps emphasizing what informal workers have in common, and poor women's issues in addition to domestic workers' issues, can help build working-class solidarity among women, and between women and men. I agree with Kathi Weeks that "focusing on work is one politically promising way of approaching class—because it is so expansive, because it is such a significant part of everyday life, because it is something we do rather than a category to which we are assigned" (2011, 20).

These women's stories identify two phenomena—cultural ideas, but also material processes—that shape their lives and those of other poor people in Ecuador. They are la situación, the collection of economic woes and social stigmas that constrain options and throw up roadblocks, and la lucha, people's creative responses to these challenges. Linking individual luchas to a larger lucha for workers' rights is one way that domestic worker organizations can build power and improve lives. It is to this collective lucha that I turn in the next chapter.

LIKE ANY OTHER JOB?

Given the low pay, social stigma, and domination by employers that domestic workers describe, what are the possibilities for improving these workers' lives by mobilizing them politically? This chapter presents some of the challenges that organizers of domestic workers in Ecuador face. I examine their rhetorical strategy of redefining domestic work as a "regular" job, a strategy that explicitly demands equal rights with other workers while downplaying the unique characteristics of domestic work.

The context in Ecuador, as in other parts of Latin America, is a patchwork quilt of legislation about paid domestic work. Although specific laws protecting domestic workers have been passed in countries including Argentina, Brazil, and Bolivia, there is not a recent comprehensive and specific law covering domestic work in Ecuador. Rather, this type of employment is governed by sometimes contradictory rules in Ecuador's Labor Code, Constitution, and the International Labor Organization (ILO) Convention 189, which Ecuador signed. Despite having legal rights, domestic workers are still often seen by employers and those tasked with enforcing labor laws as inferior to other workers. Achieving not just legal recognition, but also a guarantee that workers can exercise their rights, requires a revaluing of social reproduction. Yet the language of labor in Latin America is that of production, not reproduction. Labor is equated with male workers (*obreros*) rather than women.

Traditionally, neither ministries of labor nor labor unions in Latin America have done much about the situation of paid domestic workers.[1] Politicians—frequently employers of domestic workers themselves—often mention what they consider the "special" and "delicate" relationship between employers and domestic workers, which granting and enforcing legal rights will disturb (Cutuli 2018). These relationships descend from cultures and customs of servitude that emerged in colonial Latin America (Maich 2014b, 85). As Mary Goldsmith writes, the private location of domestic employment, and ideas about the home as sacrosanct and outside the purview of the state, feed into this discourse. In describing the encounter that produced the first-ever international labor convention on domestic work, ILO Convention 189, Goldsmith recounts: "Employers, and to a lesser extent, some governments, emphasized that it was not possible to bring domestic workers' rights completely in line with the rights of the rest of the workers, because their activities were undertaken in a home for a family" (2013, 241). Here the gap between social reproduction and capitalist production is used to justify domestic workers' inferior treatment.

Because of this exceptionalism, even when new labor codes have been instituted or existing codes reformed, paid domestic workers were often left out of laws expanding workers' rights and protections (Blofield 2012). In some cases, labor laws specific to domestic employment cement their lower status: the law passed in Peru in 2003, for example, codified domestic workers' right to *exactly half* the overtime pay, vacation time and bonuses of other workers. Domestic workers have often existed outside of the labor law framework, and the rights they do have are frequently violated. Thus, despite the existence of laws regulating domestic employment, it makes sense to study it as part of the informal economy in Latin America (Lautier 2003). Indeed, the efforts of domestic worker organizations and allies often aim to formalize this type of employment by bringing it in line with labor laws.

The social movement for domestic workers' rights in Ecuador shares many of the challenges facing similar movements in other Latin American countries. As in other places, some progress has been made, particularly in domestic workers' sense of dignity and pride in the work they do, and in the public's awareness of their legal rights. For more than a decade, a president who embraced the label of socialist, and now his successor and former vice president, have governed Ecuador. Socialist parties and politicians generally pay lip service, and sometimes offer concrete forms of support, to working people. Yet working conditions for Ecuador's domestic workers do not live up to the promise of decent work, and in fact domestic employment in a supposedly "post-neoliberal" Ecuador looked and looks remarkably similar to the situation in neighboring Peru and Colombia, which have had right-leaning, conservative political regimes in recent years. While the political context in Ecuador is unique, then, the challenges and struggles of domestic worker organizing are similar to those in many other Latin American countries.

In thinking about resistance and collective organizing in capitalist societies, we need to be clear about what workers are fighting against. Is it exploitation, the simple fact that their labor is being sold to someone else? Is it also domination, in which members of higher social classes oppress and subjugate others? Here I find the work of Aníbal Quijano on the "coloniality of power" to be useful: "There is a clear relationship between exploitation and domination: not all domination implies exploitation" (2000, 379). But he goes on to argue that exploitation is not possible without domination. Exploitation in domestic employment builds on preexisting relations of domination. Differences between employers and domestic workers are seen as natural and immutable, which stymies efforts toward equality. Quijano identifies echoes of the colonial period in contemporary Latin American social and economic hierarchies. The "naturalization" or unquestioning acceptance of categories of inferiority and superiority based on race, gender, or occupation, is "a naked historico-social product" and "an effective indicator that power, all power, requires this subjective mechanism to reproduce itself" (Quijano 2000, 373). Labor unions and workers' organizations usually focus their energies on exploitation—how workers are used and abused in production—yet in domestic work, the relations and subjective experiences of domination that underlie the labor arrangement also must be combatted. This is the biggest challenge facing domestic workers' movements, because it involves changing cultural norms, identities, and worldviews.

This chapter's discussion of domestic worker organizing touches on the three major themes of my book: social reproduction (seen as inferior or not-work when compared to production), informal arrangements that render domestic work invisible, and class relations that degrade and dehumanize workers. Workers' engagement in long hours of paid and unpaid social reproduction makes them difficult to reach and organize. Informal arrangements, and lack of political will and political effectiveness to change these arrangements, combine to make the enforcement of existing laws difficult. And relationships with the left-leaning state,[2] embedded in traditional assumptions about who constitutes the working class—assumptions that leave out women and informal workers—have been fraught. My purpose here is to show how domestic workers and their advocates have been organizing, what strategies they have used to demand the rights of these workers, and what the implications of these strategies are for political action and change.

Previous Research on Domestic Worker Organizing

The rich and varied studies on the organization and mobilization of paid domestic workers in Latin America have excluded Ecuador as a research site (Acciari 2016; Bernardino-Costa 2011; Brites 2013; Cabezas Fernández 2012; Cornwall, Oliveira, and Gonçalvez 2013; Goldsmith 2017, 2007, 2006; Hutchison 2011;

Magliano, Perissinotti, and Zenklusen 2017; Maich 2014b; Tizziani 2011b; the exception is a brief overview, Vervecken 2013). Why is Ecuador largely absent from the sizable body of literature on domestic employment in Latin America, much of which focuses on other South American nations, such as Argentina, Brazil, and Chile? First, Ecuador is understudied relative to other Latin American countries. Second, until recently its main domestic workers' organization, the ATRH (Asociación de Trabajadoras Remuneradas del Hogar), worked primarily in one city, Guayaquil. Even within Ecuadorian studies, Guayaquil is rarely the site of social research. Ecuador, though a relatively small country, is similar to others in the region in its lack of enforcement of existing labor laws affecting domestic workers, historically low rates of immigration from other countries,[3] shrinking numbers of domestic employees, and hierarchical social and economic relations shaped by colonial and neocolonial power structures. Domestic worker activism in Ecuador also shares many commonalities with that seen in other Latin American countries.

Depending on the laws of each country, domestic workers and their advocates may set up labor unions, social service organizations, or workers' associations.[4] This diversity in types of organizations is typical of other informal workers' movements throughout the world (Agarwala 2013, 259). Many organizations— including the one I focus on here—have dual goals of providing services to individual workers and encouraging collective mobilization. The idea is that providing services will get workers in the door, where they can then be encouraged to engage in activism (Tizziani 2011b). Research shows that the actual content of the courses, workshops, and other services provided to domestic workers may be less important than the opportunity to socialize and bond with other workers, a kind of camaraderie they don't get at the workplace (Tizziani 2011b). Yet these organizations can be fragile and depend on a population whose energies are stretched thin, so sustaining them is always a concern (Jiang and Korczynski 2016; Tizziani 2011b). International organizations and networks for domestic workers are often dedicated to supporting and "nourishing" these smaller local or national organizations (Goldsmith 2013). Even with all the difficulties they face, domestic workers' organizations exist in nearly every Latin American country (Tizziani 2011b, 91). The workers most involved with these organizations represent a small proportion of paid domestic workers, who may be more "privileged" than others, as they have the freedom to commit time to the organization and to travel to its locations and events (Tizziani 2011b, 94).

Domestic workers' organizations almost always endeavor to get workers involved in politics, to inculcate in them an awareness of themselves as political subjects (Garcia Castro 1993; Goldsmith 2006; Magliano, Perissinotti, and Zenklusen 2017). A Peruvian domestic worker in Argentina who became an activist after many years of working in exploitative conditions is quoted as saying,

"Well, I went through that because I didn't know . . . then I woke up [*me avivé*]." This waking up or getting wise, *avivarse* in Spanish, is "a transformation of her subjectivity as a worker that makes possible a re-reading of her own life history. It is precisely this '*avivarse*' that allows her to see herself as a subject with rights, and as such, with the power to demand them and struggle for them" (Magliano, Perissinotti, and Zenklusen 2017, 316). Organizations use different strategies for "waking up" domestic workers. Raising awareness and collective identity among workers is an important first step, while not guaranteeing that political action or concrete changes in working conditions will follow.

Domestic workers' organizations are not alone in pushing for social change and making demands on the state: they operate alongside other nongovernmental actors, such as labor unions (usually representing workers in formal employment) and identity-based social movements such as feminist movements and indigenous movements. Although "alliances among 'the dominated' are not easily built" (Garcia Castro 1993, 4), successful domestic workers' movements in Latin America have forged strong ties with other social movements. In Brazil, black social movements and domestic workers' movements have worked together, as most domestic workers in that country are black women (Bernardino-Costa 2014). Although feminist movements might seem like natural allies, many are led by and oriented toward middle-class women, who as employers of domestic workers may not share their interest in improving working conditions or wages (Bernardino-Costa 2014). On the other hand, domestic worker activists are aware of some of the negative perceptions of feminism as an ideology imported from other countries or as hostile to men, leading some to resist identifying as feminist or joining with feminists (Garcia Castro 1993). The feminist groups who advocate for domestic workers are usually those that focus on women of color or the intersections of gender, race, and class (Bernardino-Costa 2014). Such alliances make sense because in many cases, domestic worker organizations are already developing intersectional explanations for the situation of these workers (Acciari 2016; Garcia Castro 1993; Gonçalves 2010), who are simultaneously oppressed as women, poor women, and nonwhite women (Bernardino-Costa 2014).

What about alliances with other labor groups? In most places, traditional labor unions are dominated by men and focus on organizing male-dominated workplaces and occupations. These labor union leaders often do not see domestic work as real work (Tizziani 2011b, 93). Beyond the case of domestic work, informal workers' organizations usually arise after these workers are rejected or ignored by existing labor unions (Agarwala 2014). Of course, some labor policies and reforms benefit different kinds of workers, so there may occasionally be openings for labor groups to collaborate on a specific law or issue even if they are not already partners.

Priorities of the Ecuadorian Domestic Workers' Movement

The organization that I studied and collaborated with, ATRH, was formed in Guayaquil in 1998. Since that time, it has worked with other local and national nonprofit organizations and NGOs and formed friendly relationships with some labor unions. It is currently affiliated with the national CUT union (Central Única de Trabajadores).[5] The association has participated in international networks and summits of domestic workers through membership in CONLAC-TRAHO, one of the largest international confederations of domestic worker organizations.[6] In 2016, ATRH helped form the first national union of domestic workers in Ecuador. It is still early to speculate on the eventual size and impact of the union, but its creation was an important step in expanding the reach of the domestic workers' movement beyond its historical base of Guayaquil.

The primary activities of ATRH over the years have included free legal advice for domestic workers who feel employers have violated their rights; workshops on labor rights and other topics (e.g., domestic violence, self-esteem); awareness-raising campaigns directed at workers, employers and the general public; and demonstrations at local offices of Social Security (IESS) and the Ministry of Labor. The organization informs workers about their legal rights to enroll in social security (with employers' contributions); vacation time; maternity leave; overtime pay; severance pay; a good work environment; and freedom from discrimination. Although there were many more members of the association who were active sporadically as time allowed, during my study there was a core group of about twenty to thirty women who regularly planned and participated in group activities. The majority were former domestic workers, motivated to change the conditions that they had experienced firsthand, but some were employed in domestic work at the time. Funding came primarily from foundations and NGOs based in Ecuador and abroad. The organization's leaders and most active members received little or no direct financial benefit from their participation. Likewise, there was only a meager budget for overhead and recurring expenses, as most of the funding was project-based and temporary.

The concrete aims of ATRH have shifted since I first started to learn about it and spend time with its members. From about 2009 to 2011, the group's focus was primarily on advocacy with national government agencies, local awareness campaigns, and providing services and popular education to workers. From 2011 to 2013, the primary advocacy activities were oriented toward urging the Ecuadorian government to sign on to ILO Convention 189.[7] Ecuador signed on to the convention in 2013, and twenty-seven countries had signed as of January 2019 (Latin America is the region with the most signatories). The signing of the convention spurred a new round of advocacy for ATRH, in which they pushed for the language of Convention 189 to be included in the new Labor Code that was supposed to be developed by the Ministry of Labor with input from labor groups. The idea of writing a new Labor Code was later scrapped, and it was reformed instead. These reforms continue intermittently, and ATRH is still working to get domestic workers' rights (as spelled out in the ILO convention) included. When I asked the president of ATRH why there was no specific domestic work legislation introduced in Ecuador, despite new laws being passed in other parts of South America, she admitted, "we have never asked for that." Their aims had been to enforce the existing laws protecting domestic workers and to get the ILO convention signed.

During the period of the study, the leadership of ATRH was increasingly successful in connecting with organizations in other Ecuadorian cities, some of which focus on domestic workers' issues, and most of which address the concerns of poor and working-class women. After several years of ATRH working to expand its reach nationally, the hope is that the national union will strengthen the collective power of domestic workers in interactions with the state.[8]

Paid Social Reproduction

As social reproduction that is performed for wages, paid domestic work complicates the rigid division between production and reproduction that often appears in theories of political economy. Paid domestic workers sell their labor power, and employers exploit them, but this situation does not correspond to the typical labor-capital relation, as I discussed in the introduction. These workers perform activities that are usually done without pay, and usually by women (Carrasquer Oto 2013; Mose Brown 2012).

From a Marxist perspective, all work that is performed for someone else's gain (within an employment relationship) is exploitative. Despite all work being exploitative in this sense, paid domestic work differs from other types of employment. Domestic employment today, like domestic service and slave labor in earlier periods, is marked by "personalized" domination, which is made possible because it is a relation between people with "asymmetrical social positions" (Toledo González 2013; see also Borgeaud-Garciandía and Lautier, 2014; Casanova 2013; Gorbán and Tizziani 2014; León 2013).

Domestic workers tend to labor alone, so there is no factory floor on which to coordinate or organize with other workers. Because Marx's ideas of class interest and class consciousness were based on factory workers involved in productive rather than reproductive labor, in leftist movements "the interests of other workers were always seen as secondary and susceptible to being subordinated to those of waged laborers and in particular the so-called industrial working class" (Quijano 2000, 372). This is still the case in Latin American labor politics (Bank Muñoz 2017), with implications for domestic worker organizing. On the other hand, union power has been decreasing in Ecuador since the 1980s (Gaussens 2016, 34), so perhaps being on the margins of the traditional unions is not that great of a disadvantage.

In this context of intimate inequality rather than public and collective exploitation, even food becomes a terrain of conflict, as shown in chapter 2. Sociologist Bruno Lautier (2003) has suggested that this very inequality, and the way it benefits elites, explain why Latin American academics specializing in labor have avoided studying the situation of domestic employees. They don't have the sufficient distance, and their findings could potentially threaten their own privileges as employers of domestic workers. For this reason, Lautier writes, domestic work is more commonly discussed by gender scholars than scholars of labor. I have also noticed that the burgeoning research on domestic work coming from Latin America in the last couple decades is written almost exclusively by women scholars.

At the macro level, domestic workers' organizations must combat the mainstream political and economic discourse that reaffirms the separation (and ranking) of productive and reproductive work, a separation that symbolically excludes paid domestic workers from the labor force. At the micro level, this definition of domestic work as nonwork is evident in employers' claims that the worker "is like part of the family" or just "helps out"; these phrases obscure the labor relation in domestic employment and distinguish it from other paid work (Rollins 1985; Wrigley 1995; Moreno Zúñiga 2013). It is not the separation between production and reproduction, but the subordination of paid reproductive work to work that produces profit (and takes place outside the home) that stigmatizes women's carework and domestic labor.

Challenges in Organizing Domestic Workers in Ecuador

In its quest to improve working conditions for paid domestic workers, ATRH faces three main challenges. Two of these—reaching workers and enforcing existing laws—are common struggles for domestic workers' advocates around the world. The third, the challenge of obtaining and maintaining state support, takes a unique form given the political structures and trends in Ecuador since 2007.

Challenge #1: Reaching and Mobilizing Workers

Many of the association's activities aim to raise awareness among workers about their rights, motivate them to mobilize to defend those rights, and involve them in the life of ATRH. These are necessary activities that make up the main work of the organization. As Maximina Salazar, president of ATRH, explained to me:

> We, the women who are following this path of trying to develop activists or peer educators in labor rights, like social security, valuing paid domestic work, [we do this] so we can send the *compañeras* to replicate these activities, yes?[9] Directly to the neighborhoods [where workers live]. If we have to go house by house, door to door, as they say, that's even better, so that we can—so that the *compañeras* can learn their rights and we can try to incentivize them [to participate in the organization], because that is another problem.

ATRH, like many domestic worker organizations, tries to create a base for social movement beginning with educational activities and services for the people they want to mobilize (León 2013). However, field outreach, going door to door, is complicated by some workers' residence in their employers' homes (*puertas adentro*) and by long workdays.

In Guayaquil, most domestic workers live apart from employers, with their children and often other family members. They tend to live in places that are poorly served by public transportation, making for long commutes from home to work (see figure 2 in chapter 2). On top of these commutes, they work long days, and full-time workers often work six days a week. Many domestic workers whom ATRH members know and want to organize live in peripheral, low-income neighborhoods in the southwestern sector of Guayaquil called La Isla Trinitaria, which is distant and disconnected from more well-to-do neighborhoods. The residents of La Trinitaria and other poor and working-class neighborhoods may travel up to two hours each way to get to work in other parts of the city (other Latin American cities have similar issues of spatial segregation and long commutes for low-income workers: Fleischer and Marín 2019).

As seen in chapters 3 and 4, most paid domestic workers are mothers (and many of them, single mothers), and their "free" time, often limited to Sundays, is for family: a chance to rest or catch up on their own household chores. When children are not in school and their mothers are working, they either stay alone or with relatives or neighbors. Several workers interviewed for this study expressed concern that they do not spend enough time with their children, and many more pointed to the difficulty of juggling motherhood and paid work, so any moments they can share are precious. The only day of the week that ATRH can expect to find domestic workers in their own homes is the day that these workers will least want to leave their families to participate in activities that will take them far from home and pay them nothing. This dilemma is not uncommon: scholars of domestic workers' movements in Brazil and Argentina note that participants said family responsibilities and lack of time constrained their ability to engage in activism (Garcia Castro 1993; Magliano, Perissinotti, and Zenklusen 2017). Unpaid social reproduction can thus directly hamper efforts to improve women's experience of paid social reproduction.

Unlike office or factory workers, many domestic workers do not see other domestic workers when they go to work in the morning, and they do not meet up during lunch. Their work is invisible—not just for the public, but for other domestic workers who are also toiling in isolation in private spaces throughout the city (for more on this invisibility, see Borgeaud-Garciandía and Lautier 2014; Brites, Tizziani, and Gorbán 2013; Gutiérrez-Rodríguez 2014; Lautier 2003; Pereyra 2013). When I asked domestic workers whether they socialized with other domestic workers in or near the homes they worked in, most of them told me that they did not. This isolation poses a challenge for ATRH and similar organizations, which must find ways to reach, educate, involve, and ultimately, mobilize workers who spend nearly all day doing physically exhausting, solitary, and socially invisible work.[10] The spaces that ATRH traverses are multiple and fragmented—it seems more likely that other informal workers who share a workplace (such as market vendors or agricultural employees) would respond to traditional organization and mobilization tactics. The lack of mass social movement in this sector in Ecuador is partly due to these logistical challenges: you cannot persuade domestic workers to participate in collective action if you cannot physically reach them and get their attention.[11] Indeed, a major issue facing domestic workers' movements in Latin America is the "low and frequently unstable level of participation of the workers [the organizations] represent" (Tizziani 2011b, 91).

Challenge #2: Enforcing Labor Laws

Given the prevalence of informal employment arrangements instead of written contracts (Moreno Zúñiga 2013; Pereyra 2013) and the invisibility of work in private homes, enforcing existing labor laws to protect paid domestic workers is nearly impossible without more investment from the government. In a large city like Guayaquil, it is impractical, or the government is unwilling, to conduct exhaustive labor inspections in homes. The inspections that the Ministry of Labor did conduct, mostly in 2009 and 2010, were sporadic and focused on just a few neighborhoods. We might expect such inspections to lead to follow-up visits, new policies, or concrete consequences for violators of labor laws, but it seems that these inspections did not produce such outcomes, according to employers and workers I interviewed. Some workers said they believed that employers bribed labor inspectors, and others told stories of employers trying to hide domestic workers or pass them off as relatives visiting from the countryside. Labor inspections that were continuous and covered all parts of the city in which domestic employment took place would have a better chance of impact. Alternatively, focused labor inspections based on anonymous complaints could also increase compliance.

However, according to the results of our survey (chapter 3; Casanova, Rodríguez, and Bueno Roldán 2018), and anecdotes from ATRH members, employers, legal and employment experts, and other Ecuadorians I spoke with, the rights of domestic workers are being respected more than in the past. More domestic employees are enrolled in social security, which gives them health coverage, retirement pay, and other resources. According to news reports, in Guayaquil social security coverage rates among domestic workers rose from 8 percent in 2005 to 12.5 percent in June 2010 and 20 percent in December 2010 (*Expreso* 2005; *El Universo* 2010a, 2010b). One survey conducted in 2014 with a sample of more than three hundred paid domestic workers found that 56 percent were enrolled in social security (Paspuel 2014; Wong 2017), although our survey conducted the same year showed less than 20 percent affiliation among a sample of four hundred paid domestic workers (chapter 3), so there is some room for debate about exactly how much enrollment has increased.[12] Some of this increase is the result of employers enrolling workers they were already employing, but it undoubtedly also results from new hires in which employers and workers are entering a labor relation conscious of the legal requirement to contribute to social security.

There have been cases of paid domestic workers (some of them associated with ATRH) suing or denouncing their former employers with the Ministry of Labor or in the courts, demanding back wages, overtime pay, or severance pay after being fired. When I began participant observation with ATRH in 2010, the association was monitoring thirteen legal cases of workers who were members of the organization. A white board on an easel in ATRH's downtown office listed the names of the claimants and sometimes the dollar value being sought. The very fact that these processes were being initiated and these cases considered by government agencies is an indicator of the recognition that domestic employees had legal rights. Although suing employers usually happens after the employment relation ends and thus does not help improve conditions during employment, it is one of the few ways in which laws may be enforced currently. We should not overestimate the change in working conditions based on these denunciations, since we do not know their rates of success.[13] The data presented in this book still show that most workers are not enjoying their legal rights, not to mention enduring the outright abuse and harassment that some encounter. It is these issues of trato (treatment), rather than economic grievances, that more often lead to legal complaints, according to one lawyer I interviewed.

The government of former president Rafael Correa implemented many new social and economic programs when it took power in the last decade. The state's efforts to formalize paid domestic work and guarantee these workers' rights seemed to peak around 2010. Although there is some public awareness about the rights of domestic workers to the minimum wage ($394 per month in 2019), and although there have been legal cases brought against noncompliant employers, there are limits to the execution of the law. Even the simple idea of having written contracts for domestic employees, which could also benefit employers, has not been adopted widely in Guayaquil (nor in Buenos Aires, Monterrey, or Lima: Toledo González 2013; Moreno Zúñiga 2013; Pérez and Llanos 2017). Despite being guaranteed specific rights, domestic workers continue to be informal, precarious workers. The problem of how to ensure respect for laws that give domestic workers labor rights has been discussed in the context of Latin America (Blofield 2012; Brites 2013; Jaramillo 2014; Pereyra 2017, 2013; Pereyra and Poblete 2015; Pérez 2015; Pérez and Hutchison 2016; Poblete 2016, 2015; Toledo González 2013) and Europe, the source of Latin American legal tradition (Abrantes 2013). As ATRH members have often told me in relation to the passage of new laws and policies by governments, "El papel aguanta todo" (You can write anything on paper). Having laws in place is one thing: changing the conditions of each workplace is another (Jaramillo 2014). The state is a key player in the enforcement of laws regulating domestic employment, yet it often remains "remarkably silent" (Maich 2014b, 77).

Challenge #3: Relations with the State

The third challenge stems from the relationship between ATRH and the Ecuadorian government. Ecuador is among a group of well-known political outliers in Latin America. Its most recent, left-leaning government under Rafael Correa, who identified as a socialist, distinguished it from its nearest neighbors, as both Peru and Colombia have been governed in recent years by conservative, explicitly procapitalist presidents. In this turn to the left, Ecuador joined other South American regimes that embraced socialist ideas and policies, including Bolivia and Venezuela, and to some extent, Uruguay. We might expect a more socialist political climate or leadership to result in better working conditions for domestic workers (Blofield and Jokela 2018). While Bolivia saw a former domestic worker elected to congress (which in itself is no guarantee of improved working conditions), domestic employment in Ecuador has not changed radically. Domestic work in Ecuador looks much like that in countries whose leaders did not proclaim allegiance to socialist ideals. The government's treatment of the domestic workers' movement during this period seems to be an example of "symbolic cooptation . . . of the demands historically formulated by social movements," a co-optation that lasted only as long as the brief "Dignified Domestic Work" campaign (Gaussens 2016, 34).

In Latin America, unions and workers' associations often represent the working class in claims against the state,[14] whether that state is friendly to labor or not, and they apply political pressure to try to reach their goals. Change in domestic work regulations can emerge from such pressure, but also from the government attempting to co-opt groups by granting them benefits (Tizziani 2011b, 90). Correa's government, which early on drew public attention to domestic workers' issues through press conferences and public awareness campaigns, later became an unreliable ally. Despite sitting at the president's side at meetings and events just a few years before, ATRH's leaders were unable to keep the state's attention during Correa's second term. The government's campaigns were increasingly less visible, did not benefit from consultation with ATRH, and then became virtually nonexistent. In 2010, the president of ATRH told me: "The government has been very generous with us [she then clarified they had not received government funding], with all of this follow-up, and the fact that the Ministry of Labor is doing the campaign is on the basis of the conversation that we had one day with him [President Correa]." Just two years later, she and her compañeras lamented not being able to communicate complaints and concerns to Correa and his staff, and they resorted to sending him e-mails and Facebook messages. These attempts to get his attention and request a meeting received no response.

It was unclear why the relationship between the organization and the government had weakened, a common experience among other Ecuadorian social movements at the time (Gaussens 2016). The leaders of ATRH seemed somewhat confused by this change. A new opening emerged with the public presentation in 2015 of the results from our survey (discussed in chapter 3), which led to a series of meetings between ATRH and representatives of the Ministry of Labor and the ILO. But it seems that these connections have so far been difficult to maintain under the new government of Correa's successor, President Lenín Moreno.

Strategically Redefining Paid Domestic Work

While the ATRH dealt with the challenges I've outlined here, it pursued strategies to build the type of political power that can create change. Some of the most difficult work the organization does with domestic employees aims to help them develop "political consciousness" (Garcia Castro 1993) or achieve "cognitive liberation" (Magliano, Perissinotti, and Zenklusen 2017; see also Acciari 2016). In this section, rather than focusing on this in-group discourse, I focus on the external discourse of the organization: the language it uses to advocate for domestic workers with government agencies, funders, and the general public.

Considering the challenges posed by the structure and invisibility of paid domestic work and its location in the undervalued sphere of social reproduction (as opposed to capitalist, "productive" work), the most interesting rhetorical tactic that these leaders use is the redefinition of paid domestic work as "regular work" or "like any other job." The most visible and vocal leaders, and also the rank-and-file members, frequently used this description. A typical example comes from a member I interviewed: "Part of our principles is to enforce [labor] rights, to be able to guarantee the rest of the domestic workers that we all have rights, like any other worker [*trabajador*-masculine], like any other worker [*trabajadora*-feminine]." Although the organization produces its own written materials and presentations, the insistence that paid domestic work be recognized *as work*, and the goal of "equality with other workers" is a transnational discourse that emerges from and is amplified by the international meetings of domestic workers' organizations, such as the summit that produced ILO Convention 189 (Goldsmith 2013).

In the organization's brochure and other printed materials, only the masculine noun *trabajador* is used in this phrase. The rhetorical strategy for valuing women's paid domestic work is to compare it with paid work done by men, which is less stigmatized. In this discourse the ideal worker is a man, as in the thinking of local labor unions (according to domestic work activists). In more frequently using the masculine form of the word *worker*, ATRH reproduces the association of men with the concepts of paid work and labor organization and unionization (Bank Muñoz 2017; Borgeaud-Garciandía and Lautier 2014). This may be a tactic of using language they think will best appeal to policy makers or the public, and the use of similar language in other Latin American countries means that some organizers find it effective.

Yet the "like any other work" comparison symbolically accepts and perpetuates the hierarchical division between productive and reproductive work, assuming that reproduction has to be seen as similar to production to be valued. While domestic workers should enjoy the same legal rights as other workers, a rhetoric equating feminized, informal work with formal work done by men misses the elements that make domestic work a bad job. Both factory work and domestic work are exploitative, but the face-to-face domination in the intimacy of a private home between a middle-class elite employer and a lower-class, usually darker-skinned, woman makes domestic work different (Borgeaud-Garciandía and Lautier 2014). Here we see how useful, even necessary, an intersectional analysis of social reproduction is in the Latin American context (Acciari 2016; Bernardino-Costa 2014; Pérez and Llanos 2017). Factory work can proceed without that intense form of personal domination and embodied inequality, but domestic work is built on it.

By using this language to shift the terms from servitude to employment, domestic worker advocates emphasize that the domestic employee is a worker who must be paid, despite the long history of calling such workers "help" or "girl," of informal arrangements, and of in-kind payments. One ATRH activist told me that "things are changing" as a result of the new social and political awareness of domestic workers' situation, so that now an employer "has to give us social security, has to give us the minimum wage, so that it is a job like any other job." She used the phrase frequently employed by ATRH: "Un trabajo igual que cualquier otro trabajo," a job like any other job. The members and leaders of this organization constantly repeated this phrase in in-group conversations, interviews with journalists, protests, and press conferences.

The strategy of redefining paid domestic work as a regular job presents a contradiction. The factors that lead to excessive exploitation of domestic workers and make organizing them difficult are not the factors that domestic work shares with other work, but rather its particularities. The specific conditions of paid social reproduction, informally arranged and based on colonial and postcolonial systems of patronage and servitude, cannot be reduced to the most common complaints of workers in capitalist production. These particularities, as I mentioned before, make it difficult for ATRH to reach workers and for the government to enforce their rights. Declaring that paid domestic workers are the same as other workers (and more specifically, male workers), a claim that has also been made in social movements in other countries (Cornwall 2013, 151; Goldsmith 2013), does not erase these particular challenges. Informality reigns in domestic employment arrangements even as consciousness of these workers' rights increases—or perhaps because of this increased awareness, which would help explain the drop in classified ads seeking domestic workers as employers avoid their legal obligations (see chapter 1).

Domestic employees are still exploited, poorly paid, and taken advantage of for many reasons. These reasons include "local custom" (la costumbre del lugar), to borrow the phrase from the Ecuadorian Labor Code, and the structural position of these workers as poor women (who may also be minors or discriminated against because of race or appearance). Other reasons for poor working conditions include the invisibility of work taking place in private homes, the devaluation of the social reproduction activities they perform, and the modest incomes of many middle-class employers, which limit their ability to pay minimum wage and legal benefits. This is a set of conditions that other types of workers do not experience.

When domestic employment is equated with other types of work, however expedient that comparison may be, the unique oppression that domestic workers experience is glossed over as a typical encounter between capital and labor. But employers in private homes are different from the prototypical employer. For one thing, many do not even see themselves as employers. They use different techniques to control workers, strategies that are more personalized and often incorporate elements of paternalism; maternalism (Borgeaud-Garciandía and Lautier 2014; Rollins 1985); or racial, gender, and class domination (Brites 2014; Gutiérrez-Rodríguez 2014; Ribeiro Corassacz 2014). In addition, many paid domestic workers do carework (Carrasquer Oto 2013; England 2005; Sarti 2014; Torns 2008), which requires a level of emotional commitment and performance not required in other types of work (Gutiérrez-Rodríguez 2014). If workers collectively claim rights from the state, then paid domestic workers can benefit from their inclusion as "regular" workers. But there is a disconnect between the insistence that paid domestic workers are the same as other workers, and the unique conditions that they endure. These conditions affect their work experiences and hamper efforts to organize these workers.

Domestic workers' movements in Brazil and Bolivia have drawn on a somewhat different strategy: highlighting the multiple oppressions that affect domestic workers and using an intersectional discourse that recognizes the gender, racialized, and class aspects that combine to exploit these women in a particular way (Acciari 2016; Bernardino-Costa 2014; Cabezas Fernández 2012). These efforts show that to equalize effective rights, something that has happened to a greater extent in those two countries than in Ecuador, it may not be necessary to omit the particularities of domestic employment. There are other differences in approach: in both Brazil and Bolivia, domestic workers' organizations have built successful partnerships with other social movement groups, and also had the backing of international NGOs. Yet the potential alliances for Ecuador's domestic workers are unclear. Ecuadorian feminist movements do not tend to spend much energy on labor issues. Unlike in Brazil or Bolivia, Ecuadorian domestic workers come from a range of racial and ethnic backgrounds and thus do not have obvious common ground for activism with indigenous or Afro-Ecuadorian movements. Traditional labor unions have been slow to reach out to informal and women workers. Given the challenges I have outlined in this chapter, the achievements of Ecuadorian domestic workers—for example, the ratification of the ILO Convention and the formation of a national union—are impressive.

As sociologist Francisca Pereyra points out, domestic workers cannot really be treated like any other workers until the organizations that defend their rights are strengthened and mechanisms effectively regulate and penalize employers' noncompliance (2013, 65). The blurring of personal and employment relationships, and the absence of protections afforded to union members in collective bargaining arrangements, mean that domestic workers often eschew activism for fear of being fired. Questions about strategy remain. What factors other than working conditions facilitate or impede organizing precarious workers such as domestic employees? Can the new national union for domestic workers, SINUTRHE, successfully unionize large numbers of Ecuador's domestic workers, and what are the advantages and disadvantages of having unions? What specific challenges do jobs that are perceived as feminine and reproductive rather than masculine and productive present for traditional labor organizing strategies? These are questions that ATRH and other Latin American domestic worker groups are grappling with in a political environment in which their needs are simultaneously publicized (by NGOs and sometimes government agencies) and ignored (by most employers and political actors). Meanwhile, individual resistance by workers in their workplaces continues.

Will domestic workers fully unionize?

CONCLUSION

This book set out to answer two main questions: (1) What makes domestic employment in contemporary Ecuador a bad job? (2) How can working conditions be improved? I explored three main themes to understand working conditions and possibilities for change: social reproduction, informality, and class. My analysis confirms previous research on Latin American domestic workers' experiences published mostly in Spanish and Portuguese, while generating new insights. One benefit of studying Ecuador is that most domestic workers are native-born rather than international migrants. Worldwide, as in Latin America, native-born workers outnumber international migrant workers in domestic employment, despite the focus of most English-language research on migrants from the Global South to the Global North.

My findings, when viewed along with research from other parts of Latin America, suggest that the experiences of nonmigrants, internal migrants, and international migrants in the region are quite similar (as Feliu 2014 also argued).[1] Their working conditions are equally dismal. Domestic workers are exploited as a subclass of worker, a subclass of human, whether they were born in the same country as their employers or not. They are always the other. In this part of the world, where fewer domestic workers are international migrants, we find working conditions similar to those in situations with more international migrants. Setting migration aside, then, as the primary variable explaining exploitation, I focus on three dimensions of oppression that act as obstacles to domestic workers' rights: social reproduction, informality, and class. Scholars and activists can target these obstacles in the effort to improve working conditions.

Social Reproduction, Informality, and Class

Social reproduction is the behind-the-scenes work of caring, socializing, and feeding the current workforce and the next generation of workers. Despite being necessary for survival, this work is devalued, which devalues people who earn incomes doing it. Occupational segregation by gender, and stereotypes about who counts as a real worker, exacerbate the hierarchy of production over reproduction. The divide between men's work and women's work has implications for domestic worker organizing, which faces challenges different from traditional trade-union organizing despite using a discourse of domestic workers being "like any other worker." Finding ways to value social reproduction, paid and unpaid, will benefit the workers whose voices this book presents, and also women and girls who have never spent a day in domestic employment. Women are usually the ones doing the work of social reproduction, so this is a question that domestic worker organizations and feminist groups can rally around: How can we assign greater social, economic, and political value to this work? Alternatively, how can women resist or reduce unpaid domestic work, and how can societies distribute it in new ways (Weeks 2011; see also Davis 1981, chap. 13)? Efforts to value social reproduction should begin at the local and household levels. Even within Ecuador, cultural norms of gender vary, making national campaigns unlikely to succeed.

Informal arrangements and the precarity of domestic work are key aspects of working conditions. Informality seems to be taking new forms as part-time work increases. We know that part-time workers are less likely to be enrolled in social security, but we know less about how their other working conditions compare. The increase in part-time work has implications for organizing, too: full-time and part-time workers may not have identical interests, and scholars should collect data to find out.[2] Formalization efforts and the part-time/multiple employer trends are connected, as employers seek to skirt the law or reduce their employees' hours, but we need more analysis of this connection.

New research with informal workers, including domestic workers, shows that sometimes they see formalization as taking away advantages and giving them less room to negotiate (Brites 2013; Inglis 2017). Rather than assuming that workers want formalization, we asked them. The workers who participated in this research find formalization appealing, but it has not been seriously pursued in

Ecuador beyond the pressure for employers to enroll workers in social security. The mechanisms and incentives in place now are too weak and depend too much on the goodwill of employers and the state. Employers should be the target of new policies (e.g., sanctions, subsidies, inspections), as most workers already know—and many demand—their rights. Also, the government has to be committed to enforcing the law.

If formalization is the goal, as it should be in Ecuador given workers' preferences, the question is how to formalize. Around the world, there are now more and more models for enforcing labor laws, with regulation reaching even workers who have long been informal. More systematic labor inspections would be helpful, as Wong (2017) hypothesizes that in-home labor inspections raise employers' rates of compliance with labor laws, and anecdotes confirm that this seems to be the case in Argentina and Uruguay. A recent debate about the wisdom of delinking employment and social security is also helpful for thinking about alternatives to current systems. While this seems like a good way to increase coverage of informal workers, if delinking means "letting employers off the hook" and degrading protections for all workers, it is not the best strategy (Alfers 2018).

Another reason that domestic work continues to be a bad job is that class relations structuring work in private homes are built on personalized forms of domination. These relations rely on categories of superiority and inferiority that are recognized as legitimate by employers, and to a lesser extent, by workers. The strong stigma and racialization of domestic work set it apart from other types of work. Because of these unequal relations, employers feel the need to promise good treatment (*buen trato*) when hiring, and workers point out "good" employers' deeds with pleasant surprise. This is the biggest challenge to asserting domestic workers' dignity, as longstanding cultural norms and local customs are resistant to change, especially when the powerful interpret that change as a threat to their privileged status. Economic exploitation, combined with class domination in intimate spaces, makes reproductive labor unlike other jobs.

Researchers' and practitioners' tendency to treat "domestic worker" as a static occupational identity limits our ability to see workers in a holistic way. Domestic workers are not just domestic workers. They cycle through domestic work, unemployment, other informal work, self-employment, and sometimes formal employment. They are women with families and dreams. They live their lives among poor people, yet see up close the luxury made possible by inequality. Rather than advocating only for domestic workers, activists and organizers could also integrate them into working-class movements.[3] This feeling of belonging to the working class is more important for domestic workers than for other workers, because their constant movement in and out of the labor market and the isolation they experience at work may lead them to have weaker social networks than other workers (García, Roco, and Larenas 2015, 16). In the meantime, my research shows that we can enrich our analyses by including former or currently unemployed domestic workers—not just those currently employed.

Each of these themes presents both a reason that domestic workers continue to struggle and a possible point of intervention to improve their lives.

Possible Ways Forward

After studying working conditions, individual work histories, and the challenges faced by Ecuador's domestic workers' movement, I see a few ways forward. These are interventions that address the issues of outreach, enforcement/regulation, and culture.

We already know that traditional methods of organizing and building labor power through workplace interactions are not a viable approach with this population; door-to-door personalized interactions work better, but require a great deal of resources. In the age of WhatsApp, a popular form of communication that is ubiquitous in Ecuador, in-person contact can be augmented in new ways. What outreach strategies might be pursued going forward? Organizers could capitalize on workers' use of cell phones to raise awareness and announce events through text messages. Even those who do not have smart phones or high levels of literacy could benefit from this form of communication.[4] The Association of Remunerated Household Workers (ATRH) has experimented with this approach. However, I have not seen a study of domestic work activists' use of phone communication, particularly text messages, to help inform and organize workers.

The local level offers opportunities for change, as cities are taking on new importance with the retrenchment of some national governments in the neoliberal era.[5] One U.S. city, Seattle, passed its own domestic worker bill of rights in 2018. Uruguay, which has implemented collective bargaining for domestic workers with representatives of employers and the state (Ferrari and Vence 2010), has roughly the same population as the city of Guayaquil. Collective bargaining could be established at the local level in Guayaquil or other Ecuadorian cities. Local arrangements could work as well as or better than a national one-size-fits-all agreement, as they would recognize Ecuador's regionalism and local ways of doing business, already enshrined in the "local custom" clause in the labor code. If nationwide labor inspections are the goal, then smaller-scale efforts at labor inspection or other mechanisms for enforcement could be tested out and then scaled up.

In research and practice, there has not been enough exploration of workers' cooperatives as a way to improve working conditions. By cooperatives, I mean cleaning and child care businesses owned and run collectively by workers themselves. Reconfiguring these activities as services rather than servitude could ameliorate the exploitation and the dehumanizing domination that workers experience. When workers—whom the cooperative would train and vouch for—rotate in and out of different homes, there is a clear labor relation rather than a form of patronage or pseudo-family connection. Rather than struggling on their own, workers would have the support of the cooperative in dealing with difficult employers or rights violations. Cooperatives could help employers with the process of enrolling workers in social security and calculating bonuses or overtime wages. Cooperatives not only give more power to workers in their dealings with employers, but also symbolically seize the means of (re)production and make the domestic work experience collective rather than isolating. More research needs to be done on the advantages, disadvantages, and legal constraints that such a collaborative model presents in different Latin American contexts (for one recent example from the Caribbean, see ILO 2018; also Goldsmith 2007).

At the macro level, the International Labor Organization (ILO) and the Ecuadorian government are now beginning to break down employment statistics to clearly show what is happening with domestic workers. Whether domestic employment is assigned its own category apart from formal and informal employment, or represented as a subcategory of informal employment, the recognition of its uniqueness by the agencies that collect and disseminate statistical information is important. Not only does this type of record keeping help researchers and advocates, but it also shows that even these authorities understand that domestic work is not "like any other job." We still need more, and more accurate, data on domestic worker populations.

A larger goal of domestic worker movements, and one that they share with many feminist movements, is a revaluing of social reproduction, both paid and unpaid. As I mentioned earlier, this project would benefit many women, not just paid domestic workers. Some progress has been made in this area, with Ecuador now permitting housewives and other unpaid caregivers to join the social security system. Valuing social reproduction means throwing out the idea that production is more socially and economically important than reproduction. This requires a cultural shift—in which people begin to believe that fathers and mothers have equal caregiving capabilities—a shift that is slow to emerge almost everywhere in the world.

Education matters, too. As this book and other research demonstrate, increasing women's education levels can increase their employment options and their knowledge of their labor rights. Identifying the ways that girls' and women's unpaid social reproduction hinders their schooling can help target interventions to those most vulnerable to interrupting their education (in the stories of domestic workers, it's those who live in rural or other high-poverty areas or in single-parent families).

Women domestic workers do reproductive labor that benefits their employers, sometimes at the expense of their own families. This transfer of reproductive labor distinguishes domestic employment from other jobs, including other informal jobs, despite domestic workers' organizations' rhetorical strategy of presenting it as just another job. Ecuadorian domestic workers are still not receiving working conditions and benefits guaranteed by law, conditions and benefits that are associated with "productive" formal work. At the same time, precarity is increasing and working conditions are tanking for even formal workers, which creates the potential for new types of cross-occupational alliances (Weeks 2011, 18).

Directions for Future Research

I began this book with a critique of research from the Global North that does not make use of the abundance of high-quality scholarship on domestic work produced in Latin America, especially since 2000. Part of my book's contribution is to make the insights of this body of research accessible to scholars outside of the region. I am critical of an academic hierarchy that values works in English that are published in the United States, the UK, and Canada more highly than those in Spanish or Portuguese that are published in Latin America. I say this as a social scientist who benefits from this unequal circulation of knowledge: enough is enough. Scholars of domestic work who are not able to directly read the Latin American research because of language barriers can seek out research assistants or collaborators with the necessary language skills, advocate for translation of these resources into English, or request feedback from reviewers with knowledge of this literature.[6]

Another goal of my book is to show how collaboration between researchers and activists can contribute to knowledge and produce rigorous social research. As social scientists, we are not often trained to do this sort of work, and we sometimes view it skeptically. I have found it to be not only personally rewarding and a source of rich data, but also an excellent check on my own assumptions and biases.

I see at least three areas that are ripe for future research.

Comparing Full-Time and Part-Time Workers

We know that part-time, hourly, and sporadic or temporary domestic employment is on the rise in Latin America, even as the overall number of workers drops. But we still don't have a good grasp on what this means for formalization efforts, collective organizing, or workers' experiences. The speculations in the published research are tantalizing: when compared to full-time workers, maybe part-time workers have better wages, maybe they are receiving fewer benefits, maybe they are more effective negotiators. Part-time workers are less likely than full-time workers to have social security, yet coverage rates are going up in most countries. Some scholars also suggest that part-time workers, who spend less time in the company of their employers, are able to be more autonomous and less likely to emulate middle-class practices or cut ties with their low-income communities of origin (García López 2012). How do we make sense of these trends, and how can knowledge inform policy, advocacy, and grassroots activism? Investigating all types of domestic work arrangements, and comparing them, as Pereyra and Tizziani (2014) have done for Argentina and Fraga (2010) has done for Brazil, can push forward a field of study that tends to focus on full-time domestic workers. More research that includes part-time or sporadic workers and unemployed workers will help us to get a better sense of women's work trajectories, multiple income-earning strategies, and work-family conflicts. Chapter 4 represents a step in this direction, and future research could be enriched by using the biogram method, in which women themselves draw or write down their work histories (Undurraga 2018).

Connecting Representation with the Real World

The hardest thing to change about domestic employment in Latin America is the predetermined set of assumptions about class and culture. While an integral part of contemporary capitalist economies, domestic work is burdened with traditional concepts of servitude and status. Artists producing everything from fictional feature-length films to documentaries to novels to hip-hop music, have told moving stories about the cross-class relations and dynamics of domination in domestic employment. Scholars have analyzed these images, their subtle and overt messages, and their audiences (Durin and Vázquez 2013; Dunstan and Pite 2018; Pite 2013; Randall 2018; Roncador 2014). We need more of this cultural production and its analysis, yet media representations of domestic work and the resulting conversations in cultural and film studies are largely divorced from the conversations that most social scientists, advocates, and policy makers are having about labor law, social security, and formalization. The task for those who are interested in both understanding and improving domestic work in Latin America is to connect these worlds: fictional and creative stories, criticism of literature and film and television, and policy making. Can we begin to bring together these diverse voices and inject the power of narrative—a necessary complement to statistics and graphs—into the world of policy and public opinion? Too much research on domestic work treats culture as a black box that we cannot change. Change needs to emerge from on-the-ground resistance and critiques of cultural norms, and scholars and artists have a role to play in creating the space for conversations about culture, class, domination, and exploitation.

The (Changing) Meanings of Work

In the nearly ten years that I have been studying domestic employment in Ecuador, and even before that in researching other informal work, I keep coming back to two questions. They are questions that my students and I discuss in the courses I teach on gender, work, and globalization, questions that only workers can answer for themselves. The answers point the way forward for labor movements and allies. The questions are: "What counts as work?" and "Is a bad job better than no job?" In countries where poverty and inequality are constant problems, la lucha, the struggle to survive economic difficulties and crises, is equally constant. Women are the architects of la lucha for their families. They may not consider all of their survival strategies to be "work." Should these strategies count as work in surveys and censuses, and be discussed in qualitative research? I think they should, but how to count and recognize all of women's contributions to their households, cities, and national economies is a real dilemma (Benería 2003). As to whether a bad job is better than no job, those of us with jobs that let us pay all our bills (and then some) are in no position to judge. But we can work to improve conditions for the most vulnerable workers, and to build social safety nets that can catch those who fall through the cracks of the increasingly precarious labor market. And we can provide research with real-world value for those who are doing the everyday work of advocacy, organizing, and collective bargaining.

We should step back and see domestic workers' lives in context. This means seeing them not just as domestic workers, but as women who cycle in and out of informal and unpaid work, as members of families, as stigmatized bodies, as people moving to and through cities, and as people who were driven or drawn out of the education system before they wanted to leave. My goal is to provide information that activists, advocates, and policy makers can use. In the meantime, as new research questions call out for attention, and scholars begin to answer those calls, domestic workers' movements will continue to push for equality. They remain, in the words of one of the indomitable and militant members of Ecuador's pioneer domestic worker organization, *en pie de lucha*, in the struggle.

EPILOGUE

This research began in 2010, and I have been fortunate enough to follow relevant developments in the intervening years. The book is ultimately a snapshot rather than a longitudinal study. However, several new factors affecting domestic employment in Ecuador today may change the landscape for workers, employers, and activists.

First is the new government. Current president Lenín Moreno campaigned on the successes of his predecessor, Rafael Correa, and promised to continue his commitment to social programs and a model of economic development that rejected dependence on foreign aid and investment. However, in his first year in power, he worked to distance himself from Correa, pursuing legal redress for alleged corruption in Correa's government. Moreno has adopted a more conciliatory stance toward international development agencies, the International Monetary Fund, the World Bank, and Ecuador's traditional oligarchs. The toning down of socialist rhetoric has accompanied the slashing of expensive government programs as oil revenues remain much lower than during the Correa boom years. What will this mean for domestic workers? If before, there was worker-friendly rhetoric and praise for humble domestic workers, but little concrete improvement in policies and conditions, today even the rhetoric is gone. The best way to reach and make claims on the new government is still unclear, and it will be difficult to obtain state funding for domestic worker initiatives. The inevitable return of international NGOs, many of them chased away by Correa, may help to fill the funding gap, but the landscape is still rearranging itself.

Second, there has been a "rupture" in the organization with which I collaborate, ATRH. A very public interpersonal conflict among the leadership led the organization to split into two groups. This situation makes organizing and advocating for domestic workers more difficult and may lead to confusion among policy makers and funders. Some previous allies are partial to one faction over the other. This conflict emerged just as major funding for the organization's projects was winding down, and its persistence has had a paralyzing effect. I do not know what the outcome will be.

Third, there has been an uptick in migration to Ecuador from Colombia and Venezuela, as people flee violence, political instability, and economic disaster. Its location close to these troubled countries, and its relatively open immigration policies, have led Ecuador to become the country that accepts the most refugees in Latin America. We need more research on these migrants and their employment patterns, but it seems that Colombians are not entering domestic work in large numbers. Venezuelan women are associated with informal selling (street vending, for example), but they have also sought out domestic work. Some online help-wanted ads I reviewed in 2018 specified a preference for a Venezuelan domestic worker, and some explicitly excluded Venezuelan applicants. According to experts I spoke with, Venezuelans will work for lower wages, making them appealing to employers, but there is a stereotype that they cannot cook Ecuadorian food, and these culinary differences have led employers to prefer native-born workers. This information is anecdotal, of course, and requires further investigation, as the influx of Venezuelan migrants is a recent development. An estimated 280,000 Venezuelans entered Ecuador in 2017 (*La Hora* 2018); many were on their way to Peru, which had promised them work permits. In 2018, Peru tried to reduce the flow by requiring passports, which could affect the numbers of Venezuelans passing through Ecuador.

Finally, some people I interviewed in 2018 claim to be witnessing growth in the proportion of live-in, full-time domestic workers. If this change is happening, it could be the result of increasing demands on middle-class working mothers, who need more assistance with the unpaid labor at home. It could also mean that more employers are paying wages and benefits below legal minimums in order to afford a domestic employee's labor. Perhaps under the new government, employers are less worried about sanctions for violating workers' rights. I have not seen convincing evidence of this trend, which would be moving in the opposite direction of the rest of Latin America, where part-time work is rising relative to full-time work. Time will tell whether the hourly or daily model of part-time work is actually giving way to a revival of the traditional full-time, live-in worker. It is up to us social scientists to find out and to understand the implications of any such shifts.

Despite changes in the context of domestic employment, workers' status has not changed much since I began this study. Social reproduction is still devalued, informal arrangements still prevail, and the class gulf between employers and domestic workers remains.

RESEARCH METHODS

This appendix describes the methods used to collect and analyze the data for each chapter.

Chapter 1: Content Analysis of Classified Advertisements

Since the Sunday edition of *El Universo* newspaper has the most extensive classified section, I collected all the ads related to domestic employment from every Sunday paper in 2010 and 2016.[1] This method yielded a total of 1,051 ads, with 795 from the earlier time period and 256 from the later time period. With the help of a research assistant, I coded the text of each ad for information about the job (tasks, salary, benefits, schedule, etc.), desired characteristics of the worker (age, experience, etc.), and information about the employer (neighborhood, family size, etc.). This approach combines both quantitative and qualitative content analysis, and both focused coding and open coding. Focused coding draws on existing research and theory to identify categories that are relevant to the research question, while open coding allows thematic categories to emerge from close readings of the texts, in this case, the classified ads (Lofland et al. 2006).

Once the text of the ads was coded, I generated descriptive statistics to draw out the most common types of information provided by the advertisers. I also conducted qualitative content analysis of the words and phrases in the ads.

Typically, job descriptions have two components: a description of the position and specifications for what kind of person the employer is seeking. I analyzed both aspects of the ads. With this sense of the content of each category for each year, I could compare the 2010 results with those from 2016. The coding was extensive, but based on themes that emerged in other parts of the research, I focused my analysis in the chapter on (1) the number of ads, which could indicate changes in how employment relationships were initiated; (2) the types of tasks and positions; (3) the preferred age range of workers; (4) the preferred geographic origins of workers; (5) the employment arrangement (live-in or live-out); and (6) salary and benefits.

The text of the ads, placed to appeal to potential workers, and the messages conveyed, are important. They illustrate norms among employers, including what to say and what not to say when recruiting workers. They also show what employers and agencies who place the ads think might appeal to workers. If the same keywords recur often, it is because they have become part of the domestic employment hiring discourse, which is relevant for all parties involved, including government and social movements.

To help provide context for the hiring process and employers' ideal requirements, I interviewed two domestic employment agency owners in Guayaquil in June 2018. In 2017 I interviewed one executive at *El Universo* by telephone to learn more about the process of placing an ad and how ads (especially those seeking domestic employees) had changed over time. I also interviewed an attorney in Guayaquil about the legal framework for domestic employment in July 2018.

Chapter 2: Interviews with Domestic Workers and Employers in Guayaquil

This chapter draws on interviews I conducted with fourteen domestic workers and three employers in Guayaquil in 2010. Because of the volatility of the domestic labor market, seven of the worker-interviewees were unemployed, though all self-identified as domestic workers and expressed interest in returning to work in private homes (two of these women had been recently hired and were negotiating start dates with new employers). Interviewees ranged in age from twenty-eight to sixty-two. Some had spent most of their working lives in domestic employment, often since adolescence. I asked women about each of their domestic work experiences, beginning with their first and ending with the most recent or current job.[2] Despite the stereotype of domestic workers as rural-to-urban migrants, eight of the fourteen workers interviewed were born in or near Guayaquil. Three hailed from the neighboring province, Los Ríos, and three were born in Esmeraldas, a northern coastal province with an Afro-Ecuadorian majority and long tradition of migration to Guayaquil. Although I did not ask about racial self-identification, three of the women would likely be identified as black by most Guayaquileans, and two others appeared to have some African ancestry but may not be considered black. All the women but one were mothers, and most were not legally married, though several were *unidas* (cohabiting with a partner).

Interviews were conducted in Spanish in locations around Guayaquil and later transcribed. Topics discussed with workers included work history, family, work experiences, and future plans. Topics covered with employers included career, family, and experiences with domestic workers. I asked both groups questions about appearance and uniforms. Other body-related topics, including health concerns, physical demands of domestic work, and employers' bodies, were raised by interviewees. I focus here on the themes of embodiment that emerged as I analyzed interview transcripts to identify patterns in participants' accounts. Because I spent more time with and interviewed more domestic workers than employers (although much of my daily life in the field takes place in the company of employers), and because their subjective work experiences are my focus, I draw more heavily on workers' accounts. I am more similar in social class and education level to the employers, so perhaps had a different sort of rapport with them. Over time, through my participation in action-oriented research and collective demonstrations, my rapport with many of the workers associated with the organization has grown since our initial contact, though I still occupy a privileged position due to my class, whiteness, and U.S. nationality. Translations from Spanish are mine, and names are pseudonyms (used to protect workers from potential threats to their employment arrangements, or retribution from past employers).

Chapter 3: Survey of Current and Former Domestic Workers in Guayaquil

We used quantitative methods to analyze data collected from surveys of four hundred employed and unemployed domestic workers, conducted between July and October 2014. The survey was developed collaboratively with members of ATRH (Asociación de Trabajadoras Remuneradas del Hogar) in Guayaquil. Before the surveying began, I led two days of training workshops with members of ATRH on social research, including discussions of ethics and data collection techniques. Having taught these topics to undergraduate students at my institution in the United States, I can say that the ATRH *compañeras* were a quick study, grasping in a profound way how power can shape research encounters.

After these workshops, we decided together which data needed to be collected and the ideal way to phrase and order the survey questions so that people would participate and give precise information. We created and tested a thirty-one-item questionnaire and decided to administer it verbally because of the generally low levels of education among household workers. This method also allowed us to include domestic workers who were illiterate.[3]

The criteria for participating in the survey were (1) being at least sixteen years old;[4] (2) being a woman (the great majority of people working in private homes are women); and (3) being a household worker at the time of the survey or in the past. We included domestic workers who were not employed at the time because this group had two types of workers we wanted in our sample: those who had worked in earlier time periods and had since withdrawn from the labor force, who could give us an idea of working conditions in the past; and those who were between jobs. Domestic employment is unstable, and it is common for workers to be fired or quit before having another job lined up. Former workers were also included because, if covered, they may still be using social security benefits even after leaving domestic employment. All participants lived in Guayaquil at the time of the survey, although many had lived, and some had also worked, in other parts of the country.

It is impossible to obtain a random (or even representative) sample of domestic workers due to the informal nature of the work and the lack of a sampling frame (a list or directory of workers). For this reason, we used a purposive sample. ATRH has conducted fieldwork with domestic workers for many years, and members also have domestic workers in their social networks. We used a double strategy to reach the greatest possible number of domestic workers. First, trained ATRH members went out to administer the survey in four neighborhoods where they know many domestic workers live: La Isla Trinitaria, Malvinas/Esmeraldas Chiquito, Socio Vivienda, and Nueva Prosperina. Two of these neighborhoods are in the northern part of Guayaquil, and two are in the southern part (north and south are meaningful divisions for city residents). The participation rate in these neighborhoods was extremely high. Of the households visited where an eligible current or former domestic worker lived, 93 percent of these women decided to participate. In many houses visited, none of the residents was employed, which gives a sense of the unemployment problem in these areas. There were at least two homes with two domestic workers each, and a couple of surveyed workers referred us to others. Second, the members of ATRH, most of them ex-domestic workers, identified potential survey participants among their friends, relatives, and neighbors.

As with any study, our methodology has limitations. Live-in workers, though rarer than live-outs, are probably underrepresented in our sample, and we did not survey workers under age sixteen (ATRH had previously conducted research and advocacy about child labor). We focused on women living in Guayaquil, which, although it is Ecuador's largest city, might differ from other cities in ways that affect working conditions or workers' experiences. Despite these limitations, participants were chosen based on ATRH's decades of experience doing outreach to domestic workers in Guayaquil; therefore, we are relatively confident that the demographic profile of the survey participants is typical of the city's domestic workers.

With the data collected and coded, we used STATA statistical analysis software to generate descriptive statistics and conduct logistical regression analysis to understand the relationships among the variables.

Figure 2: Mapping Domestic Workers' Commutes

In the survey whose results are discussed in chapter 3, we asked workers and former workers where they lived, and where they worked currently or most recently. A total of 405 survey respondents provided this information. Using a GIS (Geographic Information Systems) program called Esri and publicly available maps of Guayaquil, urban planner Juliana Sarmento da Silveira created a map that links the workers' neighborhoods of residence with the neighborhoods in which workplaces (employers' homes) are located. The map does not show the exact routes that women take to work, but it gives a sense of the spatial inequality in the city—where wealth and poverty are concentrated—and the distances traversed.

Chapter 4: Interviews with Domestic Workers in Four Cities

For this part of the study, we chose to conduct interviews with more open-ended questions rather than surveys, since we wanted to elicit narratives from research participants about their working lives from their first employment to the present. ATRH was working to create a national union for domestic workers, a goal that has since been realized, and I wanted to collect data beyond Guayaquil, their home and my main research site. In order to represent different regions of the country, we conducted interviews in the cities of Quito (Ecuador's capital, in the Andean *sierra*), Esmeraldas (on the northern coast), Jipijapa (in Manabí, the province just to the north of Guayas, where Guayaquil is located), and Guayaquil.

In the summer of 2015, I spent three days training members of ATRH on research ethics and interview techniques. We then designed the interview guide together, with some questions for all research participants, some tailored to those who were currently domestic workers, and some tailored to those who had left domestic work for some other type of work (or who were out of the labor force but had done domestic work in the past). Once we drafted the questions, the research team members practiced interviewing each other to pretest the interview guide, which we revised based on their feedback. Interviews were conducted by seven members of ATRH, most of whom are former domestic workers themselves. They recruited interview participants during the organization's activities, and those of their partner organizations in other cities. Interviews took place in 2015 and 2016, with a total of fifty-two participants: twenty from Guayaquil, thirteen from Quito, twelve from Esmeraldas, and seven from Manabí (Jipijapa). Interviews were recorded and transcribed in Spanish, and I analyzed them to look for common themes, particularly around our main research questions about labor trajectories, decisions about work, and mobility. All translations from Spanish are mine.

The demographics of the sample were typical of the general profile of domestic workers in Ecuador. All four cities in which interviews were conducted had samples with similar demographic characteristics except for some slight differences in education level and racial self-identification. The average age was forty-three, and nearly all were mothers, with 3.6 children per participant on average. Those who identified themselves as single made up 48 percent of the sample, followed by those in civil unions (*unidas*) with 16 percent. About the same percentage was legally married as *unida*. Nine women were divorced or separated, two were widows, and one did not answer the marital status question: when asked, "What is your marital status?" she answered, chuckling, "*aish, de lamentarse* [ay, it's lamentable]," which leads me to believe that she was unmarried.

The average participant had finished elementary school and started but not graduated from high school. There was variation in education levels across the four cities, with Quito having the highest average education level and Jipijapa having the lowest. Samples included college-educated women in every city except for Jipijapa, the site with the fewest interviews.

We asked participants what race or ethnicity they identified with, using an open-ended question rather than asking interviewees to choose from a list. Nearly two-thirds said they were *mestiza* (mixed race or ethnicity), the most common racial self-identification among Ecuadorians. About 9.6 percent said that they were Afro-Ecuadorian or *negra* (black), and another 7.7 percent said they were *chola* (mixed race with indigenous descent). A bit less than 6 percent identified as *mulata* (mixed race with African descent). One person each identified with these racial categories: *rubia* (blond), *india* (Indian), *blanca* (white). Three people chose not to answer this question (5.8 percent of the sample), and of those who did answer, four expressed some confusion or doubt about what to answer, sometimes asking the interviewer for help. It is worth noting that the greatest variety of racial/ethnic terminology appeared among the Guayaquil subsample. This may simply be because the largest proportion of interviewees were from this city, but the varied self-identification confirms previous research conducted in Guayaquil, where multiple, vague, and overlapping racial and skin color categories abound (Casanova 2004).

All the interviewees were either current domestic workers or had worked in domestic employment in the past. Seven were in full-time domestic employment at the time of the interviews; fourteen were in part-time domestic employment. Several of these domestic workers had other means of earning income as well. Some of the part-time workers reported working very few hours per week or per month, exemplifying what the ILO has called "mini-jobs" (ILO 2016b). Low pay was common among these part-time workers, some of whom earned as little as five or ten dollars per day. Of those who were not working in private homes at the time of the interview, nineteen told us they were unemployed. Only one of these women did not have plans to return to paid work in the future. Others who were not engaged in paid domestic work were in informal self-employment (ten people), mostly selling goods or food. One was in the formal labor market at the time of the interviews (and a handful of others had previously been in formal employment), one was an informal employee of a retail store, and one was studying in addition to doing informal selling. Almost a third of our sample, 29 percent, were second-generation domestic workers. These are typical demographic and employment characteristics of domestic workers and other low-income working women in Ecuador.

Although the interviewers were all women and had similar class backgrounds to the research participants, rapport was sometimes hard to establish. Several women questioned the purpose or the usefulness of the interview, saying, for example, "I would like to know what benefits we get from this" or asking "Who is this interview for?" or how the interview would help "all of us mothers who are out of work." One interviewee said, "I would like to know why you are asking me so many questions: are you going to help me in some way?" When asked whether she had any questions at the end of the interview, another woman said "I have questions about my future, about how to survive and support myself on my own." They understood that they were offering something of value to the research team by sharing their experiences and wanted to know what we would give them in exchange. One woman directed the interviewer: "Write it down there that I want a job." Even when researchers and research participants are matched on some dimensions of social identity, participants may still be suspicious of the research. And when dealing with participants living in poverty, we can only promise a vague, long-term return rather than an immediate payoff. Interviewers did the best they could in handling questions about the point of the research and assertions by participants about their needs.

Chapter 5: Researching the Domestic Workers' Movement in Ecuador

There are many ways to study social movement organizations' strategies and challenges. For this case study of one domestic workers' organization, I employed various data collection methods, including participant observation (ethnography), analysis of documents produced by and about ATRH (i.e., brochures, news articles), and group and individual interviews with members. Participant observation took place in 2010, 2012, 2014, and 2015, when I spent time with ATRH members in and outside the office, attending formal and informal meetings, educational workshops, press conferences, social and fundraising events (e.g., bingos), and demonstrations. I formally interviewed fourteen current and former workers who participated in ATRH activities (these interviews also formed the basis of chapter 2 in this book, Casanova 2015b, 2013). I agree with sociologist Rebeca Moreno Zúñiga that case studies are useful for studying domestic work, since they "consist of a detailed description of a particular situation or of actors that converge in that situation, in order to understand their actions in concrete circumstances" (2013, 92). We should be careful about overgeneralizing from a case study, but it can allow us to comprehend the social reality of a specific time and place. Although there have been a couple of case studies of domestic work in Ecuador (Casanova 2013; Radcliffe 1999), aside from my recent article, there is no academic research published on domestic worker organizations and advocacy in the country (Casanova 2015b). Despite a healthy literature on domestic worker organizing in Latin America, most of it published since 2000, the Ecuadorian case had not been represented.

Notes

INTRODUCTION

1. The sketch also inverts the patterns of international migration: the audience will know that it is Ecuadorians who migrate to the United States because of financial hardship rather than the reverse.

2. The domestic work advocates I know in Ecuador prefer not to use the term *domestic worker* or *domestic* because, as they say, they are politically aware and actively defending their rights rather than being "domesticated." Like other researchers (Durin 2017), I struggled over which term to use in my research, because language matters, and demeaning terms can help support existing hierarchies. I considered using an English translation of Ecuadorian activists' preferred term, "remunerated household worker," but in the end I decided to follow the precedent set by other scholars writing in English and use "domestic work/er" and "paid domestic work/er" throughout the book. Using the standard term will help make my work here intelligible and searchable in the academic universe, and I also like the conciseness of "domestic work." Because I believe it is important to highlight the labor relation, I refer to the families that hire domestic workers as employers, although they may prefer to call themselves *patrones* (Durin 2017). In this book, I use "paid domestic work" and "domestic work" interchangeably. When I refer to the work of social reproduction that is not exchanged for wages, I use the descriptor "unpaid."

3. This decline in unionized, industrial labor creates a perverse situation in which domestic workers are just beginning to get basic labor rights as other workers in the formal economy are losing theirs.

4. The terms *developing* and *developed* are less-than-ideal descriptors for countries that are differently positioned in the global economy, because they imply a simple, linear trajectory toward economic development that is based on Western (U.S./European) models. Even when I don't place these terms in quotation marks, the reader should know that I question them. The terminology of Global North/Global South has become popular, and I use these terms, though they lack specificity. Myrdal (1957) simply used "rich" and "poor" to denote countries' status; this can be effective, but masks the inequality within national economies. For example, while Brazil is increasingly a "rich" country by the numbers, it is plagued by extreme economic inequality. There is no perfect way to describe inequalities among nations, which are shaped by historical relationships of domination such as imperialism and colonialism. The World Bank places Ecuador in the "upper-middle income countries," and poverty has decreased over the past decade. But Ecuador remains in the bottom half of GDP among Latin American and Caribbean countries, for example, with per capita GDP about half that of Chile.

5. Gorbán and Tizziani (2014) suggest that focusing on international migration does not help to explain asymmetrical power relations in domestic employment in Latin America.

6. The service sector includes nonagricultural, nonindustrial occupations that produce use value but no tangible commodities. Teachers, hairdressers, and hospitality and retail workers are all employed in the service sector. Employment in this sector is expanding in both developing and developed countries.

7. For Marx, an object has use value for the person who needs it and uses it; use value is separate from exchange value, which is what something is worth in kind or in money. Domestic services that have use for the members of a household do not involve exchange value or surplus value (profit).

8. In Latin America, many countries (including Ecuador) have labor laws that require these employers to share a portion of profits with employees.

9. There are exceptions in which domestic workers are kin of employers: Baptista Canedo (2010) on Bolivia; Haydocy, Yotebieng, and Norris (2015) on Haiti; Hordge-Freeman and Harrington (2015) on Brazil. These workers are usually compensated only in room and board.

10. For Marx, the bourgeoisie or capitalists are those who own the means of production (everything that is needed to produce commodities). Laborers, the proletariat, work for the bourgeoisie because the only thing they have to sell is their labor power.

11. Empirical research does not bear out Engels's ([1884] 1978) theory that proletarian families are more egalitarian and exhibit less patriarchal domination than bourgeois families.

12. This is true except in the case of formalized household services provided by a company rather than an individual worker hired by the household. For example, cleaning companies (e.g., Merry Maids in the United States) do generate profit. They are part of the service sector. Such companies in Ecuador focus on cleaning offices and nonresidential buildings rather than private homes.

13. Brazilian scholar Heleieth Saffioti considers domestic workers to be part of the reserve army of labor, since they move in and out of domestic work positions and graduate from domestic work to jobs in the service sector when they can (see also Beechey 1978; Tizziani 2011a). This reserve army provides crucial flexibility to help maintain the capitalist mode of production.

14. For examples of different formalization strategies for occupations other than domestic work see http://www.wiego.org/informal-economy/rethinking-formalization-wiego-perspective.

15. Informal economic activities exist in wealthy nations too, where domestic employment is generally arranged informally. The informal economies of developed countries are not equivalent to those in Latin America, however, because economic and social conditions are different (Connolly 1985; Cortés 2000). What does it mean to do informal work when that type of work is seen as the norm rather than the exception? Informal employment is a larger proportion of all employment in developing countries, and discussions of domestic employment in the Global South are more likely to address how this context shapes women workers' choices.

16. The International Labor Organization, whose Convention 189 lays out the rights to which domestic workers should be entitled, published the report *Formalizing Domestic Work* in 2016.

17. Peru's law is controversial, because it gives domestic workers exactly half the rights (in terms of minimum wage, vacation time, etc.) that other workers are entitled to; with the country's recent signing of Convention 189, however, the days of this discriminatory system may be numbered.

18. ILO conventions become binding when they are ratified by member countries. Ratification means that these countries need to bring their national labor laws into line with the convention as soon as possible. The full text of the convention and the list of the twenty-five countries who have ratified it to date can be found at http://www.ilo.org/dyn/normlex/en/f?p=NORMLEXPUB:12100:0::NO::p12100_instrument_id:2551460.

19. Information from the United Nations: https://esa.un.org/unpd/wup/Country-Profiles/.

20. Informal employment dropped in the recent petroleum boom (roughly 2009–12), but it is unclear whether there will be a lasting impact. There were similar reductions in other Latin American countries, and the variation in proportion of informal workers across Latin America is quite large, so the situation is in flux.

21. Though domestic work has developed differently and takes different forms throughout the world, "it is rooted in the global history of slavery, colonialism, and other forms of servitude" (ILO 2010).

22. For a discussion of these demeaning stereotypes in Argentina, see Gorbán and Tizziani 2014.

23. The most recent code was drafted in 1997, but the document is continually being updated through addenda.

24. This development contradicted the previously predicted demise of domestic work as an occupation (Coser 1973).

25. There are three primary modes of domestic employment. With live-in work arrangements (called *puertas adentro* in Ecuador), workers reside in the employers' home. In live-out work arrangements (*puertas afuera*), they live separately. The third mode, which is increasingly popular, is hourly or daily part-time work, sometimes called *por horas* in Spanish (and "job work" in English; Hondagneu-Sotelo 1994).

26. The exceptions to this pattern are well known: Argentina (with many workers from Bolivia, Peru, and Paraguay), Chile (with many Peruvian workers), Costa Rica (Nicaraguan workers), and the Dominican Republic (Haitian workers). Prior to its recent economic collapse, Venezuela formerly had many Colombian workers, but now that migratory flow has reversed. Still, only 4.5 percent of domestic workers in the region are international migrants, and even the countries with the highest rates of migrant domestic workers have mostly native-born domestic workers. For example, Costa Rica has the biggest proportion of international migrant domestic workers in Latin America, with 17 percent (Blofield and Jokela 2018, 533).

27. In an article on "Southern Theory," or ways of understanding society that are not rooted in the Global North, Julian Go discusses Raewyn Connell's suggestion that "paying attention to the concerns and experiences of those in the Global South would lead us to different starting points, such as experiences of colonial subjugation" (Go 2016, 11; Connell 2007). We should not automatically or uncritically reproduce the dichotomies of social theory that come from the United States and Europe, such as structure versus agency or public versus private. I attempt to follow the lead of Southern theorists rather than extending Northern theory to analyze the case of domestic work in Ecuador.

1. IN SEARCH OF THE IDEAL WORKER

1. Domestic work advocates and people who work in employment agencies told me in 2018 that they had seen a resurgence in live-in domestic employment in Guayaquil over the past few years, but it is too early to know if this is a trend across the sector and if so, what its causes may be.

2. For more information about the methods used to select and analyze the classified ads, see the appendix.

3. By 2011, the Dignified Domestic Work campaign had "expanded to include all workers and was renamed 'Dignified Work,'" meaning that the government was already moving on from its interest in domestic workers' unique situation (ILO 2014a).

4. This downward trend began in 2011 and accelerated between 2014 and 2016. For details see https://data.worldbank.org/indicator/NY.GDP.PETR.RT.ZS?locations=EC and http://repositorio.cepal.org/bitstream/handle/11362/40826/35/1601259BP_Ecuador_en.pdf.

5. Bergot (2017), with an analysis of Chilean newspaper announcements related to domestic service in the year 1895, is an exception.

6. There are other limitations to this methodology. Staff from *El Universo* confirmed that agencies do not always identify themselves in the ads, and estimated that ads from agencies account for 80 to 90 percent of the classified ads for domestic employment. (Employment agency owners disputed this, saying that hardly any agencies advertised in the classifieds anymore.) Another limitation is that people who place the ad may misrepresent themselves or the job. They may advertise a salary they are not willing to pay, or say they have one child instead of three, or mention tasks different from what they expect a worker to do once hired. As sociological research and our own everyday experiences show, people routinely bend and hide the truth to achieve desired outcomes. In classified ads, we might expect to see these types of face-saving or impression-managing moves.

7. This is a likely scenario: "Jobs listed by agencies are the best jobs of many of the same occupation and are selected to attract a large flow of applicants.... If one high-quality listing attracts fifty well-qualified applicants, for example, private agencies will try to place the other 49 perhaps less attractive but still desirable individuals in its less desirable, more difficult-to-fill jobs which were not advertised" (Walsh, Johnson, and Sugarman 1975, 41). Thus, if a large proportion of ads are placed by agencies, it is likely that the job details are less meaningful than the descriptions of what type of worker they are seeking.

8. For a study of a Latin American location in which employment agencies play a larger role in placing domestic workers, see Durin (2017) on Monterrey, Mexico.

9. Or they may be discouraged from placing ads. The *El Universo* executive I spoke with told me that advertisers have legal obligations to follow labor laws, so if a potential employer tried to advertise an illegally low salary or specifically exclude legal benefits, the newspaper staff would tell them that they could not place such an ad. An employment agency representative confirmed that this enforcement has driven agencies away from the classifieds.

10. Ecuador has the highest Internet usage rate of any Latin American country, according to a recent study, at 77 percent of the population (Espinoza 2018).

11. It is especially easy to tell when only women are being sought for a position, as both men-only and mixed-gender positions are described with masculine plural nouns. The increasing use of the gender-neutral word ending "x" to replace gendered "o" and "a" word endings, particularly in academic circles, seems not to have affected language usage in job advertisements or other mainstream journalistic texts in Latin America.

12. Though I have not found data specific to Ecuador, throughout Latin America the domestic worker population is aging as younger women avoid entering the occupation (Ferrari and Vence 2010), which implies a mismatch between these employers' insistence on youth and the pool of available workers.

13. In contrast, while Venezuelan migrants will often work for lower wages than Ecuadorian workers, the agency representatives I spoke with said that employers had become disillusioned with these workers because they did not know how to prepare Ecuadorian dishes.

14. For a discussion of how different modes of employment relate to working conditions in Argentina, see Pereyra and Tizziani 2014.

15. When we interviewed current and former domestic workers (see chapter 4), most said that they had learned about their job from friends, relatives, or acquaintances. Almost none mentioned using the newspaper's classifieds section or websites. However, we don't have a large enough sample to effectively compare the ways that workers got live-in versus live-out jobs.

16. In their study of help wanted ads in two U.S. cities, Walsh, Johnson, and Sugarman found that more than 85 percent of ads provided no information on what the job paid (1975, 39).

17. Seven ads from 2016 listed a salary of $360 rather than the mandated $366, but I think this is just a shorthand rather than an illegally low salary.

18. I would not want to generalize too much from these data, though, especially since there were so few ads mentioning salary in the more recent sample.

19. As one historical study of domestic workers in Colombia puts it, "more [important] than the servitude was the belonging; more than the salary, the affection" (García López 2012, 166).

2. EMBODIED INEQUALITY

1. Aside from its symbolic aspects, habitus can be a source of identification and meaning-making for individuals.

2. Research on domestic work in Brazil discusses the Portuguese equivalent, *boa aparência* (Goldstein 2003, 60). This term also operates as a form of racial and skin-color discrimination.

3. In her study of domestic work in South Africa, King identified the uniform as a "symbolic representation of the regulation of their [workers'] constructed role" (King 2007, 36). For uniforms' role in society see Joseph 1986.

4. In a study of the impact of washing machine technology in Chile, Katharine French-Fuller writes: "Many of the wealthier women I spoke with said they did not allow their maids to use the machine or that their maids did not want to be responsible for the operation of the machine. . . . [One employer named] Cecilia still did not trust her maid to use this expensive appliance. Cecilia was exercising power within the household by controlling the technology, but still left the grunt work to the maid. The most labor-intensive and tedious parts of the washing cycle—hanging the clothes to dry and then ironing everything—was left to the maid . . . however, the washing machine could also be a site for acts of resistance; a maid could profess ignorance about how to use the machine or intentionally misunderstand directions about how to wash clothes as a way to express that she was already overwhelmed with responsibilities within the household. Or if the maid felt she had been badly treated . . . she might 'accidentally' shrink the husband's work shirts or turn all the white towels pink. . . . In other words, daily practices surrounding the washing machine highlight already existing class tensions in the relationship between employer and maid" (French-Fuller 2006, 92).

5. I met the domestic worker interviewees through fieldwork at ATRH, and employer interviewees through referrals from my personal contacts. For more information about the methods of data collection and analysis, see the appendix.

6. Other themes included sexual harassment, violence, and caring for employers' bodies. Since much attention is paid to harassment in popular, NGO, and scholarly reports, and there were few mentions of carework, my analysis excludes these topics.

7. The legal monthly minimum wage in Ecuador, to which domestic workers were legally entitled, was $240 at the time of these interviews (plus benefits: Social Security, overtime, vacation, etc.). The members of the association told me that most domestic workers in Guayaquil were paid around $200 per month, with unpaid overtime and no benefits.

8. For more information on domestic workers' movements in and out of the labor force, see chapter 4.

9. Rojas-García and Toledo-González (2018) discuss domestic workers' health problems and lack of health-care options in Mexico.

10. In Ecuador (as in many developing countries), most drugs are available in pharmacies without a prescription. Rojas-García and Toledo-González (2018) also reported self-medication as a strategy among Mexican domestic workers they studied.

11. See Auyero's (2011) excellent ethnography of "poor people's waiting" in government benefits offices in Argentina; Sutton's interviews with domestic workers in Argentina

also highlighted long waits to see doctors as a reason that women "neglected signs of illness in their bodies" (Sutton 2010, 56). One domestic worker Sutton interviewed said, "I know I cannot get sick" (ibid.).

12. Domestic worker advocates would rightly point out that, if these workers were guaranteed health benefits, they would not have to depend on the generosity of employers to have their health-care needs met.

13. Historian Shailaja Paik notes the similar embodied exclusion of Dalit people in India, particularly in educational settings (personal communication).

14. Thanks to Tamara R. Mose for highlighting this point (personal communication).

15. Some domestic workers in studies of Latin America report preferring not to eat with employers, because different eating styles can highlight the differences in class and habitus between employer and worker, and also because they may have to eat quickly so that they can clear the table and wash the dishes (Gorbán 2013; Toledo González 2013). It is worth noting, as does sociologist Francisca Pereyra in writing about Argentina, that the very assertion by employers that they believe their domestic workers are human shows the uniqueness of domestic work in comparison to other occupations (2015, 95).

16. A major theme and object of critique in domestic work research. There are too many sources to cite on the subject, but in the Latin American context, I would note Camus and de la O 2014; Canevaro 2014; Toledo González 2013.

17. For a discussion of ideals of beauty and appearance in Latin America, and how these intertwine with class and race, see Casanova 2018.

18. Patty offered clothes lending as an example of how a "good employer" behaves.

19. Rollins argues that gifts from employer to domestic workers, which were not expected to be reciprocated and often used or worn, highlight employees' inferior status, symbolically defining them as "needy" and "dependent" (1985, 192–94).

20. The employers I interviewed were middle-class, working professionals in their thirties, just starting their families. Thus, their opinions on uniforms may differ from older or wealthier employers.

21. This worker favored uniforms, yet criticized the quality and appearance of those typically offered by employers, and thus preferred to buy or make her own (at her expense). One of the employment agency owners interviewed said that workers were less resistant to uniforms now than in the past, partly because of what she perceived as the rising status of the occupation, and partly because more attractive uniforms were available, even some with—as she put it—cute Mickey Mouse prints.

22. In a recent study, domestic workers in Bogotá, Colombia, "admitted having been made fun of or pointed at when moving around the neighborhoods they work in while wearing their uniform" (Fleischer and Marín 2019, 42).

23. An example of a worker shaping her working conditions by stating what she "doesn't like" doing. For more on this type of negotiation with employers, see Goldstein 2003; Tizziani 2011.

24. For discussions of the sexualization and sexual harassment of domestic workers, see Durin 2014.

25. For analysis of similar class and gender dynamics in another time and place (twentieth-century Argentina) see Inés Pérez's discussion of clothing, cosmetics, and jewelry as the most common items domestic workers stole from their employers. These items were the key to embodying a respectable femininity based on modern consumption practices. As a result, the thefts of these types of items were the most vexing to employers, who wanted to maintain class boundaries by degrading working-class women who tried to achieve this type of appearance (Pérez 2016).

26. Lautier has also discussed Brazilian domestic workers' beautifying practices, but argues that it is a way of "denying what they are," that is, making their occupation as domestic workers invisible (2003, 806).

3. INFORMED BUT INSECURE

1. This funder, FOS, is a Belgian socialist solidarity organization that promotes social change, workers' rights, and poverty reduction in the Global South: https://fos.ngo/en-fos/.

2. Ecuadorian domestic workers' situation, for example, is quite similar to that of domestic workers in neighboring Peru and Colombia, both of which had right-conservative governments during the period under study.

3. Employers can enroll workers through the IESS website or in person at an IESS office. They are required to present their (employer's) identity documents and indicate the date employment began. IESS calculates the contribution amounts for employers and employees based on salaries that must be minimum wage or above, and then bills the employer. Employers can also enroll part-time employees in this way. Online calculators allow them to see in advance what the contribution amounts will be. This process has become easier in recent years, as Correa's government made its agencies more accessible.

4. The penal code (Article 244) states that employers who are notified of overdue contributions have forty-eight hours to pay or else they could be put in jail for three to seven days (the penal code can be found online at http://www.justicia.gob.ec/wp-content/uploads/2014/05/c%C3%B3digo_org%C3%A1nico_integral_penal_-_coip_ed._sdn-mjdhc.pdf).

5. Worldwide, most domestic workers are part-time and have multiple employers (ILO 2016a), though among respondents to this survey employed as domestic workers, there were slightly more full-time workers.

6. For more information on the methods of data collection and statistical analysis used in this chapter, see the appendix.

7. This percentage is higher than that reported for Argentina, where 33 percent of domestic workers are heads of household (Gorbán 2013).

8. Colombians migrate to Ecuador escaping violence and Venezuelans to escape political and economic chaos; because of its location and its relatively generous immigration policies, Ecuador takes in more refugees than any other Latin American country (*La Hora* 2018).

9. In planning the survey, we had spirited debates over whether to include a question about race/ethnicity. The members of ATRH who would be conducting the survey ultimately decided not to ask about race, as they thought it was a question that some participants would be offended by or reluctant to answer. In interviews for the following chapter, however, we did include a question on racial identity.

10. While one earlier study (Wong 2017) found large variations in social security enrollment rates by neighborhood, we did not find this relationship to be statistically significant.

11. In Wong's (2017) study, 6.3 percent of survey respondents were live-in workers.

12. Live-in workers are often internal migrants, and in addition to their already-limited local networks, they lack time and opportunity to make connections with people outside their home-workplace. Research on domestic work confirms these disadvantages (Borgeaud-Garciandía and Lautier 2014; Lan 2006; Lautier 2003; León 2013). We also know that the rates of live-in domestic employment are falling in Latin America (Brites, Tizziani, and Gorbán 2013; Brites 2013; ILO 2016a; Moreno Zúñiga 2013), although a few of my informants say it is making a comeback in Ecuador, a claim I don't have the data to evaluate. Domestic workers who live with their employers tend to work longer hours and have less vacation time than those who live out. Their capacity to negotiate with employers and openness to activism may also be constrained because losing their job means losing a place to live.

13. "Full time, and then some!"

14. In her study of domestic workers in Guayaquil, Wong (2017) found that part-time workers tended to work for two employers, and in many cases these employers were members of the same family.

15. Ecuador's official currency has been the U.S. dollar since 2000.

16. The *décimo tercero* is equivalent to one month of the monthly minimum wage, and the *décimo cuarto*, which is calculated based on number of days worked in the year, is also tied to the minimum wage (http://www.ecuadorlegalonline.com/laboral/decimo-cuarto-sueldo/).

17. In a study of domestic workers in Monterrey, Mexico, participants were much more likely to receive health coverage and benefits, with the majority reporting that they had access to these entitlements (Moreno Zúñiga 2013).

18. It is worth noting, since some research claims that internal migrant women are more vulnerable to exploitation than nonmigrants, that we did not find a significant difference between natives of Guayaquil and migrants to the city in their knowledge of this right.

19. Wong's (2017) survey found an enrollment rate of nearly 56 percent. Her sample was purposely drawn from neighborhoods where labor inspections had been conducted by the government, in order to oversample enrolled workers. Wong's participants were overwhelmingly full-time workers, and we found in our survey that full-time workers were more likely to be covered. The Ecuadorian Census Institute reports that 33 percent of domestic workers are enrolled in social security (Wong 2017, 29). Such divergent results mean that we need more comprehensive research on social security coverage rates among domestic workers in Guayaquil and Ecuador.

20. Wong (2017) asked enrolled domestic workers in Guayaquil about social security service use. On average, 11.6 percent had used a service; the most popular was personal medical care, which 44.4 percent said they had used. Thus our figures for usage—when asking a general question about whether any social security services or programs had been used—are much higher than Wong's.

21. Some of these women mentioned not wanting to lose or jeopardize their welfare benefits (*bono de desarrollo humano*) by joining IESS.

22. Because education is used as a dummy variable, the effect has to be interpreted in comparison with the other (omitted) category, in this case, "no schooling," or zero years of formal education.

23. The major important difference between civil unions (cohabitation) and marriage is that only legally married spouses have a right to access social security benefits through their spouse's employment. Yet married and unida respondents did not show different patterns on this variable. In the neighborhoods we studied, formal employment rates are relatively low for men, so there were likely not many women eligible for IESS through their husbands.

24. Indeed, Mexican sociologist Rebeca Moreno Zúñiga argues that many times, a domestic worker is hired in moments of "marital problems, exhaustions and difficulties," which means that domestic workers are often present during and after the dissolution of their employers' marriage (2013, 102).

4. PATHWAYS THROUGH POVERTY

1. Many women moved between domestic work, self-employment, and contributing to family income-earning activities, all in the informal economy: these three modes of work "account for 60% of non-agricultural informal employment in the country" (ILO 2014a).

2. Quitting the job is the "ultimate form of resistance," and sometimes the only one workers feel they have (Goldsmith 2007; Thornton Dill 1998, 41; Tizziani 2011a).

3. Seven were in full-time domestic employment at the time of the interviews; fourteen were in part-time domestic employment; nineteen were unemployed; the rest were working in other types of jobs. Nearly a third of the interviewees had mothers who had worked in domestic employment. For more information about the sample and methods for data collection and analysis, see the appendix.

4. As one interviewee put it: "Now at my age, you can say that it is difficult to keep working; they always look for someone—and if you're young, they say you don't have experience, but if you are older, they tell you you can't continue with the job."

5. When I conducted research on direct selling in Guayaquil in 2007–9 (Casanova 2011a, 2011b), women from poor and working-class neighborhoods often told me that they chose direct sales because the only other employment alternative was domestic work. There is significant overlap between these two populations of workers, and some women do domestic work and direct sales simultaneously. In my fieldwork with ATRH, when members of the organization (current and former domestic workers) found out about my research on direct selling, they often asked me how it worked and whether women were able to make money doing it.

6. No women mentioned training geared specifically to domestic workers. As they suspected and the research shows, even with professionalization and new skills there is little possibility for upward mobility in domestic employment (Hondagneu-Sotelo 1994; Tizziani 2011b).

7. Of course, migrants or not, city dwellers find themselves having to work. As one internal migrant to Quito put it, "Obviously, living in the capital is no joke, your choice is to work or to work—at whatever—but you have to see how you will support yourself."

8. Cultural and social incentives may promote intentional early childbearing, which many young women see as the only way to become independent from parents or achieve adult status. We need more research on these cultural norms in order to design appropriate and sensitive interventions.

9. In addition to the literature on Latin America (Pérez and Llanos 2017; Tizziani 2011a), this pattern of cycling in and out of domestic work has been noted in the case of Spain (García Sainz, Santos Pérez, and Valencia Olivero 2014).

5. LIKE ANY OTHER JOB?

1. For a historical perspective on the uneven legal treatment of domestic workers over time and the selective incorporation of domestic work into labor law, see Hutchison 2015; and Pérez and Canevaro 2016. Unfortunately, similar analysis is not available for the Ecuadorian case.

2. The government of President Lenín Moreno, who took office in 2017, so far appears to be more moderate and less invested in socialist and anti-neoliberal rhetoric than the previous regime of Rafael Correa.

3. For example, the three most populous countries in Latin America have historically had relatively small percentages of foreign-born domestic workers: Brazil, Colombia, and Mexico. The Colombian situation may be changing somewhat with the recent influx of Venezuelan migrants, though I have not seen statistics on this.

4. The differences between unions and workers' associations are not always clear. Unions require recognition by employers, which is difficult due to the fragmentation of domestic employers. Most Latin American countries do not have national unions of domestic workers that bargain collectively with employers: one exception is Uruguay (Goldsmith 2017). In general, associations tend to be more local and smaller, although there are local unions of domestic workers in Brazil. Sometimes, legal restrictions on who can unionize lead workers to call their organizations "associations"—even if they play a role similar to that of unions. These associations often combine advocacy and political

activities with services and training for workers (Tizziani 2011b). In Ecuador, unionization requires a minimum number of employees with the same employer, which was initially an obstacle to forming a national domestic workers' union. A special dispensation from the Ecuadorian government allowed domestic workers to overcome this obstacle (Jo Vervecken, personal communication). For a discussion of domestic work activists' decisions about creating unions versus associations outside of Latin America, see Jiang and Korczynski 2016.

5. This federation of more than five hundred unions and workers' groups was created in 2014 with the backing of supporters of then-president Correa, and is one of three such large unions in Ecuador today (*El Universo* 2018).

6. Founded in 1988, CONLACTRAHO focuses on issues of domestic work in Latin America and the Caribbean, and hosts international summits to plan advocacy campaigns and connect organizations across the hemisphere (Goldsmith 2013).

7. ILO Convention 189 spells out a complete set of rights for domestic workers, including the right to minimum wage, weekly rest periods, social security and maternity benefits, and protection from unhealthy or unsafe conditions, abuse, and harassment. The idea is that once a country has signed the convention, it can be held to account for bringing its national laws in line with the convention. Conventions like this one thus provide leverage to activists. The full text of Convention 189 can be found online at http://www.ilo.org/dyn/normlex/en/f?p=1000:12100:0::NO::P12100_ILO_CODE:C189.

8. For more information about the research methods used in this chapter, see the appendix.

9. The Spanish word *compañera* translates roughly to "comrade," but has a weaker unionist or socialist tinge than the English term.

10. This is a challenge shared by groups looking to organize other types of informal and precarious workers (Agarwala 2014; Kabeer, Sudarshan, and Milward 2013).

11. Some of these challenges have been discussed in recent research about domestic worker mobilization in Brazil and India, but in those cases, there were factors that helped the organizations, such as the success of recruitment at night schools for workers who had not completed high school, links with powerful labor unions or other social movements, and the establishment of an employment agency (Bernardino-Costa 2014; Cornwall 2013; Menon 2013).

12. Reporting bias by the workers surveyed in the first study may be partly responsible for this higher rate, as they were surveyed in the neighborhoods of their employers. Given this setting, they may have felt more pressure to present a positive image of their employers as complying with the law than the respondents in our survey, who were surveyed in their own homes and neighborhoods with no risk of their answers being exposed to their employers. In addition, the neighborhoods that were the focus of Wong's study had been the targets of labor inspections, so we would expect rates of coverage to be higher in those locations. Another main difference between the two surveys is that ours included employed and unemployed (former) domestic workers.

13. The attorney I interviewed said he thinks most cases brought by domestic workers have positive outcomes for the workers; he sees the law as leaning in their favor and said that the process is less subject to manipulation by employers than in the past.

14. According to theories of "new social movements" in Latin America, the national government is an entity to which workers can appeal and express their concerns; often these concerns are communicated through claims to common identity based on race or gender (Escobar and Álvarez 1992).

CONCLUSION

1. International migrants and non-migrants do have different work experiences and labor trajectories in Spain, according to recent research (García, Santos Pérez, and Valencia Olivero 2014, 117). But in Latin America, class distinctions and racialization of domestic employment seem more important for working conditions than migration status.

2. See Poblete (2016), Ally (2009), and especially Pereyra and Tizziani (2014) for good discussions of how mode of employment matters.

3. A recent study on domestic worker organizing in Spain makes a powerful argument about the need for greater working-class solidarity (García, Roco, and Larenas 2015).

4. Sociologists Pei-Chia Lan (2006) and Tamara Mose Brown (2011) researched the use of cell phones among domestic workers in Taiwan and New York City, respectively. They found that workers use phones to avoid employer surveillance and to stay connected to friends and family in the city and back in their home countries.

5. For example, after the United States withdrew from the international environmental agreement signed in Paris, many U.S. cities said they would still honor its terms. See also the work of the Rockefeller Foundation and its NGO partners to bypass national-level initiatives and build "resilient cities" through local models of economic and human development.

6. Knowledge exchanges should ideally work in multiple directions. For example, I have published parts of this study in Spanish and written reports in Spanish for the domestic workers' organization with which I collaborate so that it can use them in its advocacy efforts.

APPENDIX

1. At least one previous study of classified ad content used the same strategy of focusing on Sunday editions "because they usually represent the highest volume of jobs in the week. . . [and] it can be assumed . . . that more job seekers scan the Sunday papers than any other edition of the week" (Walsh, Johnson, and Sugarman 1975, 14–15). These researchers thought that Sunday ads, though more numerous, were similar in other ways to those published during the week, something I confirmed in the case of the domestic employment ads in *El Universo*.

2. All workers interviewed were connected to the domestic worker advocacy organization (ATRH) where I conducted ethnographic fieldwork. This may bias my sample: interviewees may be more committed to domestic workers' rights or more politically informed and active than other domestic workers.

3. Wong (2017) administered surveys verbally to this population for the same reason.

4. Fifteen-year-olds can legally work in Ecuador, and it is well known that some domestic workers start earlier. There are some restrictions on the types of work and the number of hours that fifteen-year-olds can work, so we decided to set the cutoff just above the legal minimum age in order to include only participants who were allowed to participate in any sector of the labor market.

References

Abrantes, Manuel. 2013. "A Matter of Decency? Persistent Tensions in the Regulation of Domestic Service." *Revista de Estudios Sociales* 45:110–22.

Acciari, Louisa. 2016. "'Foi difícil, mas eu sempre falo que nós somos guerreiras'—O movimento das trabalhadoras domésticas entre a marginalidade e o empoderamento." *Mosaico* 7(11): 125–47.

Adair, Vivyan C. 2001. "Branded with Infamy: Inscriptions of Poverty and Class in the United States." *Signs* 27:451–71.

Agarwala, Rina. 2013. *Informal Labor, Formal Politics, and Dignified Discontent in India.* Cambridge: Cambridge University Press.

Alfers, Laura. 2018. "How the Draft WDR 2019 Got It Wrong: Rethinking and 'Relinking' Social Protections for the Future of Work." WIEGO blog: http://www.wiego.org/blog/how-draft-wdr-2019-got-it-wrong-rethinking-and-"relinking"-social-protections-future-work?platform=hootsuite. Accessed July 31, 2018.

Ally, Shireen. 2009. *From Servants to Workers: South African Domestic Workers and the Democratic State.* Ithaca, NY: ILR / Cornell University Press.

América Economía. 2015. "Ecuador: La informalidad e ingresos de US$452 al mes marcan el empleo." April 27. https://www.americaeconomia.com/economia-mercados/finanzas/ecuador-la-informalidad-e-ingresos-de-us452-al-mes-marcan-el-empleo. Accessed February 5, 2019.

Ampudia, Marina. 2016. "Participatory Action Research in Argentina: New Expressions at the Field of Social Movement's Militant Action." *International Journal of Action Research* 12(2): 191–215.

Anderson, Bridget. 2000. *Doing the Dirty Work? The Global Politics of Domestic Labour.* London: Zed Books.

Arango Gaviria, Luz Gabriela. 2001. "Democratización de las relaciones de género y nuevas formas de dominación de clase en América Latina: Reflexiones a partir del caso colombiano." *Revista Colombiana de Sociología* 6(2): 7–37.

Arnado, Janet M. 2003. "Maternalism in Mistress-Maid Relations: The Philippine Experience." *Journal of International Women's Studies* 4:154–77.

Arriagada, Irma, and Rosalba Todaro. 2012. *Cadenas Globales de Cuidados: El papel de las migrantes peruanas en la provisión de cuidados en Chile.* Santo Domingo: ONU Mujeres.

Auyero, Javier. 2011. "Patients of the State: An Ethnographic Account of Poor People's Waiting." *Latin American Research Review* 46:5–29.

Ávila, Maria Betânia. 2008. "Algumas questões teóricas e políticas sobre emprego doméstico." In *Reflexões Feministas sobre Informalidade e Trabalho Doméstico,* edited by Maria Betânia Ávila, Milena Prado, Tereza Souza, Vera Soares, and Verônica Ferreira, 65–72. Recife: SOS Corpo.

Bahnisch, Mark. 2000. "Embodied Work, Divided Labour: Subjectivity and the Scientific Management of the Body in Frederick W. Taylor's 1907 'Lecture on Management.'" *Body and Society* 6:51–68.

Bakker, Isabella. 2007. "Social Reproduction and the Constitution of a Gendered Political Economy." *New Political Economy* 12(4): 541–56.

Bank Muñoz, Carolina. 2017. *Building Power from Below: Chilean Workers Take on Walmart*. Ithaca, NY: ILR / Cornell University Press.

——. 2008. *Transnational Tortillas: Race, Gender, and Shop-Floor Politics in Mexico and the United States*. Ithaca, NY: ILR / Cornell University Press.

Baptista Canedo, Rosario. 2010. "Trabajo doméstico: Experiencias sobre regulación y sindicalización en Bolivia." In *Hacia un fortalecimiento de derechos laborales en el trabajo del hogar: Algunas experiencias de América Latina*, edited by Mary Rosaria Goldsmith Connelly, Rosario Baptista Canedo, Ariel Ferrari, and María Celia Vence, 25–54. Montevideo: Friedrich Ebert Stiftung.

Barrett, Michèle. (1980) 2014. *Women's Oppression Today: The Marxist/Feminist Encounter*. London: Verso.

Bastos, Santiago. 2014. "Presentación: Servicio doméstico, etnicidad y racismo." In Durin, de la O, and Bastos, *Trabajadoras en la sombra*, 347–53.

Beauvoir, Simone de. (1949) 2011. *The Second Sex*. New York: Vintage Books.

Beechey, Veronica. 1978. "Women and Production: A Critical Analysis of Some Sociological Theories of Women's Work." In *Feminism and Materialism: Women and Modes of Production*, edited by Annette Kuhn and AnnMarie Wolpe, 155–97. London: Routledge and Kegan Paul.

Benavides Passos, José Luis. 2010. "La diversidad en la composición demográfica del recurso humano en América Latina." *Revista Finanzas y Política Económica* 2(1): 53–66.

Benería, Lourdes. 2003. *Gender, Development, and Globalization: Economics as If All People Mattered*. New York: Routledge.

——. 1979. "Reproduction, Production and the Sexual Division of Labor." *Cambridge Journal of Economics* 3:203–25.

Benston, Margaret. 1969. "The Political Economy of Women's Liberation." *Monthly Review* 21(4): 13–27.

Bergot, Solène. 2017. "Caracterización y mapeo del servicio doméstico en Santiago de Chile. Una radiografía en 1895 a través del diario 'El Chileno.'" *Historia* 1:11–41.

Bernardino-Costa, Joaze. 2014. "Intersectionality and Female Domestic Workers' Unions in Brazil." *Women's Studies International Forum* 46:72–80.

——. 2011. "Destabilizing the National Hegemonic Narrative: The Decolonized Thought of Brazil's Domestic Workers' Unions." *Latin American Perspectives* 38(178): 33–45.

Blackett, Adelle. 1998. *Making Domestic Work Visible: The Case for Specific Regulation*. Geneva: International Labor Office.

Blofield, Merike. 2012. *Care Work and Class: Domestic Workers' Struggle for Equal Rights in Latin America*. University Park: Penn State University Press.

Blofield, Merike, and Merita Jokela. 2018. "Paid Domestic Work and the Struggles of Care Workers in Latin America." *Current Sociology* 66(4): 531–46.

Borgeaud-Garciandía, Natacha, and Bruno Lautier. 2014. "La personalización de la relación de dominación laboral: Las obreras de las maquilas y las empleadas domésticas en América Latina." *Revista Mexicana de Sociología* 76(1): 89–113.

Bourdieu, Pierre. (1984) 2007. *Distinction: A Social Critique of the Judgment of Taste*. Translated by R. Nice. Cambridge, MA: Harvard University Press.

——. 1990. *The Logic of Practice*. Cambridge: Polity.

——. 1977. *Outline of a Theory of Practice*. Cambridge: Cambridge University Press.

Brites, Jurema. 2014. "Domestic Service, Affection and Inequality: Elements of Subalternity." *Women's Studies International Forum* 46:63–71.

———. 2013. "Trabajo doméstico en Brasil: Transformaciones y continuidades de la precariedad." *Trayectorias* 15(36): 3–19.

Brites, Jurema, Ania Tizziani, and Débora Gorbán. 2013. "Trabajo doméstico remunerado: Espacios y desafíos de la visibilidad social." *Revista de Estudios Sociales* 45:226–28.

Bruthiaux, Paul. 1994. *The Discourse of Classified Advertising: Exploring the Nature of Linguistic Simplicity.* New York: Oxford University Press.

Brydon-Miller, Mary. 1997. "Participatory Action Research: Psychology and Social Change." *Journal of Social Issues* 53(4): 657–66.

Bryson, Valerie. 2005. "Production and Reproduction." In *Marx and Other Four-Letter Words*, edited by Georgina Blakely and Valerie Bryson, 127–42. Ann Arbor, MI: Pluto.

Cabezas Fernández, Marta. 2012. "10 años de lucha por la ley, 11 en el parlamento: Las reivindicaciones de las trabajadoras asalariadas del hogar en Bolivia durante la etapa neoliberal." *Íconos: Revista de Ciencias Sociales,* 44:85–100.

Camus, Manuela, and María Eugenia de la O. 2014. "El encanto de la colonialidad tapatía: Notas sobre la cultura de la servidumbre." In Durin, de la O, and Bastos, *Trabajadoras en la sombra,* 145–69.

Canevaro, Santiago. 2014. "Afectos, saberes y proximidades en la gestión del cuidado de niños: Empleadas y empleadoras del servicio doméstico de Buenos Aires, Argentina." In Durin, de la O, and Bastos, *Trabajadoras en la sombra,* 173–99.

———. 2008. "Empleadoras del servicio doméstico en Buenos Aires: Orden, afecto, y umbrales de 'modernidad.'" IX Congreso Argentino de Antropología Social. Facultad de Humanidades y Ciencias Sociales. Universidad Nacional de Misiones, Posadas.

Carrasco Bengoa, Cristina. 1991. *El trabajo doméstico: Un análisis económico.* Madrid: Ministerio de Trabajo y Seguridad Social, Colección Tesis Doctorales.

Carrasquer Oto, Pilar. 2013. "El redescubrimiento del trabajo de los cuidados: Algunas reflexiones desde la sociología." *Cuadernos de Relaciones Laborales* 31(1): 91–113.

Carrasquer, Pilar, Teresa Torns, Elisabet Tejero, and Alfonso Romero. 1998. "El trabajo reproductivo." *Papers: Revista de Sociología* 55:95–114.

Casanova, Erynn Masi. 2018. "Beauty Ideology in Latin America." *Dobras* 11(23).

———. 2015a. *Buttoned Up: Clothing, Conformity, and White-Collar Masculinity.* Ithaca, NY: ILR / Cornell University Press.

———. 2015b. "'Como cualquier otro trabajo': Organizando a las trabajadoras remuneradas del hogar en Ecuador." *Revista Economía* 67(106): 37–52.

———. 2013. "Embodied Inequality: The Experience of Domestic Work in Urban Ecuador." *Gender & Society* 4(27): 561–85.

———. 2011a. *Making Up the Difference: Women, Beauty, and Direct Selling in Ecuador.* Austin: University of Texas Press.

———. 2011b. "Multiplying Themselves: Women Cosmetics Sellers in Ecuador." *Feminist Economics* 17(2): 1–29.

———. 2004. "No Ugly Women: Concepts of Race and Beauty among Adolescent Women in Ecuador." *Gender & Society* 18:287–308.

Casanova, Erynn Masi, Leila Rodríguez, and Rocío Bueno Roldán. 2018. "Informed but Insecure: Employment Conditions and Social Protection among Paid Domestic Workers in Guayaquil." *Latin American Perspectives* 45(1): 163–74.

Castillo, Juan José. 2000. "La sociología del trabajo hoy: La genealogía de un paradigma." In de la Garza Toledo, *Tratado latinoamericano de sociología del trabajo,* 39–64.

Ceballos López, María Elí. 2014. "'El trabajo de hombre' en lo doméstico: La inclusión del género masculino en el servicio doméstico." In Durin, de la O, and Bastos, *Trabajadoras en la sombra*, 319–40.

Chaney, Elsa M., and Mary Garcia Castro, eds. 1991. *Muchachas No More: Household Workers in Latin America and the Caribbean*. Philadelphia: Temple University Press.

Chang, Grace. 2016. *Disposable Domestics: Immigrant Workers in the Global Economy*. 2nd ed. San Francisco: Haymarket Books.

Chatterjee, Anindita, and Anne Schluter. Forthcoming. "Maid to Maiden: The Promise of English for Domestic Workers and Their Daughters within a Postcolonial Setting." *International Journal of the Sociology of Language*.

Connell, Raewyn. 2007. *Southern Theory: The Global Dynamics of Knowledge in Social Science*. New York: Polity.

Connolly, Priscilla. 1985. "The Politics of the Informal Sector: A Critique." In *Beyond Employment: Household, Gender and Subsistence*, edited by Nanneke Redclift and Enzo Mingione, 55–91. Oxford: Basil Blackwell.

Cornwall, Andrea, with Creuza Maria Oliveira and Terezinha Gonçalves. 2013. "'If You Don't See a Light in the Darkness, You Must Light a Fire': Brazilian Domestic Workers' Struggle for Rights." In *Organizing Women Workers in the Informal Economy: Beyond the Weapons of the Weak*, edited by Naila Kabeer, Ratna Sudarshan, and Kristy Milward, 149–80. London: Zed Books.

Cortés, Fernando. 2000. "La metamorfosis de los marginales: La polémica sobre el sector informal en América Latina." In de la Garza Toledo, *Tratado latinoamericano de sociología del trabajo*, 592–618.

Coser, Lewis A. 1973. "Servants: The Obsolescence of an Occupational Role." *Social Forces* 52(1): 31–40.

Cumes, Aura. 2014. "La casa como espacio de 'civilización.'" In Durin, de la O, and Bastos, *Trabajadoras en la sombra*, 371–97.

Cutuli, Romina Denisse. 2018. "Representatividad y desigualdades interseccionales: Un análisis del debate legislativo del Régimen Especial de Contrato de Trabajo para el Personal de Casas Particulares, Argentina, 2013." *Revista Latinoamericana de Antropología del Trabajo* 2(4). Accessed at http://www.ceil-conicet.gov.ar/ojs/index.php/lat/article/ view/411/308 on February 7, 2019.

Dalla Costa, Mariarosa, and Selma James. 1975. *The Power of Women and the Subversion of the Community*. Bristol, UK: Falling Wall.

Davis, Angela Y. 1981. *Women, Race, and Class*. New York: Vintage Books.

Davolos, Patricia. 2012. "Nuevas tendencias en el mundo del trabajo: Las huellas de más de una década de reformas estructurales." In *El mundo del trabajo en América Latina*, edited by María Julia Soul, Julia Polessa Maçaira, Anahí Durand Guevara, Anabel Rieiro, Catalina Alejandra Chamorro Ríos, Gustavo Antonio das Neves Bezerra, Verónica Barrera, and Cristian Pérez Muñoz, 11–37. Buenos Aires: Ediciones Ciccus / CLACSO.

de Barbieri, M. Teresita. 1978. "Notas para el estudio del trabajo de las mujeres: El problema del trabajo doméstico." *Demografía y Economía* 12(1): 129–37.

Defensoría del Pueblo [Lima, Peru]. 2013. "Las trabajadoras del hogar en el Perú: Supervisión a los sectores encargados de la promoción y la defensa de sus derechos." Serie Informes de Adjuntía, No. 007–2013-DP/ADM. Defensoría del Pueblo.

de la Garza Toledo, Enrique, ed. 2000. *Tratado latinoamericano de sociología del trabajo*. Mexico City: El Colegio de México.

de la Garza Toledo, Enrique, and Juan Manuel Hernández. 2000. "Fin del trabajo o trabajo sin fin." In de la Garza Toledo, *Tratado latinoamericano de sociología del trabajo*, 755–74.

de la Torre, Carlos, and Steve Striffler, eds. 2008. *The Ecuador Reader: History, Culture, Politics*. Durham, NC: Duke University Press.

Delphy, Christine. 1980. "The Main Enemy." *Feminist Issues*, Summer 1980.

de Oliveira, Orlandina, and Marina Ariza. 2000. "Trabajo femenino en América Latina: Un recuento de los principales enfoques analíticos." In de la Garza Toledo, *Tratado latinoamericano de sociología del trabajo*, 644–63.

de Oliveira, Orlandina, and Bryan Roberts. 1993. "La informalidad urbana en años de expansión, crisis y reestructuración económica." *Estudios Sociológicos* 11(31).

de Soto, Hernando. 1987. *El otro sendero: La revolución informal*. Bogotá: La Oveja Negra.

DeVault, Marjorie L. 1994. *Feeding the Family: The Social Organization of Caring as Gendered Work*. Chicago: University of Chicago Press.

Dunstan, Inés, and Rebekah Pite. 2018. "Mistress vs. Maid: Race, Class, Nation, and Boundaries between Women in Argentine Fiction since the Mid-nineteenth Century." *Gender & History* 30(2): 401–22.

Durin, Séverine. 2017. *Yo trabajo en casa: Trabajo del hogar de planta, género, y etnicidad en Monterrey*. Mexico City: CIESAS / Publicaciones de la Casa Chata.

———. 2014. "Etnización y estratificación étnica del servicio doméstico en el área metropolitana de Monterrey." In Durin, de la O, and Bastos, *Trabajadoras en la sombra*, 399–423.

Durin, Séverine, María Eugenia de la O, and Santiago Bastos, eds. 2014. *Trabajadoras en la sombra: Dimensiones del servicio doméstico latinoamericano*. Mexico City: CIESAS / Publicaciones de la Casa Chata.

Durin, Séverine, and Natalia Vázquez. 2013. "Heroínas-Sirvientas: Análisis de las representaciones de trabajadoras domésticas en telenovelas mexicanas." *Trayectorias* 15(36): 20–44.

Ehrenreich, Barbara, and Arlie Russell Hochschild, eds. 2002. *Global Woman: Nannies, Maids, and Sex Workers in the New Economy*. New York: Metropolitan Books.

Engels, Friedrich. (1884) 1978. "The Origin of the Family, Private Property, and the State." In *The Marx-Engels Reader*, 2nd ed., edited by Robert C. Tucker. New York: W. W. Norton.

England, Paula. 2005. "Emerging Theories of Care Work." *Annual Review of Sociology* 31:381–99.

Escobar, Arturo, and Sonia E. Álvarez. 1992. *The Making of Social Movements in Latin America: Identity, Strategy, and Democracy*. Boulder, CO: Westview.

Espinoza, Giannella. 2018. "Ecuador 2.0 en Cifras." *El Expreso*, January 25, 2018. http://www.expreso.ec/ciencia-y-tecnologia/ecuador-2-0-en-cifras-DC1985720. Accessed July 31, 2018.

Esquivel, Valeria. 2011. *La economía del cuidado en América Latina: Poniendo a los cuidados en el centro de la agenda*. Panama: PNUD/United Nations.

Estrada, Daniela. 2009. "Strides and Setbacks for Domestic and Rural Workers." Inter Press Service, September 27. http://ipsnews.net/news.asp?idnews=48613. Accessed October 10, 2009.

Expreso. 2005. "El IESS sólo registra 4.037 afiliados del servicio doméstico." February 27. www.explored.com.ec/wphoy-imprimir.php?id=198677. Accessed October 10, 2009.

Fanon, Frantz. 1967. *Black Skin, White Masks*. New York: Grove.

Feliu, Verónica. 2014. "Chilean Domestic Labor: A Feminist Silence." In *Translocalities/Translocalidades: Feminist Politics of Translation in the Latin/a Américas*, edited by Sonia E. Álvarez, Claudia de Lima Costa, Verónica Feliu, Rebecca J. Hester, Norma Klahn, and Millie Thayer, 240–57. Durham, NC: Duke University Press.

Ferguson, Susan. 2008. "Canadian Contributions to Social Reproduction Feminism, Race, and Embodied Labor." *Race, Gender, and Class* 15(1–2): 42–57.

Ferrari, Ariel, and María Celia Vence. 2010. "Avances del sector doméstico uruguayo." In *Hacia un fortalecimiento de derechos laborales en el trabajo del hogar: Algunas experiencias de América Latina*, edited by Mary Rosaria Goldsmith Connelly, Rosario Baptista Canedo, Ariel Ferrari, and María Celia Vence, 55–91. Montevideo: Friedrich Ebert Stiftung.

Fleischer, Friederike, and Keren Marín. 2019. "Atravesando la ciudad: La movilidad y experiencia subjetiva del espacio por las empleadas domésticas en Bogotá." *EURE* 45(135): 27–47.

Floro, María, and John Messier. 2006. "Tendencias y patrones de crédito entre hogares urbanos pobres en Ecuador." In *La Persistencia de la Desigualdad: Género, trabajo y pobreza en América Latina*, edited by Gioconda Herrera, 225–49. Quito: FLACSO Ecuador.

FORLAC (Programme for the Promotion of Formalization in Latin America and the Caribbean). http://lawsdocbox.com/Immigration/80307723-Transition-to-formality.html. Accessed on August 13, 2018.

Fraga, Alexandre Barbosa. 2010. "De empregada a diarista: As novas configurações do trabalho doméstico remunerado." Master's thesis, Universidade Federal do Rio de Janeiro, Instituto de Filosofia e Ciências Sociais.

Francisco-Menchavez, Valerie. 2018. *The Labor of Care: Filipina Migrants and Transnational Families in the Digital Age*. Urbana-Champaign: University of Illinois Press.

Freeman, Carla. 2000. *High Tech and High Heels in the Global Economy: Women, Work, and Pink-Collar Identities in the Caribbean*. Durham, NC: Duke University Press.

French-Fuller, Katharine. 2006. "Gendered Invisibility, Respectable Cleanliness: The Impact of the Washing Machine on Daily Living in Post-1950 Santiago, Chile." *Journal of Women's History* 18(4): 79–100.

Gachet, Iván, Diego F. Grijalva, Paúl Ponce, and Damián Rodríguez. 2017. "The Rise of the Middle Class in Ecuador during the Oil Boom." *Cuadernos de Economía* 36(72): 327–52.

Gammage, Sarah. 2012. "Identidades y mercados laborales: La economía del cuidado y el papel del Estado." In *¿Qué es el trabajo hoy? Cambios y continuidades en una sociedad global*, edited by Ana Cárdenas, Felipe Link, and Joel Stillerman, 175–90. Santiago: Catalonia.

García, Oihane, Josefina Roco, and Angie Larenas. 2015. "De la atomización a la colectivización: Una experiencia de intervención colaborativa en el sector doméstico." *Aposta: Revista de Ciencias Sociales* 64:1–22.

Garcia Castro, Mary. 1993. "The Alchemy between Social Categories in the Production of Political Subjects: Class, Gender, Race, and Generation in the Case of Domestic Workers' Union Leaders in Salvador-Bahia, Brazil." *European Journal of Development Research* 5(2): 1–22.

García López, Ana Camila. 2012. "Trabajo a cambio de pertenencia, empleadas domésticas en Bogotá, 1950–1980." *Revista Grafía* 9:159–74.

García Sainz, Cristina, M. Lourdes Santos Pérez, and Nelcy Y. Valencia Olivero. 2014. "La construcción social del mercado laboral doméstico en España a comienzos del siglo XXI." *Cuaderno de Relaciones Laborales* 32(1): 101–31.

Gatens, Moira. 1996. *Imaginary Bodies: Ethics, Power, and Corporeality*. London: Routledge.

Gaussens, Pierre. 2016. "¿El fin del trabajo o el trabajo como fin? Proceso constituyente y reformas laborales en el Ecuador de la 'Revolución Ciudadana.'" *Revista Latinoamericana de Derecho Social* 23:31–55.

Gill, Lesley. 1994. *Precarious Dependencies: Gender, Class, and Domestic Service in Bolivia.* New York: Columbia University Press.

———. 1990. "Painted Faces: Conflict and Ambiguity in Domestic Servant-Employer Relations in La Paz, 1930–1988." *Latin American Research Review* 25:119–36.

Giménez, Martha E. 1990. "The Dialectics of Waged and Unwaged Work: Waged Work, Domestic Labor, and Household Survival in the United States." In *Work without Wages: Domestic Labor and Self-Employment within Capitalism*, edited by Jane L. Collins and Martha E. Giménez, 25–46. Albany: SUNY Press.

Gimeno, Beatriz. 2010. "El debate sobre el trabajo doméstico." *Trasversales* 20. Accessed at www.trasversales.net/t20beatd.htm on June 8, 2017.

Gimlin, Debra. 2007. "What Is 'Body Work'? A Review of the Literature." *Sociology Compass* 1:353–70.

Go, Julian. 2016. "Globalizing Sociology, Turning South: Perspectival Realism and the Southern Standpoint." *Sociologica* 2.

Goffman, Erving. 1963. *Stigma: Notes on the Management of Spoiled Identity.* New York: Simon & Schuster.

———. 1959. *The Presentation of Self in Everyday Life.* Garden City, NY: Doubleday.

Goldsmith, Mary R. 2017. "Domestic Workers in Uruguay: Collective Bargaining Agreement and Legal Protection." In *Informal Workers and Collective Action: A Global Perspective*, edited by Adrienne E. Eaton, Susan J. Schurman, and Martha A. Chen, 96–119. Ithaca, NY: ILR / Cornell University Press.

———. 2013. "Los espacios internacionales de la participación política de las trabajadoras remuneradas del hogar." *Revista de Estudios Sociales* 45:233–46.

———. 2006. "Política, trabajo y género: La sindicalización de las y los trabajadores domésticos y el estado mexicano." In *Orden social e identidad de género, México, siglos XIX–XX*, 217–46. México City: CIESAS.

———. "Disputando fronteras: La movilización de las trabajadoras del hogar en América Latina." *Amérique Latine: Histoire & Mémoire. Les Cahiers ALHIM* 27. https://journals.openedition.org/alhim/2202#text

Goldsmith Connelly, Mary Rosaria, Rosario Baptista Canedo, Ariel Ferrari, and María Celia Vence. 2010. *Hacia un fortalecimiento de derechos laborales en el trabajo del hogar: Algunas experiencias de América Latina.* Montevideo: Friedrich Ebert Stiftung.

Goldstein, Donna M. 2003. *Laughter Out of Place: Race, Class, Violence, and Sexuality in a Rio Shantytown.* Berkeley: University of California Press.

Gonçalves, Terezinha. 2010. "Crossroads of Empowerment: The Organisation of Women Domestic Workers in Brazil." *IDS Bulletin* 41(2): 62–69.

Gorbán, Débora. 2013. "El trabajo doméstico se sienta a la mesa: La comida en la configuración de las relaciones entre empleadores y empleadas en la ciudad de Buenos Aires." *Revista de Estudios Sociales* 45:67–78.

Gorbán, Débora, and Ania Tizziani. 2018. *¿Cada una en su lugar? Trabajo, género, y clase en el servicio doméstico.* Buenos Aires: Editorial Biblos.

———. 2014. "Inferiorization and Deference: The Construction of Social Hierarchies in the Context of Paid Domestic Labor." *Women's Studies International Forum* 46:54–62.

Gregson, Nicky, and Michelle Lowe. 1994. *Servicing the Middle Classes: Class, Gender, and Waged Domestic Labour in Contemporary Britain.* London: Routledge.

Grosz, Elizabeth. 1994. *Volatile Bodies: Toward a Corporeal Feminism*. Bloomington: Indiana University Press.

Gutiérrez-Rodríguez, Encarnación. 2014. "Domestic Work-Affective Labor: On Feminization and the Coloniality of Labor." *Women's Studies International Forum* 46:45–53.

Hall, Alex, Jenny Hockey, and Victoria Robinson. 2007. "Occupational Cultures and the Embodiment of Masculinity: Hairdressing, Estate Agency, and Firefighting." *Gender, Work, and Organization* 14:534–51.

Hartmann, Heidi I. 1979. "The Unhappy Marriage of Marxism and Feminism: Towards a More Progressive Union." *Capital and Class* 3(2): 1–33.

Hatton, Erin. 2011. *The Temp Economy: From Kelly Girls to Permatemps in Postwar America*. Philadelphia: Temple University Press.

Haydocy, Kelci E., Marcel Yotebieng, and Alison Norris. 2015. "Restavèk Children in Context: Wellbeing Compared to Other Haitian Children." *Child Abuse and Neglect* 50:42–48.

Hochschild, Arlie R. 1983. *The Managed Heart: The Commercialization of Human Feeling*. Berkeley: University of California Press.

Hondagneu-Sotelo, Pierette. 2007. *Doméstica: Immigrant Workers Cleaning and Caring in the Shadows of Influence*. Berkeley: University of California Press.

——. 1994. "Regulating the Unregulated? Domestic Workers' Social Networks." *Social Problems* 41(1): 50–64.

Hondagneu-Sotelo, Pierette, and Ernestine Ávila. 1997. "'I'm Here, but I'm There': The Meanings of Latina Transnational Motherhood." *Gender & Society* 11(5): 548–71.

La Hora. 2018. "Ecuador acoge más refugiados que toda América Latina." June 20. https://www.lahora.com.ec/quito/noticia/1102165248/ecuador-acoge-mas-refugiados-que-toda-america-latina. Accessed July 31, 2018.

Hordge-Freeman, Elizabeth, and Jaira J. Harrington. 2015. "Ties that Bind: Localizing the Occupational Motivations that Drive Non-union Affiliated Domestic Workers in Salvador, Brazil." In *Towards a Global History of Domestic and Caregiving Workers*, edited by Dirk Hoerder, Elise van Nederveen Meerkerk, and Silke Neunsinger, 137–57. Leiden: Brill.

Humez, Alexander, Nicholas Humez, and Rob Flynn. 2010. *Short Cuts: A Guide to Oaths, Ring Tones, Ransom Notes, Famous Last Words, and Other Forms of Minimalist Communication*. New York: Oxford University Press.

Hutchison, Elizabeth Quay. 2015. "The Problem of Domestic Service in Chile, 1924–1952." In *Towards a Global History of Domestic and Caregiving Workers*, edited by Dirk Hoerder, Elise van Nederveen Meerkerk, and Silke Neunsinger, 512–29. Leiden: Brill.

——. 2011. "Shifting Solidarities: The Politics of Household Workers in Chile, 1967–1988." *Hispanic American Historical Review* 91(1): 129–62.

IESS (Instituto Ecuatoriano de Seguridad Social). N.d. "Asegurados del IESS ya superan los 8.4 millones de personas." www.iess.gob.ec/en/web/afiliado/noticias. Accessed March 16, 2017.

——. N.d. "Aumenta el número de afiliados a la Seguridad Social." www.iess.gob.ec/en/web/afiliado/noticias. Accessed March 16, 2017.

ILO (International Labor Organization). 2018. "Advancing Domestic Workers' Rights through Cooperatives in Trinidad and Tobago: An ILO, NUDE, and SWCC Initiative." http://www.ilo.org/global/topics/cooperatives/publications/WCMS_626009/lang--en/index.htm. Accessed August 1, 2018.

——. 2016a. *Formalizing Domestic Work*. Geneva: International Labor Office.

——. 2016b. *Non-standard Employment around the World: Understanding Challenges, Shaping Prospects*. Geneva: International Labor Office.

——. 2014a. *Trends in Informal Employment in Ecuador: 2009–2012*. Regional Office for Latin America and the Caribbean: FORLAC.

——. 2014b. *Women and Men in the Informal Economy: A Statistical Picture*. Geneva: International Labor Office.

——. 2013. *Domestic Workers across the World: Global and Regional Statistics and the Extent of Legal Protection*. Geneva: International Labor Office.

——. 2011. "Coverage of Domestic Workers by Key Working Conditions Laws." Domestic Work Policy Brief No. 5. Geneva: International Labor Office.

——. 2010. *Decent Work for Domestic Workers*. Geneva: International Labor Office.

INEC (Instituto Nacional de Estadística y Censos, Ecuador). 2016. *Compendio estadístico 2016*. http://www.ecuadorencifras.gob.ec/compendio-estadistico-2016/. Accessed January 25, 2019.

——. 2014. "La mujer ecuatoriana en números." www.ecuadorencifras.gob.ec/la-mujer-ecuatoriana-en-numeros/. Accessed on February 22, 2017.

——. 2013. *Encuesta Nacional de Empleo, Desempleo y Subempleo* [ENEMDU]. Quito: INEC.

——. 2012. *E-Análisis: La Mujer como Jefa de Hogar*. Quito: INEC.

Inglis, Patrick. 2017. "The 'Caddie Question': Why the Golf Caddies of Bangalore Reject Formal Employment." *Journal of Contemporary Ethnography* 47(5): 579–608.

Jaramillo, Verónica. 2014. "En los papeles: De servidoras domésticas a trabajadoras. El caso argentino." *Estudios de Derecho* 71(158): 197–217.

Jiang, Zhe, and Marek Korczynski. 2016. "When the 'Unorganizable' Organize: The Collective Mobilization of Migrant Domestic Workers in London." *Human Relations* 69(3): 813–38.

Jiménez, Diana Marcela. 2012. "Búsqueda de empleo y duración del desempleo en el área metropolitana de Cali: Un recuento para los segundos trimestres de 2009 y 2010." *Sociedad y Economía* 22:163–86.

Joseph, Nathan. 1986. *Uniforms and Nonuniforms: Communication through Clothing*. New York: Greenwood.

Kabeer, Naila, Ratna Sudarshan, and Kristy Milward, eds. 2013. *Organizing Women Workers in the Informal Economy: Beyond the Weapons of the Weak*. London: Zed Books.

Kalleberg, Arne L. 2009. "Precarious Work, Insecure Workers: Employment Relations in Transition." *American Sociological Review* 74(1): 1–22.

Kang, Miliann. 2010. *The Managed Hand: Race, Gender, and the Body in Beauty Service Work*. Berkeley: University of California Press.

Karides, Marina. 2002. "Linking Local Efforts with Global Struggle: Trinidad's National Union of Domestic Employees." In *Women's Activism and Globalization: Linking Local Struggles and Transnational Politics*, edited by Nancy Naples and Manisha Desai, 1156–71. New York: Routledge.

Kessler, Sarah. 2018. *Gigged: The End of the Job and the Future of Work*. New York: St. Martin's.

King, Alison Jill. 2007. *Domestic Service in Post-Apartheid South Africa: Deference and Disdain*. Burlington, VT: Ashgate.

Kofman, Eleonore. 2012. "Rethinking Care through Social Reproduction: Articulating Circuits of Migration." *Social Politics: International Studies in Gender, State, and Society* 19(1): 142–62.

Lan, Pei-Chia. 2006. *Global Cinderellas: Migrant Domestics and Newly Rich Employers in Taiwan*. Durham, NC: Duke University Press.

Lautier, Bruno. 2003. "Las empleadas domésticas latinoamericanas y la sociología del trabajo: Algunas observaciones acerca del caso brasileño." *Revista Mexicana de Sociología* 65(4): 789–814.

Lehdonvirta, Vili. Forthcoming. "Flexibility in the Gig Economy: Managing Time on Three Online Piecework Platforms." *New Technology, Work, and Employment.*

León, Magdalena. 2013. "Proyecto de investigación-acción: Trabajo doméstico y servicio doméstico en Colombia." *Revista de Estudios Sociales* 45:198–211.

Lerussi, Romina. 2014. *La retórica de la domesticidad: Política feminista, derecho, y empleo doméstico en la Argentina.* Buenos Aires: CONICET.

Lind, Amy. 2005. *Gendered Paradoxes: Women's Movements, State Restructuring, and Global Development in Ecuador.* University Park: Penn State University Press.

Lobato, Mirta Zaida. 1997. "Women Workers in the 'Cathedral of Corned Beef': Structure and Subjectivity in the Argentine Meatpacking Industry." In *The Gendered Worlds of Latin American Women Workers: From Household and Factory to the Union Hall and Ballot Box,* edited by John D. French and Daniel James, 53–71. Durham, NC: Duke University Press.

Lofland, John, David Snow, Leon Anderson, and Lyn H. Lofland. 2006. *Analyzing Social Settings: A Guide to Qualitative Observation and Analysis.* Belmont, CA: Cengage.

Lupton, Deborah. 1994. "Food, Memory, and Meaning: The Symbolic and Social Nature of Food Events." *Sociological Review* 42:664–85.

Magliano, María José, María Victoria Perissinotti, and Denise Zenklusen. 2017. "Las luchas de la migración en contextos laborales: La experiencia de sindicalización de una trabajadora doméstica peruana en Córdoba, Argentina." *Trabajo y Sociedad* 28:309–26.

Maich, Katherine. 2014a. "Geographies of Racism and Inequality: Peruvian Household Workers Navigate Spaces of Servitude." In *Critical Cities: Ideas, Knowledge, and Agitation from Emerging Urbanists,* vol. 4, edited by Deepa Naik and Trenton Oldfield, 104–23. London: Myrdle Court.

——. 2014b. "Marginalized Struggles for Legal Reform: Cross-Country Consequences of Domestic Worker Organizing." *Social Development Issues* 36(3): 73–91.

Marx, Karl. (1867) 1990. *Capital.* Vol. 1. Translated by Ben Fowkes. New York: Penguin Classics.

——. (1844) 1978. "Economic and Philosophic Manuscripts of 1844." In *The Marx-Engels Reader.* 2nd ed., edited by Robert C. Tucker. New York: W. W. Norton.

McDowell, Linda. 1997. *Capital Culture: Gender at Work in the City.* Oxford: Blackwell.

McTaggart, Robin. 1998. "Is Validity Really an Issue for Participatory Action Research?" *Studies in Culture, Organizations, and Societies* 4(2): 211–37.

Menon, Geeta. 2013. "The Challenge of Organizing Domestic Workers in Bangalore: Caste, Gender, and Employer-Employee Relations in the Informal Economy." In *Organizing Women Workers in the Informal Economy: Beyond the Weapons of the Weak,* edited by Naila Kabeer, Ratna Sudarshan, and Kristy Milward, 181–204. London: Zed Books.

M.I. Municipalidad de Guayaquil. 2016. http://www.guayaquil.gob.ec/. Accessed October 24, 2016.

Mies, Maria. 1998. *Patriarchy and Accumulation on a World Scale.* London: Zed Books.

Miles, Ann. 2013. *Living with Lupus: Women and Chronic Illness in Ecuador.* Austin: University of Texas Press.

——. 1998. "Women's Bodies, Women's Selves: Illness Narratives and the 'Andean' Body." *Body and Society* 4:1–19.

Milkman, Ruth, Ellen Reese, and Benita Roth. 1998. "The Macrosociology of Paid Domestic Labor." *Work and Occupations* 25(4): 483–510.

Molyneux, Maxine. 1979. "Beyond the Domestic Labour Debate." *New Left Review* 116:3–27.

Moreno Zúñiga, Rebeca. 2013. "Las Empleadoras del Área Metropolitana de Monterrey: Interacciones sociales y acuerdos de contratación del servicio doméstico a tiempo parcial." *Trayectorias* 15(37): 90–111.

Mose Brown, Tamara. 2012. "Who's the Boss? The Political Economy of Unpaid Care Work and Food Sharing in Brooklyn, USA." *Feminist Economics* 18(3): 1–24.

———. 2011. *Raising Brooklyn: Nannies, Childcare, and Caribbeans Creating Community.* New York: NYU Press.

Myrdal, Gunnar. 1957. *Rich Lands and Poor Lands: The Road to World Prosperity.* New York: Harper.

Nencel, Lorraine. 2008. "'Que viva la minifalda!': Secretaries, Miniskirts and Daily Practices of Sexuality in the Public Sector in Lima." *Gender, Work, and Organization* 17:69–90.

OIT (Organización Internacional del Trabajo). 2018. *Panorama Laboral Temático: Presente y futuro de la protección social en América Latina y el Caribe.* Peru: OIT.

Orozco, Mónica. 2016. "El IESS aumenta el aporte del afiliado." *El Comercio*, n.d. http://www.elcomercio.com/actualidad/negocios/iess-aumenta-aporte-del-afiliado.html#.WMko9hsyWRc.email. Accessed March 24, 2017.

PAHO (Pan-American Health Organization). 2011. *Población Económicamente Activa, 2001.* http://www.paho.org/ecu/index.php?option=com_docman&view=d ocument&layout=default&alias=267-poblacion-economicamente-activa-2001&category_slug=sala-de-situacion-ecu&Itemid=599 Accessed March 1, 2017.

Parreñas, Rhacel Salazar. 2001. *Servants of Globalization: Women, Migration, and Domestic Work.* Stanford, CA: Stanford University Press.

Paspuel, Washington. 2014. "El 44% de las trabajadoras domésticas de Guayaquil no están afiliadas, según una encuesta." *El Comercio*, November 28. www.elcomercio.com/actualidad/trabajadoras-domesticas-guayaquil-afiliacion-iess.html. Accessed September 29, 2017.

Pereyra, Francisca. 2017. *Trabajadoras domésticas y protección social en Argentina: Avances y desafíos pendientes.* Argentina: Organización Internacional del Trabajo.

———. 2015. "El servicio doméstico y sus derechos en Argentina: Un abordaje exploratorio desde la perspectiva de empleadas y empleadoras." *Nueva Sociedad* 256:89–102.

———. 2013. "El acceso desigual a los derechos laborales en el servicio doméstico argentino: Una aproximación desde la óptica de las empleadoras." *Revista de Estudios Sociales* 45:54–66.

Pereyra, Francisca, and Lorena Poblete. 2015. "¿Qué derechos? Qué obligaciones? La construcción discursiva de la noción de empleadas y empleadores en el debate de la Ley del Personal de Casas Particulares (2010–2013)." *El Trabajo Doméstico: Entre Regulaciones Formales e Informales. Cuadernos del IDES* 30:73–102.

Pereyra, Francisca, and Ania Tizziani. 2014. "Experiencias y condiciones de trabajo diferenciadas en el servicio doméstico: Hacia una caracterización de la segmentación laboral del sector en la ciudad de Buenos Aires." *Trabajo y Sociedad* 23:5–25.

Pérez, Alba, and Claudio Gallardo. 2005. *Mujeres y hombres del Ecuador en Cifras II*. Quito: CONAMU.

Pérez, Inés. 2016. "Hurto, Consumo, y Género en el Servicio Doméstico (Mar del Plata, 1950–1980)." *Anuario IEHS* 31(2): 57–78.

———. 2015. "Un 'régimen especial' para el servicio doméstico. Tensiones entre lo laboral y lo familiar en la regulación del servicio doméstico en la Argentina, 1926–1956." *Cuadernos del IDES* 30:44–67.

Pérez, Inés, and Santiago Canevaro. 2016. "Derechos laborales y narrativas morales en las disputas entre empleadores y trabajadoras domésticas." *Política y Sociedad* 53(1).

Pérez, Inés, and Elizabeth Hutchison. 2016. "Domestic Service and Labor Laws in Chile and Argentina, 1931–1956." *Oxford Research Encyclopedia of Latin American History*. New York: Oxford University Press.

Pérez, Leda M., and Pedro M. Llanos. 2017. "Vulnerable Women in a Thriving Country: An Analysis of Twenty-First-Century Domestic Workers in Peru and Recommendations for Future Research." *Latin American Research Review* 52(4): 552–70.

Picchio, Antonella. 1992. *Social Reproduction: The Political Economy of the Labour Market*. Cambridge: Cambridge University Press.

Pite, Rebekah. 2013. "¿Así en la tele como en la casa? Patronas y empleadas en la década del sesenta en Argentina." *Revista de Estudios Sociales* 45:212–24.

Poblete, Lorena. 2016. "Empleo y protecciones sociales, ¿dos caras de la misma moneda? Reflexiones en torno a la regulación del servicio doméstico en Argentina." *Revista Latinoamericana de Derecho Social* 22:153–80.

———. 2015. "New Rights, Old Protections: The New Regulation for Domestic Workers in Argentina." McGill Labor Law and Development Research Laboratory, Working Paper Series No. 5.

Polanyi, Karl. (1944) 2001. *The Great Transformation*. Boston: Beacon.

Portes, Alejandro, Manuel Castells, and Lauren Benton. 1989. *The Informal Economy: Studies in Advanced and Less Developed Countries*. Baltimore: Johns Hopkins University Press.

Prassl, Jeremias. 2018. *Humans as a Service: The Promise and Perils of Work in the Gig Economy*. Oxford: Oxford University Press.

Quijano, Aníbal. 2000. "Colonialidad del poder y clasificación social." *Journal of World-Systems Research* 11(2): 342–86.

Radcliffe, Sarah. 1999. "Race and Domestic Service: Migration and Identity in Ecuador." In *Gender, Migration, and Domestic Service*, edited by Janet H. M. Momsen, 81–94. New York: Routledge.

Rahier, Jean Muteba. 1998. "Blackness, the 'Racial'/Spatial Order, Migrations, and Miss Ecuador 1995–1995." *American Anthropologist* 100:421–30.

Randall, Rachel. 2018. "'It Is Very Difficult to Like and to Love, but Not to Be Respected or Valued': Maids and Nannies in Contemporary Brazilian Documentary." *Journal of Romance Studies* 18(2): 275–300.

Ray, Raka, and Seemin Qayum. 2009. *Cultures of Servitude: Modernity, Domesticity, and Class in India*. Stanford, CA: Stanford University Press.

Razavi, Shahra, and Silke Staab. 2010. "Underpaid and Overworked: A Cross-National Perspective on Care Workers." *International Labour Review* 149(4): 407–22.

Redclift, Nanneke. 1985. "The Contested Domain: Gender, Accumulation and the Labor Process." In *Beyond Employment: Household, Gender and Subsistence*, edited by Nanneke Redclift and Enzo Mingione, 92–125. Oxford: Basil Blackwell.

Revista Líderes. 2015. "La informalidad laboral, una condición arraigada en Ecuador." July 26, 2015. https://www.revistalideres.ec/lideres/informalidad-laboral-condicion-ecuador.html. Accessed February 5, 2019.

Reyes Salazar, Natacha, and Gloria Camacho Zambrano. 2001. *Violencia contra las mujeres y los niños: Situación del Ecuador (1995–1999)*. Quito: CONAMU.

Ribeiro Corossacz, Valeria. 2014. "Abusos sexuais no emprego doméstico no Rio de Janeiro: A imbricação das relações de clase, gênero, e 'raça.'" *Temporalis* 14(28): 299–324.

Roberts, Elizabeth F. S. 2012. *God's Laboratory: Assisted Reproduction in the Andes*. Berkeley: University of California Press.

Rojas-García, Georgina, and Mónica Patricia Toledo-González. 2018. "Paid Domestic Work: Gender and the Informal Economy in Mexico." *Latin American Perspectives* 45(1): 146–62.

Rollins, Judith. 1985. *Between Women: Domestics and Their Employers*. Philadelphia: Temple University Press.

Romero, Mary. 2002. *Maid in the U.S.A.* 10th anniversary ed. New York: Routledge.

Romo, María Paula. 2013. "Revisión del marco jurídico sobre trabajo infantil doméstico en el Ecuador." Unpublished report on behalf of ATRH to OIT Ecuador.

Roncador, Sônia. 2014. *Domestic Servants in Literature and Testimony in Brazil, 1889–1999*. New York: Palgrave Macmillan.

Rosenbaum, Susanna. 2017. *Domestic Economies: Women, Work, and the American Dream in Los Angeles*. Durham, NC: Duke University Press.

Saffioti, Heleieth Iara Bongiovani. 1978. *Emprego doméstico e capitalismo*. Petrópolis: Editora Vozes.

Saldaña-Tejeda, Abril. 2015. "Un/Identifying Reflexive Subjects: The Case of Women in Paid Domestic Work in Mexico." *Current Sociology* 63(7): 943–60.

———. 2013. "Racismo, proximidad y mestizaje: El caso de las mujeres en el servicio doméstico en México." *Trayectorias* 15(37): 73–89.

———. 2012. "'Why Should I Not Take an Apple or a Fruit If I Wash Their Underwear?' Food, Social Classification, and Paid Domestic Work in Mexico." *Journal of Intercultural Studies* 33(2): 121–37.

Salzinger, Leslie. 2003. *Genders in Production: Making Workers in Mexico's Global Factories*. Berkeley: University of California Press.

Sarti, Raffaella. 2014. "Historians, Social Scientists, Servants, and Domestic Workers: Fifty Years of Research on Domestic and Care Work." *IRSH* 59:279–314.

Sassen, Saskia. 2001. *The Global City*. Princeton, NJ: Princeton University Press.

Schurman, Susan J., Adrienne E. Eaton, and Martha A. Chen. 2017. "Expanding the Boundaries of Labor Organizing and Collective Bargaining." In *Informal Workers and Collective Action: A Global Perspective*, edited by Adrienne E. Eaton, Susan J. Schurman, and Martha A. Chen, 217–37. Ithaca, NY: ILR / Cornell University Press.

Seccombe, Wally. 1974. "The Housewife and Her Labour under Capitalism." *New Left Review* 83:3–24.

Seoane Vázquez, Pilar. 2011. *Manual de equidad de género en el trabajo*. Honduras: Secretaría de Trabajo y Seguridad Social.

Shilling, Chris. (1993) 2003. *The Body and Social Theory*. 2nd ed. London: Sage.

Silva, Elizabeth. 2010. "Maids, Machines, and Morality in Brazilian Homes." *Feminist Review* 94:20–37.

Skeggs, Beverly. 2004a. "Context and Background: Pierre Bourdieu's Analysis of Class, Gender, and Sexuality." *Sociological Review* 52:19–33.

———. 2004b. "Exchange, Value, and Affect: Bourdieu and the 'Self.'" *Sociological Review* 52:75–95.

Smith, Paul. 1978. "Domestic Labour and Marx's Theory of Value." In *Feminism and Materialism: Women and Modes of Production*, edited by Annette Kuhn and AnnMarie Wolpe, 198–219. London: Routledge and Kegan Paul.

Sutton, Barbara. 2010. *Bodies in Crisis: Culture, Violence, and Women's Resistance in Neoliberal Argentina.* New Brunswick, NJ: Rutgers University Press.

Tamez González, Silvia, and Pedro Moreno Salazar. 2000. "Seguridad Social en América Latina." In de la Garza Toledo, *Tratado latinoamericano de sociología del trabajo*, 471–508.

Thornton Dill, Bonnie. 1988. "'Making Your Job Good Yourself': Domestic Service and the Construction of Personal Dignity." In *Women and the Politics of Empowerment*, edited by Ann Bookman and Sandra Morgen, 33–52. Philadelphia: Temple University Press.

Tinsman, Heidi. 1992. "The Indispensable Services of Sisters: Considering Domestic Service in United States and Latin American Studies." *Journal of Women's History* 4(1): 37–59.

Tizziani, Ania. 2011a. "De la movilidad ocupacional a las condiciones de trabajo: Algunas reflexiones en torno a diferentes carreras laborales dentro del servicio doméstico en la ciudad de Buenos Aires." *Trabajo y sociedad* (17): 19–20.

———. 2011b. "Estrategias sindicales e iniciativas estatales en el sector del servicio doméstico en la ciudad de Buenos Aires: El impulse y sus límites." *Sociedad y Cultura* 14(1): 87–97.

Tokman, Víctor. 2007. "Modernizing the Informal Sector." DESA Working Paper No. 42. New York: United Nations Department of Economic and Social Affairs.

Toledo González, Mónica Patricia. 2013. "El papel de la confianza en los arreglos particulares del trabajo doméstico." *Trayectorias* 15(36): 45–64.

Tomei, Manuela. 2011. "Decent Work for Domestic Workers." *Canadian Journal of Women and the Law / Revue Femmes et Droit* 23:185–211.

Torns, Teresa. 2008. "El trabajo y el cuidado: Cuestiones teórico-metodológicas desde la perspectiva de género." *Empiria: Revista de Metodología de Ciencias Sociales* 15:53–73.

Undurraga, Rosario. 2018. "El trabajo y la vejez: Trayectorias laborales de mujeres en Chile." Paper presented at Latin American Studies Association Annual Congress, Barcelona.

———. 2011. "Between Family and Work: Women's Participation in the Labour Market in Chile." Doctoral thesis in sociology, University of Warwick.

El Universo. 2018. "En los últimos 16 meses, se constituyeron 52 sindicatos en Ecuador." Política, May 1, 2018. https://www.eluniverso.com/ noticias/2018/05/01/nota/ 6739662/ultimos-16-meses-se-constituyeron-52-sindicatos. Accessed July 31, 2018.

———. 2010a. "Campaña para afiliarlas al IESS no se mantiene, dicen empleadas." December 3. http://www.eluniverso.com/2010/12/03/1/1445/campana-afiliarlas-iess-mantiene-dicen-empleadas.html. Accessed September 29, 2017.

———. 2010b. "Jornada parcial, opción más acogida para las domésticas." June 6. http://www.eluniverso.com/2010/06/06/1/1445/jornada-parcial-opcion-mas-acogida-domesticas.html. Accessed September 29, 2017.

Valentine, Gill. 1999. "Eating In: Home, Consumption, and Identity." *Sociological Review* 3:491–524.

Valenzuela, María Elena, and Claudia Mora, eds. 2009. *Trabajo doméstico: Un largo camino hacia el trabajo decente*. Santiago: Organización Internacional del Trabajo.

Valenzuela, María Elena, and Solange Sanches. 2012. "Trabajo doméstico e identidad: Las trabajadoras domésticas remuneradas en Chile." In *¿Qué significa el trabajo hoy? Cambios y continuidades en una sociedad global*, edited by Ana Cárdenas, Felipe Link, and Joel Stillerman, 149–62. Santiago: Catalonia.

Vega, Cristina. 2009. *Culturas del cuidado en transición: Espacios, sujetos, imaginarios en una sociedad en migración*. Barcelona: UOC.

Vervecken, Jo. 2013. "La mano invisible de las trabajadoras remuneradas del hogar en el Ecuador." *Trabajo y Derecho* 50:95–100.

Vogel, Lise. 2014. *Marxism and the Oppression of Women: Toward a Unitary Theory*. Chicago: Haymarket Books.

Walsh, John, Miriam Johnson, and Marged Sugarman. 1975. *Help Wanted: Case Studies of Classified Ads*. Salt Lake City: Olympus.

Ward, Paul, John Coveney, and Julie Henderson. 2010. "Editorial: A Sociology of Food and Eating." *Journal of Sociology* 46:347–51.

Warde, Alan, and Kevin Hetherington. 1994. "English Households and Routine Food Practices." *Sociological Review* 42:758–78.

Weeks, Kathi. 2011. *The Problem with Work: Feminism, Marxism, Antiwork Politics, and Postwork Imaginaries*. Durham, NC: Duke University Press.

Wrigley, Julia. 1995. *Other People's Children*. New York: Basic Books.

Whyte, William F. 1989. "Advancing Scientific Knowledge through Participatory Action Research." *Sociological Forum* 4(3): 367–86.

Wolkowitz, Carol. 2006. *Bodies at Work*. London: Sage.

Wong, Sara. 2017. "Maids' Opinions about Social Security Benefits in Guayaquil-Ecuador." *Documentos de Trabajo: Serie Economía y Negocios*, no. 11. Guayaquil, Ecuador: ESPAE-ESPOL.

Young, Iris Marion. 2005. *On Female Body Experience: "Throwing Like a Girl" and Other Essays*. New York: Oxford University Press.

Index

Afro-Ecuadorians, 41, 62, 138
age
  and awareness regarding right to social
    security, 73, 73*f*, 76–77
  discrimination based on, 93, 149n4
  and discussing social security with
    employer, 75, 76–77
  of ideal worker, 26–28
  and likelihood of social security coverage,
    76–77
  of surveyed domestic workers, 60, 151n4
  at time of entry into workforce, 86
annual bonuses, 66, 68*f*, 78
appearance
  and domestic workers as sexual threat,
    50–51
  and embodied inequality, 47–48, 54
  as employment requirement, 32
appliances, 42, 145n4
Argentina, 146n25
Asociación de Trabajadoras Remuneradas del
  Hogar (ATRH), ix, 19–20, 26, 55, 85–86,
  110–20, 125, 132, 137–38

back wages, 90, 115–16
bad job, domestic work as, 40, 99, 118–19,
  122–24
Bastos, Santiago, 52
benefits. *See* employment benefits
Bergot, Soléne, 144n5
birthplace
  of ideal worker, 28
  of surveyed domestic workers, 61–62
Black Ecuadorians, 41, 62, 138
body/bodies
  of employers as more valuable, 45–48
  implicated in domestic food practices, 39,
    45–47, 146n15
  as resource, 43–44, 52
  as symbol, 37, 45–48
  theoretical perspectives on, 36–38
  See also embodied inequality
body work, 37–38, 44
Bolivia, 39, 46, 116–17, 120
bonuses, 66, 68*f*, 78

Bourdieu, Pierre, 37, 46
Brazil, 120, 146n26, 149n3
buena presencia, 32, 41. *See also* appearance;
  race

capitalism
  domestic work in contemporary, 4
  and embodied inequality, 36–37
  production and reproduction in, 5
  and social reproduction, 6–8
cell phones, 125, 151n4
Chatterjee, Anindita, 38
child labor, 86
children
  hopes for, 99
  and mobilization of domestic workers,
    113–14
  rewards of spending time with, 101
  sacrifices for, 102
  See also family and family situations;
    mothers; pregnancy; single mothers
civil unions. *See* marriage
class. *See* social class
classified ads, 21–22
  change in, over time, 23–24
  characteristics of ideal worker given in,
    26–28, 144n11
  content analysis of, 133–34
  decrease in, 25–26
  employment arrangements given in, 28–30
  and enforcement of labor laws, 144n9
  household tasks enumerated in, 33–34
  limitations to methodology, 144n6
  listed by agencies, 144n7
  salary and benefits given in, 30–32
  scholarship on, 24
  in study of ideal worker, 24–25, 34
clothes
  and embodied inequality, 47–51, 52, 145n3,
    146nn21–22
  and embodiment of respectable femininity,
    146n25
  washing, 42, 44, 145n4
Código del Trabajo, 13–14, 30, 105, 111
cohabitation. *See* marriage

Colombia, 132, 143n26, 147n8, 149n3
colonialism, 12–13, 17–18, 53, 107
coloniality of power, 18, 107
commutes, 62–64, 136–37
CONLACTRAHO, 150n6
Connell, Raewyn, 143n27
contracts
    lack of formal, 13–14, 36, 40, 54, 56, 83–84,
        90–91, 114
    verbal, 90
    written, 90, 91, 116
cooperatives, 126
Correa Delgado, Rafael, 14, 23, 40–41, 116, 117
Costa Rica, 143n26
credit/microcredit, 98, 100

décimos (décimo terceros, décimo cuartos).
    See annual bonuses
developing/developed countries, 141n4
Dignified Domestic Work campaign, 23, 117,
    143n1
dignity, 54
direct selling, 95–96, 149n5
domestic labor debates, 7–8
domestic work
    as bad job, 40, 99, 118–19, 122–24
    chances of upward mobility by leaving,
        97–100
    in contemporary capitalism, 4
    decrease in, 14–16, 25, 29–30, 40, 89–90
    defined, 2
    enforcement of labor laws concerning,
        40–41, 79, 114–16
    exploitation of paid, 8, 11, 19, 91–93, 111,
        118–20, 122–25
    female workforce in, 3
    future research on, 127–30
    history of, 2–3
    increase in full-time, in United States, 16
    invisibility of, 2, 9, 36, 52, 107, 114, 118–19
    as invisible, 114
    key elements of, 1–2
    laws governing, 105–6, 144n9
    and local, colonial, and precapitalist histo-
        ries of Ecuador, 12–16
    media representations of, 1–2, 128–29
    methods for finding, 21
    multiple roles and disparate tasks included
        in, 91
    new factors affecting, 131–32
    paid and unpaid, 6, 7–8, 100–101
    physical labor in, 43–44, 52
    possible interventions for improving,
        125–27
    primary modes of, 143n25

racialization of, 1–2, 12–13, 52–53, 124
    reasons for choosing, 86–87, 88–89
    rejection of, as bad job, 40
    research methods in study of, 133–40
    and reserve army of labor, 142n13
    scholarship on, 3–4, 7, 17
    social class and, 16–17
    social reproduction and, 5–8
    strategically redefining paid, 117–20
    tasks encompassing, 65
    terminology for, 26, 141n2
    unique nature of, 120
    upward mobility in, 149n6
    and urban informal economy, 8–11
    worldwide employment in, 2
    See also domestic worker organizing;
        full-time work; indigenous domestic
        workers; internal migrant domestic
        workers; international migrant domestic
        workers; live-in workers; live-out workers;
        mobilization of domestic workers;
        part-time work; survey on domestic
        work; trajectories of domestic workers
domestic worker organizing, 105–7, 120–21
    challenges in, 112–17
    and paid social reproduction, 111–12
    previous research on, 107–9, 112
    and priorities of ATRH, 110–11
    research methods for, 140
    and revaluing of social reproduction, 126
    and strategically redefining paid domestic
        work, 117–20
    strategies for, 125–27
domination, 4, 18, 72, 85, 106–7, 111,
    118–19, 124

earthquake, 23–24
Ecuador
    economic ranking of, 141n4
    history of social security in, 58–59
    increased migration to, 132
    local, colonial, and precapitalist histories
        of, 12–16
    relationship between ATRH and, 116–17
    and scholarship on domestic
        employment, 17
education
    and awareness regarding right to social
        security, 73–74, 77, 79
    and improved employment opportunities,
        103–4, 126–27
    and leaving school to enter workforce,
        86–87
    of surveyed domestic workers, 61
    through vocational training, 99–100

embodied inequality, 13, 35–36, 51–54
 and body as resource, 43–44
 and body as symbol, 37, 45–48
 and local structures of class, race, and labor, 40–43, 146n15
 and scholarship on workers' embodiment, 38–39
 and theoretical perspectives on working bodies, 36–38
 uniforms and, 42, 48–51, 52, 145n3, 146nn21–22
embodiment. *See* body/bodies
employment
 availability of other, 88
 education and improved opportunities in, 103–4
 occupation in other, 94–99
 statistics and improving domestic work, 126
 See also mode of employment
employment benefits, 30–32, 57–60, 66–67, 68*f*, 78
Engels, Friedrich, 142n11
exhaustion, 43–44, 52
exploitation
 collective organization and fight against, 106–7
 lawsuits contesting, 115–16
 of paid domestic work, 8, 11, 19, 91–93, 111, 118–20, 122–25

factory work, 118–19
family, domestic worker "like part of the," 18, 32, 47, 70, 112
family and family situations
 commute's impact on time with, 64
 as reason for leaving jobs, 93–94
 as reason for taking jobs, 86–88
 of surveyed domestic workers, 60
 See also children
feminist movements, 109
feminist political economy, 4, 6, 7
food, and social distinction, 39, 45–47, 146n15
formalization, 5, 9–11, 23, 56, 80–81, 123–24
French-Fuller, Katharine, 145n4
full-time work
 commute and, 113
 employment arrangements concerning, 28
 and enrollment in social security, 59
 future research on, 128
 reduction in, 32
 wages for, 31

gender
 and embodied inequality, 37
 of ideal worker, 26, 144n11

and social reproduction, 6, 22, 87, 123
 and upward mobility through leaving domestic work, 98
 and urban informal economy, 10
Gill, Lesley, 39
Gimlin, Debra, 44
Go, Julian, 143n27
Goffman, Erving, 83
Goldsmith, Mary, 106
Goldstein, Donna M., 53
Gorbán, Débora, 47, 48, 141n5
grandchildren, 101

habitus, 37, 52, 54, 145n1
heads of households, women as, 80, 147n7
health care, 45, 58, 59, 145–46nn11–12
health problems, 45, 54, 92, 93
home-based work, 4, 95–96, 98
household appliances, 42, 145n4

ideal worker, 21–22, 34
 change in, over time, 23–24
 characteristics of, 26–28, 144n11
 classified ads in study of, 24–25
 and decrease in classified ads, 25–26
 employment arrangements of, 28–30
 household tasks of, 33–34
 salary and benefits of, 30–32
identity, domestic work as, 82–83, 84
indigenous domestic workers, 41
informality and informal employment, 8–11
 decrease in, 143n20
 and ideal worker, 22
 increase in, 3
 as obstacle to domestic workers' rights, 123–24
 and treatment of workers by employers, 31–32
 in wealthy nations, 142n15
informal self-employment, 95–99
Instituto Ecuatoriano de Seguridad Social (IESS), 58, 59, 68–72, 147n3. *See also* social security
internal migrant domestic workers, 9, 11, 13, 16, 17, 28, 34, 61–62, 122, 147n12, 148n18
internal migrants, 9, 13, 28, 34, 61, 101–2, 122, 147n12
International Labor Organization (ILO), 2, 9–10, 105, 142n18
International Labor Organization Convention 189, 11, 30, 105, 106, 110–11, 118, 120, 150n7
international migrant domestic workers, 16, 143n26

interventions for improving domestic workers' situations, 125–27
invisibility of domestic work, 2, 9, 36, 52, 107, 114, 118–19
isolation of domestic workers, 114, 124–25

King, Alison Jill, 38–39, 145n3

Labor Code, 13–14, 30, 105, 111
labor markets, 4, 9, 11, 17, 24, 40, 82–85, 88, 104, 129, 149n5
labor unions, 8, 108, 117, 149n4
Lan, Pei-Chia, 151n4
Lautier, Bruno, 112, 146n26
lawsuits, 115–16
liquidación. *See* severance pay
live-in workers, 29, 65, 92, 132, 143n1, 147n12
live-out workers, 23, 28–29, 43, 64, 65, 101–2, 137, 143n25, 144n15
loans, 93
lucha, la, 83, 102–4, 129

marriage
    and accessibility of social security benefits, 148n23
    compared to civil unions and cohabitation, 60, 74–75, 148n23
    and discussing social security with employer, 74–75, 77–78, 79
    dissolution of employers', 148n24
Marx, Karl, 4, 5, 7, 36–37, 44, 142nn7,10
media representations of domestic work, 1–2, 128–29
middle class, precarious status of, 42
minimum wage, 31, 145n7, 148n16
mobilization of domestic workers, 106–10, 113–14, 117, 119–20, 125–27
mode of employment, 29, 151n2. *See also* full-time work; live-in workers; live-out workers; part-time work
modesty, 50–51, 52
Moreno, Lenín, 131, 149n2
Moreno Zúñiga, Rebeca, 140, 148n24
mothers
    appeal of sales jobs to, 96
    domestic workers as, 60, 87, 101, 128
    and mobilization of domestic workers, 113–14
    stay-at-home, 96
    See also children; family and family situations; pregnancy; single mothers
movements of domestic workers. *See* mobilization of domestic workers
Myrdal, Gunnar, 141n4

neighborhoods. *See* residence

occupational habitus, 37, 52, 54
occupational inheritance, 16, 88, 99, 149n3
outreach strategies, 113, 125
overtime pay, 67f, 78, 115–16
overwork, 44, 91. *See also* exhaustion; exploitation

part-time work
    and eligibility for social security, 59, 71
    and enrollment in social security, 75–76
    and face-to-face contact between employer and employee, 32
    future research on, 128
    hiring process for, 25
    increase in, 23, 33, 34, 65, 123
    for multiple employers, 15, 28, 65, 148n14
patronage relationships, 22, 93
Pereyra, Francisca, 54, 121, 146n15
Pérez, Inés, 146n25
perol, 1–2
Peru, 17, 28, 106, 132, 142n17
Polanyi, Karl, 18
poverty, 1–2, 8–10, 32, 35, 40, 54, 86, 97, 99, 103–4, 141n4, 145n11
pregnancy
    changing perspectives on, 102
    independence and adult status through, 149n8
    and maternity leave, 14, 60, 93, 110, 150n7
    as reason for leaving jobs, 93
    See also children
primary education, 73–74, 77
production
    and domestic employment in Latin America, 17–18
    formal employment within, 5
    and social reproduction, 7
puertas adentro, 65. *See also* live-in workers
puertas afuera, 65. *See also* live-out workers

Qayum, Seemin, 38, 39
Quijano, Aníbal, 17, 18, 53, 107

race
    and characteristics of ideal worker, 32
    in domestic work survey, 147n9
    and embodied inequality, 40–43, 47, 53
    and history of domestic work in Ecuador, 12–13
    social construction of, 41–42
    See also Afro-Ecuadorians; *buena presencia*; indigenous domestic workers

racialization of domestic work, 1–2, 12–13, 52–53, 124
Ray, Raka, 38, 39
recommendations. *See* word of mouth
Redclift, Nanneke, 10
residence
    of employers, 22, 40, 61–62
    of ideal worker, 28
    of surveyed domestic workers, 61–62, 136–37
Rollins, Judith, 6, 38, 146n19

sacrifice, 102–4
Saffioti, Heleieth, 142n13
salary. *See* wages
Salazar, Maximina, ix, 113
sales, self-employment in, 95–96, 149n5
Sarmento da Silveira, Juliana, 64
Schluter, Anne, 38
school, reasons for leaving, 86–87
secondary education, 73–74, 77
self-employment, informal, 95–99, 149n5
severance pay, 93, 94, 115–16
sexual threat, domestic workers as, 50–51
single mothers
    and discussing social security with employer, 77–78, 79
    domestic workers as, 60
    domestic workers as children of, 86
    employers as, 80
    and mobilization of domestic workers, 113–14
    and unpaid social reproduction, 80
"Sin peroles no hay paraíso," 1–2
SINUTRHE, 121
situación, la, 104
social class
    as aspect of domestic work, 16–17
    as basis for mobilization, 18, 83, 107, 112, 117, 124, 151n3
    and embodied inequality, 35–36, 39–43, 45–47, 51–54, 146n15
    and gifts from employer to employee, 48, 146n19
    and ideal worker, 22
    as obstacle to domestic workers' rights, 124–25
    uniforms and, 49
social mobility, through leaving domestic work, 97–100. *See also* trajectories of domestic workers
social movements, 106, 109, 110–11, 117, 120. *See also* Asociación de Trabajadoras Remuneradas del Hogar (ATRH);

feminist movements; mobilization of domestic workers
social networks, and finding employment, 21, 84, 87, 144n15
social reproduction, 5–8
    and choosing domestic work, 88
    and domestic employment in Latin America, 17–18
    domestic worker organizing and paid, 111–12
    efforts to value, 123
    and embodied inequality, 36
    and home-based work, 96
    and ideal worker, 22
    as obstacle to domestic workers' rights, 123
    revaluing of, 126
    and rights denied of domestic workers, 56
    single mothers and unpaid, 80
    social security and, 58
    as women's work, 87
social security, 56–60
    awareness regarding right to, 69, 73–74, 76
    discussed with employers, 71–72, 74–75, 77–79
    employers' stance on, 76
    enforcement of laws concerning, 79
    enrollment in, 115, 147n3, 148n19
    and formalization, 80
    as intervention point, 79
    knowledge, enrollment, and use, 69t
    likelihood of enrollment in, 75–76
    making use of benefits of, 70
    marriage and accessibility of, 148n23
    overdue contributions to, 147n4
    as reason for leaving jobs, 91
    reasons for not enrolling in, 70–71
    reported in domestic worker survey, 68–72, 74–79
    research participants enrolled in, 69–70
    and social reproduction, 5
    and trajectories of domestic workers, 100–102
    unenrolled workers' desire to enroll in, 72
    use of, 69t, 148n20
    and vulnerability of domestic workers, 72–76
    See also Instituto Ecuatoriano de Seguridad Social (IESS)
"Southern Theory," 143n27
struggle. *See* lucha, la
survey on domestic work, 55–56, 76–81
    demographics of workers surveyed, 60–62, 147n9, 151n4

survey on domestic work *(continued)*
    domestic worker commutes, 62–64
    research methods for, 135–36, 137–40
    social security, 68–72, 74–79
    vulnerability of domestic workers, 72–76
    working conditions, 64–68, 78
symbolic interactionism, 37

technology, 42, 125, 145n4, 151n4
Tizziani, Ania, 48, 141n5
trajectories of domestic workers, 82–84, 104
    chances of upward mobility by leaving
        domestic work, 97–100
    entrance into workforce, 86–87
    interviewees' work histories, 89f
    other employment, 94–97
    previous research on, 84–86
    reasons for choosing domestic work,
        88–89
    reasons for leaving jobs, 89–94
    and social reproduction, 100–102
    struggle, work, and sacrifice in, 102–4
    trato (treatment of workers), 22, 31–32,
        92–93

ugliness, and embodied inequality, 50
underemployment, 3, 98
underpayment, 90
unemployed workers, in domestic worker sur-
    vey, 66–68
unemployment, paths to, 89–94
uniforms, 42, 48–51, 52, 145n3, 146nn21–22
unionization, 8, 108, 117, 149n4
unión libre. *See* marriage
unpaid back wages, 90, 115–16

unpaid domestic work/unpaid social repro-
    duction, 5–8, 10, 17, 34, 57–58, 60, 70, 78,
    80–81, 83, 87, 91, 93, 96, 100–104, 114,
    123, 126–27, 141n2
unplanned pregnancy, 102
urban areas, 8–9, 17, 34, 62–64, 82, 94–95
urbanization, 9, 12, 17, 58

vacation time, 66, 67f, 78
Valentine, Gill, 39
value, Marx on, 142n7
Venezuela, 132, 143n26, 144n13, 147n8
vocational training, 99–100
vulnerability of domestic workers, 8, 14,
    72–76, 77, 129

wages
    of ideal worker, 30–32
    minimum, 31, 145n7, 148n16
    for overtime, 67f, 78, 115–16
    as reason for leaving jobs, 90
    unpaid, 90, 115–16
washing machines, 42, 145n4
Weeks, Kathi, 104
Wolkowitz, Carol, 37
Wong, Sara, 124, 148nn14,19,20
word of mouth, 21, 84, 87, 144n15
work
    activities considered as, 96–97
    changing meanings of, 129
    See also domestic work
workers' associations, 108, 117, 149n4
workers' cooperatives, 126
working conditions, 57–60, 64–68, 78
written contracts, 90, 91, 116